The
Mediterranean
Cookbook

The
Mediterranean
Cookbook

Joanna Farrow
& Jacqueline Clarke

LORENZ BOOKS

First published by Lorenz Books in 2001

© Anness Publishing Limited 2001

Lorenz Books is an imprint of Anness Publishing Limited
Hermes House, 88–89 Blackfriars Road, London SE1 8HA

Published in the USA by Lorenz Books, Anness Publishing Inc.
27 West 20th Street, New York, NY 10011

www.lorenzbooks.com

This edition distributed in Canada by Raincoast Books
9050 Shaughnessy Street, Vancouver, British Columbia V6P 6E5

A CIP catalogue record for this book is available from the British Library.

Publisher: Joanna Lorenz
Managing Editor: Linda Fraser
Editor: Susannah Blake
Jacket and Text Design: Chloë Steers
Typesetting: Jonathan Harley
Illustrations: Angela Wood
Recipes: Katherine Atkinson, Carla Capalbo, Jacqueline Clarke, Carole Clements,
Joanna Farrow, Silvana Franco, Rebekah Hassan, Soheila Kimberley, Sarah Lewis,
Jennie Shapter, Elizabeth Wolf-Cohen, Jeni Wright

1 3 5 7 9 10 8 6 4 2

NOTES

Bracketed terms are intended for American readers.

For all recipes, quantities are given in both metric and imperial measures and,
where appropriate, measures are also given in standard cups and spoons. Follow
one set, but not a mixture, because they are not interchangeable.

Standard spoon and cup measures are level.
1 tsp = 5ml, 1 tbsp = 15ml, 1 cup = 250ml/8fl oz

Australian standard tablespoons are 20ml. Australian readers should use 3 tsp in
place of 1 tbsp for measuring small quantities of gelatine, flour, salt, etc.

Medium (US large) eggs are used unless otherwise stated.

CONTENTS

INTRODUCTION

When you think of the Mediterranean, you think of sunshine and vibrant colours reflected in the countryside, the clothes, the buildings, and in the wonderful displays of flowers, fruits and vegetables for sale in the markets. The area comprises fifteen countries in all – Spain, France, Italy, Greece, Turkey, Syria, Lebanon and Israel, plus Egypt, Libya, Tunisia, Algeria, Morocco, and the islands of Malta and Cyprus. In many ways these countries are completely different from each other, but they all have something in common too – the love of good food.

Centuries before the time of Christ, the area surrounding the Mediterranean sea was colonized by the Phoenicians, Greeks and Romans, who shared a basic cultivation of wheat, olives and grapes. These, in turn, became bread, oil and wine, three components that are still very important in today's Mediterranean diet. With the building of ships came import and export, and the various countries began a cross-pollination of crops, ingredients and recipes. Spices and flavourings were introduced through North Africa and Arabia, and saffron, cloves, chillies, ginger and allspice continue to be popular all over the Mediterranean region, appearing in sweet and savoury dishes. Nuts, too, are an ingredient common to many of the countries, with almonds, pistachio nuts and pine nuts being perhaps the most popular as they are native to the region.

When thinking of Mediterranean food, however, it is the fresh fruit, vegetables and herbs that immediately spring to mind. Open-air markets from Marseilles down to Morocco are a feast for the senses. Fabulous arrays of tomatoes, aubergines (eggplant), courgettes (zucchini), peaches, figs, garlic and pungent herbs such as basil and thyme are tantalizingly displayed; the experience being made complete by the hot sun, drawing out the depth of flavour and aroma. Mediterranean cooking depends on the freshest of ingredients; it is honest, simple food, prepared with respect.

Research in recent years has proved the Mediterranean diet to be a very healthy one, thus increasing its popularity. Olive oil is at the heart of this theory; it contains a high proportion of mono-unsaturated fats. Olive oils vary in colour, from the golden Spanish varieties to the deep greens of some Greek, Provençal and Italian oils. Colour is not an indication of quality; the oils have to be tasted, and flavour, like colour, varies immensely from rich and fruity to mild or nutty.

The people of the Mediterranean have known great hardship. Although we have holiday images of sunny days, the weather can be wild and unjust. Lack of rain, terrible winds and a capricious sea ruin crops and the fishermen's haul; in the past, foreign domination and disease caused poverty and death. Because of this, the most basic foods are, even today, a great celebration of life to the Mediterranean people. Bread is an important staple and it is always served at a meal, be it a bowl of soup or a platter of grilled fish.

Perhaps Mediterranean food could be described as peasant food, not in any derogatory sense, but as a homage to the people who have provided and inspired us with such a vast and wonderful repertoire of recipes, ancient and new. In this book, we give you just a few of the countless dishes that can be found around the Mediterranean shores. Some such as Gazpacho soup, Ratatouille, Greek Salad and Provençal Beef and Olive Daube are very traditional, while others are more contemporary, using Mediterranean ingredients but creating something new. Amongst these recipes are Mushroom and Pesto Pizza, Pan-fried Red Mullet with Basil and Citrus Sauce, and Turkish Delight Ice Cream.

As in the Mediterranean, ingredients should be fresh and of the highest quality, even if this means waiting for some of them, such as clams or figs, to be in season. We hope to bring you a true taste of the Mediterranean.

FISH & SHELLFISH

The waters of the Mediterranean offer an abundant source of food to the countries surrounding it. Fish and shellfish are often cooked simply, perhaps drizzled with olive oil and lemon juice and grilled (broiled) or roasted with herbs and garlic. Rich seafood stews such as bouillabaisse are also popular and are enjoyed throughout the region.

RED MULLET
This pretty fish is very popular along the coasts of the Mediterranean. It is usually treated simply by grilling over a wood fire, often with the liver still inside as this imparts a wonderful flavour. It can also be filleted and pan-fried, or included in fish stews and soups.

SEA BASS
This is quite an expensive fish and is usually sold and cooked whole. The flesh is soft and delicate and needs careful attention when cooking. It is very good poached, steamed, grilled (broiled) and baked.

MONKFISH
These very ugly fish are found throughout the Mediterranean. Usually only the tail is eaten and, as a general rule, the larger the tail, the better the quality. It can be studded with herbs and garlic and roasted whole, or grilled, made into kebabs, pan-fried, poached or braised.

TUNA
This oily fish belongs to the same family as the mackerel. The flesh, which is sold in steaks or large pieces, is dark red and very dense. It needs careful cooking as the flesh has a tendency to dry out. Marinating helps to keep the flesh moist, as does basting while cooking. Tuna can be baked, fried, grilled or stewed.

SARDINES
These silvery fish are abundant throughout the Mediterranean. They tend to be small – only about 13cm/5in long – and are cooked and eaten whole. They are good grilled, barbecued or pan-fried and are often added to pasta sauces.

DRIED AND PRESERVED FISH
Since early times, fish has been preserved by salting and/or drying in the sun. Today, this continues and these fish are widely used in Mediterranean cooking.

Tarama *This is salted grey mullet roe. It is regarded as a great delicacy and is the traditional ingredient of the Greek dip taramasalata. Tarama is quite expensive so smoked cod's roe is often used instead.*

Salt Cod *Most salt cod is caught and prepared in the waters around Norway, Iceland and Newfoundland, but it is very popular in Mediterranean cooking. The fish are caught, gutted, cleaned, soaked in brine, then dried. The end result has a pungent smell and looks unappetizing but, after soaking in water for 48 hours and cooking, it is delicious.*

Mojama *This salted, dried tuna is very popular in Spain and Sicily. It is eaten as a nibble with a glass of fino sherry, or served on slices of baguette rubbed with garlic and drizzled with olive oil.*

CRAB

There are literally thousands of different species of crab around the world. In the Mediterranean countries, brown and spider crabs are the most commonly found. The meat of the crab is divided into two sorts – brown and white. Crabs are often sold cooked and dressed, which means that the crab has been prepared and is ready to eat. When buying, choose crabs that feel heavy; they should have a lot of meat in them.

MUSSELS

These pretty shellfish can be blue-black or dappled brown, and vary in size. They are available throughout the Mediterranean from September to April. They usually need to be scrubbed and have the "beard" removed. Any open mussels that do not close when sharply tapped with the back of a knife should be discarded before cooking. The easiest way to cook mussels is to steam them for a few minutes in a covered pan. They can then be eaten steamed as they are, stuffed and grilled, or added to pasta sauces, soups and stews.

CLAMS

These attractive bivalves can vary greatly in colour and size. They have a fine, sweet flavour and a firm texture. Like mussels, open clams that do not close when tapped should be discarded. Clams can be steamed open and are delicious served in pasta sauces, stews and soups.

PRAWNS/SHRIMP

These small crustaceans vary enormously in size. The classic Mediterranean prawn is large, about 20cm/8in, reddish brown in colour when raw, and pink when cooked. When prawns are cooked over a fierce heat, such as a barbecue, the shell is often left on to protect the flesh from charring.

PREPARING A LIVE CRAB

Place the crab in the freezer for 2 hours until it is comatose. When the crab is no longer moving, plunge it into a large pan of boiling salted water, quickly bring the water back to the boil, then cook for about 10 minutes.

Alternatively, place the crab in a large pan of cold salted water, bring it slowly to the boil, then cook for about 10 minutes.

Time cooking from the moment the water boils and never cook a crab for more than 12 minutes, whatever its size.

SQUID

These are popular throughout the region, particularly in Spain, Italy and Portugal. Squid vary in size from the tiny ones that can be eaten whole, to the larger varieties that are good for stuffing, grilling or stewing. The flesh is sweet and tender, when cooked for only a short time. Long cooking will also produce succulent results. Squid ink is added to sauces and risottos, and is used to colour pasta.

OCTOPUS

These can be found throughout the region. Octopus needs long, slow cooking and it is often a good idea to blanch or marinate them first. It is good stewed slowly with Mediterranean vegetables or a robust red wine, or stuffed and baked. Smaller ones can be cut into rings and sautéed.

Meat, Poultry & Game

Although fish and shellfish are probably considered central to Mediterranean cooking, meat, poultry and game are also enjoyed all around the region and they play an important role in its cuisine. Slow-cooked stews and casseroles are favoured throughout the whole region, while quick-grilled kebabs are popular in Turkey. Poultry and game is often roasted.

Meat

The countryside around the Mediterranean can be harsh. Animals are often slaughtered young and baby lamb and goat are very popular. Young animals are often roasted whole on a spit, flavoured with wild herbs. Cattle are a rare sight and beef was once considered a great luxury. Pork is another popular meat, though this is not eaten in Jewish and Muslim countries or regions.

In the past, older animals often produced tough and stringy meat, so marinating the meat in wine or yogurt and slow-cooking was favoured. Pulses, rice and potatoes were often added to make the meat go further. Despite the fact that meat is now of better quality, the traditional casseroles and stews are still very popular.

Meat is also grilled (broiled), particularly in Greece and the Middle East, where it is often threaded on to skewers with onion and other vegetables. Minced (ground) meat is also used extensively throughout the region, in the form of patties, meatballs, sausages, fillings and sauces.

Poultry and Game

These have always played an important role in Mediterranean cooking, largely due to the dry and rugged land, which does not produce good pasture for sheep and cows. Chickens and ducks have always been particularly popular as peasants were able to raise them on their own land.

Chicken is the most widely used type of poultry, although many excellent duck and goose recipes can be found throughout the region. Poultry is often cooked with fresh, dried or preserved fruits, nuts and spices. In the Middle East, where chickens were kept for their eggs, only older birds were eaten so long, slow cooking with highly flavoured sauces and stuffings is favoured.

Rabbit is widely eaten and game birds such as partridge, quail and pigeon are typical of the region. They are often lightly cooked in rich sauces, served with polenta (in Italy) and cooked in pies.

Cured Meats and Sausages
The various regions of the Mediterranean have their own cured meats, hams and sausages, each with a unique appearance, taste and texture. Most are made from pork and are preserved with salt and air-dried. They may be eaten raw, cooked in hearty stews and casseroles or added to dishes to give extra flavour.

Popular cured meats and sausages include pancetta, prosciutto and salami from Italy, and spicy chorizo from Spain.

DAIRY PRODUCE

The countries of the Mediterranean produce a diverse range of cheeses and yogurt, made from cow's, goat's, sheep's and, in the case of Italian mozzarella, buffalo's milk. The flavour of the cheese or yogurt depends on the type of milk used and varies from mild and creamy ricotta to sharp and tangy feta, strong and salty halloumi and distinctively flavoured Greek yogurt.

CREAM CHEESE

Many countries produce their own version of this cheese. Each one varies according to the milk used and method of preparation.

RICOTTA

This soft white Italian cheese has a solid yet grainy consistency. Commercially produced ricotta is made from cow's milk, but in rural areas sheep's or goat's milk is sometimes used. Ricotta is widely used for both savoury and sweet dishes. It has very little flavour, so makes a perfect vehicle for flavourings such as herbs, nutmeg or honey.

MOZZARELLA

This white Italian cheese has a moist, springy texture and a very mild, milky flavour. The best mozzarella is made from buffalo's milk, but cow's milk cheeses are also available. Fresh mozzarella is delicious served in salads, particularly with fresh tomatoes and basil, and is perfect for topping pizzas. Smoked mozzarella is good in sandwiches or as part of antipasti.

FETA

This crumbly, white Greek cheese is made from sheep's milk. It tends to be rather salty and has a very distinctive, sharp, tangy flavour. It is probably best known for its use in Greek salad, where it is combined with tomatoes, cucumber and olives and dressed with lemon juice and olive oil.

HALLOUMI

This creamy-white cheese from Cyprus is slightly firmer than mozzarella and has a rubbery texture. It was originally made from sheep's or goat's milk, but is now more commonly made from cow's milk. It is packed in brine and has a very strong, salty flavour with a distinctive, sharp tang. Chopped mint is added to the curds and this helps to give the cheese its wonderful flavour. It is one of the few cheeses that holds its shape on cooking and is delicious fried or grilled.

YOGURT

This is made from pasteurized sheep's, cow's or goat's milk combined with two beneficial bacteria. It is perhaps most associated with the Middle Eastern countries, where it is used extensively in cooking. Greek yogurt is thick and creamy, and French yogurt is traditionally of the set variety. It is used as a marinade, a dip and to enrich soups and stews. It is also served as an accompaniment to savoury dishes.

PULSES, GRAINS & PASTA

Throughout the Mediterranean region, these important staple ingredients are used in almost every meal. They may be added to hearty soups or meat and vegetable stews such as Moroccan tagines, used in salads such as Middle Eastern tabbouleh, or served as accompaniments to meat dishes. They are incredibly versatile, healthy, nutritious and delicious.

PULSES

Originally, many pulses came from the Middle East, but they are now used across the Mediterranean region, from Spain to Turkey, Israel and Tunisia.

CHICKPEAS

This pulse looks like a pale golden hazelnut and is sold either dried or ready-cooked in cans. Chickpeas have a nutty flavour and firm texture and are used in stews in every Mediterranean country, from Spain to the Lebanon. They can also be served cold as a salad, dressed with freshly squeezed lemon juice, chopped fresh herbs and extra virgin olive oil. In the Middle East they are made into flour, and in Greece and Turkey they are puréed to make a dip.

Dried and canned chickpeas are readily available. Dried chickpeas should be soaked overnight before cooking.

HARICOT BEANS

There are several varieties of these beans, including red- and cream-speckled borlotti, pale green flageolet, small white cannellini and navy, and black-eyed beans (peas). These small plump beans, which are quite soft when cooked, are often added to casseroles and soups. They are also good served as a side dish or added to salads.

Haricot beans are available dried or canned. Dried beans should be soaked overnight before cooking.

LENTILS

These come in different sizes and can be yellow, red, brown or green. Tiny green Puy lentils are favoured in France and the brown and red ones in the Middle East where they are cooked with spices. They are also used in soups. Lentils need no soaking and take less than an hour to cook.

COOKING DRIED CHICKPEAS AND HARICOT BEANS

Dried pulses such as chickpeas and haricot beans should be soaked in a large bowl of cold water for at least 8 hours before cooking.

1 Drain the soaked pulses, then place in a large pan of cold water and bring to a rapid boil. Continue to boil rapidly for about 10 minutes. Reduce the heat and simmer gently for 1–2 hours, depending on the size and freshness of the pulses.

2 To flavour the chickpeas or beans, add whatever herbs or spices you wish to the cooking liquid, but do not add salt or any acidic ingredients, such as tomatoes or vinegar, until the beans are cooked, or the beans will toughen and remain hard.

To make a hearty stew, *after the initial boiling (step 1), place the pulses in an ovenproof dish with pancetta, garlic and herbs, pour over water to cover and cook in a low oven for 1–2 hours.*

GRAINS

These staples are popular throughout the Mediterranean region and are either served as accompaniments to other dishes such as stews and casseroles, or are used to form the basis of dishes such as salads, risottos and paellas. They can also be added to soups.

COUSCOUS

These tiny yellowish grains are made from semolina. The grains are rolled, dampened and coated with fine wheat flour. Couscous has a light and fluffy texture and a rather bland flavour, which makes it the perfect accompaniment for richly flavoured stews. It is a staple in North Africa and is usually served with a spicy meat or vegetable stew, but it can also be used as a stuffing for vegetables or in salads.

Traditionally, the preparation of couscous was time-consuming as it required lengthy steaming. However, the commercial variety available today is pre-cooked and is quick and simple to prepare. Either pour over just enough boiling water to cover and leave to soak for about 10 minutes, or moisten the couscous with water and steam for about 15 minutes to swell the grains.

BULGUR WHEAT

Also called cracked wheat, this cereal has a delicious nutty flavour and light texture. It is best known for its use in Middle Eastern *tabbouleh*, where it is combined with raw cucumber, tomatoes, chopped mint and parsley, and then dressed with lemon juice and olive oil. It can be used in place of rice as an accompaniment to grilled (broiled) meats and fish, as a stuffing, and mixed with minced (ground) meat to make patties. Cracked wheat has been processed, and so cooks quickly. It can be either soaked in boiling water for 20 minutes, then drained, or cooked in boiling water until tender.

RICE

This grain is a staple throughout the world and there are many different varieties. In Italy there are at least four short-grained types, including Arborio and Carnaroli, which are used for rich and creamy risotto. In Spain, Valencia rice is used for paella. In the Middle East rice is served with every meal, either plainly boiled or cooked with saffron and spices to create fragrant pilaus.

PASTA

This is simply the Latin word for paste – the flour- and egg-based dough from which pasta is made. Although pasta is actually a staple of Italian cooking, it is widely used throughout the Mediterranean region and has much in common with Chinese noodles, which filtered from China via the Middle Eastern trade routes.

In Italy today there are countless varieties, from flat sheets of lasagne and ribbon noodles to pressed and moulded shapes, specifically designed to pocket substantial amounts of the sauce with which they are served. Dried pasta shapes make a good standby. When buying dried pasta, always choose a good quality Italian variety.

Both fresh and dried pasta can be bought flavoured with tomato, olive, spinach or mushroom paste. Black pasta, made with the addition of squid ink, is increasingly popular. Fresh pasta is very easy to make, particularly if using a pasta machine for rolling out the dough.

VEGETABLES

Throughout the Mediterranean, market stalls are piled high with a wonderful array of vibrantly coloured, sun-ripened vegetables. This locally-grown produce, including plump, red tomatoes, purple aubergines (eggplant) and shiny, green courgettes (zucchini), plays an essential role in the dishes of the region. They are added to almost every savoury dish, from salads to hearty stews.

ONIONS

These strongly flavoured vegetables are an essential component of virtually all savoury Mediterranean dishes. There are many varieties of onion, differing in colour, size and strength of flavour. Red- or white-skinned varieties have a sweet, mild flavour and are good used raw in salads. Large, Spanish onions are also mild and are a good choice when a large quantity of onion is called for in a recipe. Baby (pearl) onions are perfect for adding whole to stews, or serving as a vegetable dish.

TOMATOES

These form the basis of many traditional Mediterranean dishes and are used widely in sauces, soups and stews. Throughout the Mediterranean region, markets are packed with ripe, fresh-tasting tomatoes of many varieties: beefsteak, plum, vine, cherry and baby pear-shaped ones. Sun-dried tomatoes are richly flavoured and are used in many dishes, from sauces and stews to salads. Canned tomatoes are a handy standby.

PEPPERS/BELL PEPPERS

These sweet-tasting vegetables come in many colours, including green, red, orange and yellow. They can be used raw in salads, added to sauces or marinated and roasted in olive oil and served on their own. To make the most of their flavour, grill (broil) until charred, then peel off the skin.

AUBERGINES/EGGPLANT

Although these originated from Asia they are widely used in Mediterranean cooking. There are many varieties, including green, white and yellow, but the plump purple variety is most commonly found. Look for firm, taut, shiny-skinned specimens with green stalks. Aubergines are sometimes salted before cooking, to extract any bitter juices and prevent them absorbing too much oil during cooking.

COURGETTES/ZUCCHINI

These summer squash are at their best when they are small. They have a delicious, subtle flavour, although the larger they become, the less flavour they have. The green variety is most common but yellow ones are sometimes available. When buying, choose firm, shiny specimens. They can be lightly cooked or eaten raw. Courgette flowers are stuffed and cooked, or deep-fried in batter.

ARTICHOKES

There are two types of artichoke: the globe, which belongs to the thistle family, and the Jerusalem, which is a tuber, belonging to the sunflower family. The globe artichoke is common throughout the Mediterranean. After boiling, the leaves and base are edible. Baby varieties can be eaten whole and are good raw. Jerusalem artichokes look like knobbly potatoes, and should be prepared in the same way.

FENNEL

This white, layered bulb has green, feathery fronds and a fresh aniseed flavour. It is very good eaten cooked or raw. Its flavour complements fish and chicken, but it is also delicious served as a vegetable course, either roasted, or baked with a cheese sauce. Choose firm, rounded bulbs, and use the fronds for garnishing. If using raw, toss the slices of fennel in lemon juice to prevent them from discolouring.

OKRA

This unusual vegetable, sometimes called lady's fingers, is a long, five-sided green pod, with a tapering end. It has a subtle flavour and a gelatinous texture, which helps to thicken and enrich dishes. It is used in Middle Eastern and Greek cookery and goes well with garlic, onion and tomatoes. Choose small, firm specimens with no dark patches, and use sliced or whole.

BROAD/FAVA BEANS

When young, these beans can be cooked and eaten, pods and all, or shelled and eaten raw with cheese, as is done in Italy. When the beans are older, they are shelled, cooked, and sometimes peeled. Dried broad beans are popular in the Middle East. They are cooked with spices or added to stews.

SPINACH

This green, leafy vegetable is very popular in the Mediterranean area. Young, tender spinach leaves can be eaten raw and need little preparation, but older leaves should be washed well, then picked over and the tough stalks removed. Spinach is used in many dishes including Middle Eastern pastries, Spanish tapas and French tarts. Eggs and fish make very good partners. Spinach wilts when cooked so allow at least 250g/9oz raw weight per person.

VINE LEAVES

These pretty leaves have been used in cooking for hundreds of years. They can be stuffed with a variety of fillings and also make perfect wrappers for meat, fish and poultry. Fresh vine leaves should be young and soft. If using brined vine leaves, soak them in hot water for 20–30 minutes before stuffing or wrapping.

RADICCHIO

This red chicory is very popular in Italy. There are several varieties, but the most common is the round variety that looks like a small lettuce. The crisp leaves taste slightly bitter and can be eaten raw or cooked. Radicchio is delicious grilled (broiled) and drizzled with olive oil and sprinkled with black pepper, or shredded and stirred into risotto or spaghetti. The raw leaves look pretty in salads.

MUSHROOMS

Popular varieties used in the Mediterranean kitchen include button (white), open cup and flat. Regional wild species such as ceps, chanterelles and oyster mushrooms are to be found in the markets during autumn.

OLIVES

These are extremely popular throughout the Mediterranean and there are literally hundreds of different varieties. Colour depends purely on ripeness – changing from yellow to green, violet, purple, brown and finally black. Fresh olives are inedible and must be soaked in water, bruised and immersed in brine before eating. They are available loose, bottled or canned and may be whole or pitted. They are sometimes stuffed with nuts, pimientos or anchovies, or bottled with flavourings such as garlic and chilli.

Fruit & Nuts

The Mediterranean region produces a wonderful array of fruits and nuts, which are used extensively in its cuisine. Fruit and nuts are used in both sweet and savoury dishes and North Africa, in particular, has a tradition of adding sweet fruit to spicy meat stews. They are also enjoyed on their own: raw fruit may be eaten as a simple dessert, and toasted almonds served as a tapas.

LEMONS

These bright yellow fruits are grown all over the Mediterranean region. They are very versatile and are used in both sweet and savoury dishes. The juice can be used as the key flavouring in dishes such as lemon tart, added to cold drinks, or sprinkled over fish, meat or vegetables. It helps to bring out the flavour of other fruits and will prevent certain fruits and vegetables, such as artichokes, from becoming discoloured when cut. The rind imparts a wonderful flavour and is added to cakes, pastries, savoury dishes and salad dressings. Choose unwaxed fruits that feel heavy for their size.

PRESERVED LEMONS AND LIMES

These are used in many Mediterranean dishes, and are particularly popular in North African countries. The lemons or limes are preserved in salt and develop a wonderfully mellow flavour.

To preserve lemons or limes, *scrub and quarter almost through to the base of the fruits and rub the cut sides with salt. Pack tightly into a large sterilized jar. Half fill the jar with salt, adding bay leaves, peppercorns and cinnamon, if you like. Pour lemon juice over the fruit to cover, then seal and store for two weeks, shaking the jar daily. Add a little olive oil and use within one to six months, washing off the salt before use.*

ORANGES

These vibrant citrus fruits are grown throughout the Mediterranean. There are many different varieties, including seedless navel oranges, red-fleshed blood oranges and bitter oranges. The rind has the best flavour and is often added to recipes using oranges. Oranges are used in both sweet and savoury dishes and combine very well with fish and game.

PEACHES AND NECTARINES

These need plenty of sun to ripen them and are grown in France, Spain and Italy. Fuzzy-skinned peaches may be yellow-, pink- or white-fleshed. Some are cling, where the flesh clings to the stone, while others are the freestone variety. Nectarines are smooth-skinned, with all the luscious flavour of the peach. They are delicious raw, but may be cooked. Look for bruise-free specimens that give when squeezed gently.

FIGS

This fruit is strongly associated with all Mediterranean countries. Different varieties vary in colour, from dark purple to green to a golden yellow, but all are made up of hundreds of tiny seeds, surrounded by soft pink flesh, which is perfectly edible. Choose firm unblemished fruit that just yields to the touch. Treat them simply, or serve with prosciutto or Greek yogurt and honey. They are highly perishable so use quickly.

MELONS

This fruit comes in a range of different varieties, sizes, shapes and colours – galia, Cantaloupe, charentais, honeydew, ogen, orange- and green-fleshed varieties, and also the pink-fleshed watermelon. Ripe melons should yield to gentle pressure at the stalk end and have a fragrant scent. Rarely used in cooked dishes, they are best eaten chilled, by the slice, or as part of a fruit salad.

POMEGRANATES

These golden, apple-shaped fruits are often associated with Mediterranean cooking. Inside the tough skin are hundreds of seeds, which are covered with a deep pink flesh that has a delicate, slightly tart flavour. They are often scattered over meat dishes and sweet dishes such as fruit salads.

DATES

Although fresh dates, which are mostly grown in Israel and California, are quite widely available, the dried variety remains a very popular addition to cakes and teabreads. Fresh dates should be plump with a slightly wrinkled skin and have a rich honey-like flavour and dense texture. They are best treated simply: try them pitted and served with thick, creamy Greek yogurt. They also go particularly well with oranges and make a good addition to fruit salads.

ALMONDS

Cultivated commercially in Spain and Italy, the almond is widely used in all the Arab-influenced countries. It is an important ingredient in sweet pastries and is often added to savoury dishes. Almonds are sold fresh in their green velvety shells in the Mediterranean markets.

PISTACHIO NUTS

This colourful nut originated in the Middle East. It has flesh ranging from pale to dark green, and a dry, papery, purple-tinged skin. Pistachio nuts have a subtle yet distinctive flavour and are used in a wide range of dishes, from pastries (both sweet and savoury) to ice creams and nougat.

WALNUTS

This very versatile nut is used in both sweet and savoury dishes. In France, walnut oil is a popular addition to salad dressings. Elsewhere, walnuts are chopped and added to pastries, ground to make sauces, or eaten fresh as "wet" walnuts.

PINE NUTS

These yellowish kernels have a resinous flavour. They are used in both sweet and savoury dishes, and are one of the principal ingredients in pesto, the basil sauce that comes from Italy.

HERBS

These grow wild all over the Mediterranean and play an essential role in the region's cuisine. Some herbs such as basil, dill and tarragon have a delicate flavour and can be used fresh in salads and dressing or added to cooked dishes at the last moment. Other pungent herbs such as rosemary and thyme are best added to slow-cooked dishes such as stews and roast meats.

BASIL

This delicious, fragrant herb is widely used in Mediterranean cooking, particularly in Italian dishes. The sweet, tender, bright green leaves have a natural affinity with tomatoes, aubergines (eggplant), courgettes (zucchini), (bell) peppers, and cheese. A handful of leaves enlivens a green salad. The leaves can also be packed into a bottle of olive oil to produce an aromatic flavour. The leaves bruise easily, so always tear rather than cut them.

CORIANDER/CILANTRO

Huge bundles of fresh coriander are a familiar sight in eastern Mediterranean markets, their warm, pungent aroma rising at the merest touch. The leaves impart a distinctive flavour to soups, stews, sauces and spicy dishes. Fresh coriander leaves are also used in salads and yogurt dishes. When adding the leaves to cooked dishes, stir them in just before serving as their flavour tends to fade with cooking. When using them raw in salads, use sparingly, as their flavour can easily become overpowering.

PARSLEY

Flat leaf parsley is far more widely used in Mediterranean cookery than the tightly curled variety. Mixed with garlic and grated lemon rind, it makes a delicious, aromatic condiment, *gremolata*, for scattering over tomato and rice dishes.

CHIVES

This grass-like herb, which produces a very pretty purplish flower, is a member of the onion family. It has a mild flavour of onion and can be snipped into salads, or added to cooked dishes.

MINT

This is one of the oldest and most widely used herbs. In Greece, chopped fresh mint accompanies other herbs to enhance stuffed vegetables and fish dishes, and in Turkey and the Middle East finely chopped mint adds a cooling tang to yogurt dishes as well as iced drinks. Very sweet mint tea is widely drunk in Morocco.

CHERVIL

This delicate, pretty leafed herb is rather like a mild parsley and needs to be used generously to impart sufficient flavour. It is widely used in French cooking and is very good in herb butters. It also makes a good partner to eggs and cheese.

DILL

Feathery, dark green dill leaves have a mild aniseed taste, and are popular in the eastern Mediterranean, particularly in Greece and Turkey. It is chopped into fish and chicken dishes, as well as stuffings and rice. Pickled gherkins and cucumbers are often flavoured with this aromatic herb.

FENNEL

This feathery, blue-green herb has a mild taste of anise. It grows wild all over the region. It has a particular affinity with fish and makes a good addition to mayonnaise, creamy sauces and salad dressings.

TARRAGON

Long, greyish-green tarragon leaves have a unique aroma and flavour, which is most widely appreciated in French cookery. It is used generously in egg and chicken dishes, and with salmon and trout. Tarragon-flavoured wine vinegar makes a very good addition to home-made mayonnaise or Hollandaise sauce.

SAGE

This pungent herb is native to the northern Mediterranean. Its soft, velvety leaves have a strong, distinctive flavour, which go very well with fatty meats and strongly flavoured game. Sage can be added to stuffings or can be pan-fried with pigeon and liver to give a delicious flavour. Sage can also be used to flavour butter, which is good drizzled over fresh stuffed pasta such as ravioli. Sage can be quite pungent so use sparingly.

THYME

A few sprigs of hardy thyme add a warm, earthy flavour to slow-cooked meat and poultry dishes as well as to pâtés, marinades and vegetable dishes. It has quite a strong flavour, so use sparingly.

MARJORAM AND OREGANO

There are several varieties of this versatile herb, which has a pungent aroma but a delicate flavour. It grows wild throughout the region, but is also cultivated. It goes well with red meats, game and tomato dishes. Oregano is a wild form of marjoram and has a slightly stronger flavour.

ROSEMARY

This pretty, flowering shrub grows well throughout the Mediterranean and is most widely used in meat cookery. Several sprigs, tucked under a chicken or joint of lamb with garlic, impart an inviting warm, sweet flavour when roasted. Its flavour can be quite pungent so use sparingly.

BAY

The hardy leaves are taken from the bay shrub or tree and are widely used to flavour slow-cooked recipes such as stocks, soups and stews. Bay leaves are also added to marinades, threaded on to kebab skewers, thrown on the barbecue to invigorate the smoky flavour, or used for decorative purposes. One or two young bay leaves, infused with milk or cream in desserts, add a warm, pungent flavour.

BOUQUET GARNI

This is a combination of herbs, tied together in a muslin (cheesecloth) bundle or with string. They are often added to soups and stews and can be easily removed before serving. Bouquet garnis are available dried and fresh but they are also very easy to make.

Tie together sprigs of parsley and thyme with a few bay leaves. Other herbs such as rosemary and marjoram can also be included. Add a few sprigs of fennel when cooking fish dishes.

SPICES

These are another essential ingredient in the Mediterranean kitchen. Chillies, pepper and saffron are used throughout the region from Italy to Morocco, adding flavour and depth to dishes. Spices such as coriander, cumin and cardamom are widely used in the eastern Mediterranean, producing the rich flavours that are so commonly associated with this area.

CHILLIES

These are the small fiery relatives of the (bell) pepper and belong to the capsicum family. Mediterranean chillies are generally milder in flavour than the extremely fiery South American ones, but should still be used with caution as their heat is difficult to gauge. It is the oil in chillies that accounts for the heat and the irritation they can cause to sensitive skin.

Chillies are often added to North African dishes such as tagines and spicy stews, but they are also widely used in many Spanish and Italian dishes. Both fresh and dried chillies are used. Whole dried chillies may be soaked first or simply crumbled into dishes. Dried chilli flakes are also used.

When buying, look for firm, unblemished chillies, avoiding any that are soft or bruised. Wrap them in kitchen paper, place them in a plastic bag and store in the salad compartment of the refrigerator. To dry chillies, thread them on string and hang them in a warm place until they are dry. Store dried chillies in an airtight jar in a cool, dark place.

PEPPER

This is one of the most versatile of all spices. There are a number of different types of peppercorns, all of which are picked from the pepper vine, a plant unrelated to the capsicum family. Black peppercorns have the strongest flavour, which is rich, earthy and pungent. Green peppercorns are the fresh unripe berries, and are bottled while soft. They are just as strong as black peppercorns but have a lighter flavour.

PREPARING CHILLIES

Always wash your hands thoroughly immediately after handling chillies. Some people prefer to wear rubber (latex) gloves while preparing them.

To prepare fresh chillies, *remove the stalks, then slice the chillies lengthways. Scrape out the white pith and seeds, then slice, shred or chop as required. The seeds can be added to the dish or discarded, depending on the amount of heat desired.*

To prepare dried chillies, *remove the stems and seeds and snap each chilli into 2–3 pieces. Put these in a bowl, pour over hot water to cover and leave to stand for about 30 minutes. Drain, then use as they are or chop finely.*

Alternatively, crush dried chillies in a mortar with a pestle and used as required, or crumble directly into dishes.

Saffron

This is by far the most highly prized spice, since it takes the hand-picked stamens of about 70,000 saffron crocuses to make up 450g/1lb of the spice.

Saffron's exotic, rich colour and flavour is indispensable in many Mediterranean dishes, particularly French fish stews, Spanish rice and chicken dishes, and Italian risottos. To accentuate the flavour, the orange strands are best lightly crushed and soaked in a little boiling water before being used. Add the soaking liquid as well.

Store saffron in its cellophane or paper sachet in an airtight jar away from strong light. Its subtle aroma and flavour will fade over time so buy in small quantities.

Coriander Seeds

The round, brown seeds of the coriander herb have an earthy, warm, burnt-orange flavour. This spice is widely used in eastern Mediterranean dishes such as falafel.

The flavour of coriander seeds can be accentuated by dry-frying in a heavy pan, then crushing with a mortar and pestle or grinding in a spice grinder. Ready-ground coriander can be bought but it quickly loses its flavour and aroma. Store whole and ground coriander seeds in an airtight jar, away from direct light.

Cumin Seeds

These dark, spindly-shaped seeds are often married with coriander when making the spicy dishes that are typical of North Africa and the eastern Mediterranean. Cumin has a strong, spicy, sweet aroma with a slightly bitter, pungent taste. Like coriander, cumin is best dry-fried before grinding. Ready-ground cumin is available but quickly loses its flavour and aroma. Store whole and ground cumin seeds in an airtight jar, away from direct light.

Cinnamon

This has an aromatic, sweet flavour that is used widely in the eastern Mediterranean to flavour meat and pilau dishes, and to infuse milk and syrups for desserts.

Cinnamon sticks, which are pieces of the thin curled bark of the cinnamon tree, have the best flavour. Ground cinnamon is used for some dishes but it lacks the fresh, sweet flavour imparted by the whole spice.

Cardamom

This spice is usually associated with Indian cookery but its use extends to the eastern Mediterranean. The green or white pods should be pounded to release the small black seeds, which can then be bruised to accentuate their warm, almost lemon-like flavour. The pods are usually discarded.

Always buy whole, unsplit pods in small quantities as they lose their flavour quite quickly. Store in an airtight jar.

Nutmeg

The beautiful, sweet, warm aroma of this spice makes it a good addition to sweet and savoury dishes. It goes particularly well with spinach, cheese and eggs, and is often used in terrines and pâtés. Buy whole nutmegs, rather than the ready-ground spice, and grate them into dishes.

Mace

This is the thin, lacy covering of nutmeg. It is available ground to a powder or as thin "blades". It has a gentler, more subtle flavour than nutmeg.

FLAVOURINGS

Around the Mediterranean, various different ingredients are added to dishes to add extra flavour or to enhance those already present. In Italy, for example, good quality olive oil is drizzled liberally over many dishes, imparting a warm, nutty flavour, while in the eastern Mediterranean rose water is sometimes added to desserts, providing a wonderfully fragrant aroma and taste.

OLIVE OIL

This is indispensable to the Mediterranean cuisine. Not only is it valued for its cooking properties but also for its fine, nutty flavour. Italy, France and Spain produce some of the best quality olive oils. Oil produced from the first cold pressing of the olives is a rich green extra virgin oil. This should be used for flavouring dishes, for example drizzling over salads and pasta. Use less expensive oil from the second pressing for cooking.

VINEGAR

This flavouring is often added to dressings and sauces. The best vinegar is made from wines, which are fermented in oak casks to give a depth of flavour. Good vinegar should be aromatic, with no trace of bitterness, and should be transparent, not cloudy. White wine vinegar is pale golden with a pinkish tinge; red wine vinegar ranges from deep pink to dark red. They are often infused with herbs such as tarragon and rosemary, which gives them a rich aroma and flavour.

Dark brown balsamic vinegar has an extremely mellow, sweet flavour and is highly prized. It is made in the area around Modena in Italy; the boiled, concentrated juice of local grapes is aged in a series of barrels over a very long period, which gives it a slightly syrupy texture. It may be added to salad dressings or offered with olive oil for dipping bread into.

GARLIC

This is one of the most vital ingredients in Mediterranean cooking, and there are few recipes in which its addition would be out of place. Used crushed, sliced or whole, garlic develops a smooth, gentle flavour with long, slow cooking. Used raw in salads, mayonnaise and sauces, garlic has a hot, fierce impact. It is sold in strings or as separate bulbs. When buying garlic, check that the cloves are plump and firm.

CAPERS

These are the pickled buds of a shrub native to the Mediterranean region. The best quality capers are those preserved in salt rather than brine or vinegar. When capers are roughly chopped, their sharp, piquant tang is used to cut the richness of fatty meat such as lamb, enliven mild fish sauces and flavour various salads, dressings and pastes such as tapenade.

PESTO

This Italian sauce is traditionally made with fresh basil, pine nuts, Parmesan or Pecorino cheese and olive oil, but you may also find versions made from red (bell) peppers or sun-dried tomatoes. It has quite a strong flavour and is delicious used as a pasta sauce, added to risottos or tomato sauces, or stirred into minestrone or tomato-based soups to add extra flavour.

HOW TO MAKE PESTO

To make enough for 4–6 servings of pasta, put 115g/4oz fresh basil leaves in a mortar with 25g/1oz pine nuts, 2 peeled garlic cloves and a large pinch of coarse salt. Crush to a paste with a pestle, then work in 50g/2oz freshly grated Parmesan. Gradually add about 120ml/4fl oz extra virgin olive oil, working it in thoroughly with a wooden spoon to make a thick, creamy sauce. Use immediately or spoon into a jar, seal and store in the refrigerator. It will keep for up to a week.

TOMATO PURÉE/PASTE

This concentrated paste made from fresh tomatoes is perfect for boosting the flavour of bland tomatoes in soups, stews and sauces. Sun-dried tomato paste has an even richer, riper flavour. Both are available in jars, cans and tubes.

HARISSA

This hot and fiery red paste is used mostly in North African cooking. It is a spicy blend of chillies, garlic, cumin, coriander and cayenne and is available in small jars.

TAHINI

This oily paste is made from ground sesame seeds. It is popular in the Middle East and is combined with mashed chickpeas, garlic and olive oil to make hummus.

ORANGE RIND

Thinly pared strips of orange rind give a fresh fragrance to dishes. They are often added to French fish stews and soups.

ORANGE FLOWER WATER

This is distilled from orange blossoms and is very popular in eastern Mediterranean cooking. It is often added to desserts to impart a delicate floral flavour. It can be strong so should be used with restraint.

ROSE WATER

This distilled essence of rose petals is used mainly in eastern Mediterranean desserts, giving a mild rose fragrance and flavour. The strength varies so add with caution.

HONEY

This has been used as a sweetener since ancient times. Its flavour depends on the flowers on which the bees have fed for its individual fragrance and flavour. The Turks and Greeks use it in their syrupy pastries such as baklava, and small quantities are added to some savoury dishes.

APPETIZERS

Many Mediterranean countries are famous for their appetizers. The Italians serve wonderful antipasti, the Greeks provide meze and the Spanish make delicious tapas. An informal appetizer, one that is shared among guests with pre-dinner drinks or at the table, can be an effective ice-breaker. Choose Aubergine and Tahini Dip, which is served with pitta bread and crudités, or Hummus from Turkey or Tzatziki from Greece. Spinach Empanadillas are little Spanish pastry turnovers and Polpettes from Greece are little fried potato and feta cheese balls – both make a delightful start to a meal.

TOMATO & GARLIC BREAD

This appetizer is so simple yet it is packed with flavour. The sugar brings out the sweetness of ripe tomatoes while lemon gives the topping a lovely tang. Make the tomato mixture ahead of time if you wish and reheat briefly, stirring, before serving.

SERVES 4–6

INGREDIENTS
4 large ripe tomatoes, roughly chopped
2 garlic cloves, roughly chopped
1.5ml/¼ tsp sea salt
grated rind and juice of ½ lemon
5ml/1 tsp soft light brown sugar
1 flat loaf of bread, such as ciabatta
30ml/2 tbsp olive oil
ground black pepper

1 Preheat the oven to 200°C/400°F/Gas 6. Place the tomatoes, garlic, salt, lemon rind and brown sugar in a small pan. Cover and cook gently for 5 minutes until the tomatoes have released their juices and the mixture is quite watery.

2 Slice the loaf in half horizontally, then cut each half widthways into 2–3 pieces. Place on a baking sheet and bake for 5–8 minutes until the bread is hot, crisp and golden brown.

3 While the bread is baking, stir the lemon juice and olive oil into the tomato mixture, then cook uncovered for a further 8 minutes, or until the mixture is thick and pulpy.

4 Spread the tomato and garlic mixture on the hot bread, grind a generous amount of black pepper over the top and serve at once.

AUBERGINE & TAHINI DIP

This Turkish variation of a popular Middle Eastern dish is said to have been invented by the ladies of the sultan's harem. Aubergines are ideal for making a dip as the cooked flesh purées beautifully into a velvety paste with a slightly smoky accent.

SERVES 4–6

INGREDIENTS
3 aubergines (eggplant)
2 garlic cloves, crushed
60ml/4 tbsp tahini paste
juice of 2 lemons
15ml/1 tbsp paprika, plus extra to garnish
salt and ground black pepper
chopped fresh parsley, olive oil, plus a few olives, to garnish
pitta bread or crudités, to serve

1 Preheat the oven to 190°C/375°F/Gas 5. Slit the skins of the aubergines, place on a baking sheet and bake in the oven for about 30–40 minutes until the skins begin to split apart.

2 Place the aubergines on a chopping board. Carefully peel away and discard the skins, using a sharp knife, and roughly chop the flesh into chunks. Place the aubergine chunks in a food processor or blender.

3 Add the crushed garlic, tahini paste, lemon juice, paprika and salt and pepper to the food processor or blender. Blend to a smooth paste, adding about 15–30ml/1–2 tbsp cold water if the paste becomes too thick.

4 Spoon the purée into a small serving dish and make a shallow dip in the centre. Garnish with paprika, chopped parsley, a drizzle of olive oil and a few olives. Serve with warmed pitta bread or crudités.

HUMMUS

Blending chickpeas with garlic, olive oil and tahini paste makes a surprisingly creamy purée that is delicious served as part of a Turkish-style meze, or as a dip with a selection of colourful, crisp vegetables.

SERVES 4–6

INGREDIENTS
150g/5oz/³⁄4 cup dried chickpeas
juice of 2 lemons
2 garlic cloves, sliced
30ml/2 tbsp olive oil
pinch of cayenne pepper
150ml/¹⁄4 pint/²⁄3 cup tahini paste
salt and ground black pepper
extra olive oil and cayenne pepper, for sprinkling
flat leaf parsley, to garnish

1 Put the chickpeas in a large bowl and pour over plenty of cold water. Leave the chickpeas to soak overnight.

2 Drain the chickpeas, place in a pan and cover with fresh water. Bring to the boil and boil rapidly for 10 minutes. Reduce the heat and simmer gently for about 1 hour until soft. Drain.

3 Process the chickpeas in a food processor to a smooth purée. Add the lemon juice, garlic, olive oil, cayenne pepper and tahini, and blend until creamy, scraping the mixture down from the sides of the bowl.

4 Season the purée with salt and pepper and transfer to a serving dish. Sprinkle with olive oil and cayenne pepper, and serve garnished with parsley.

TZATZIKI

This refreshing yogurt and cucumber dish is served all over the eastern Mediterranean. It makes a good choice for an appetizer if the main course is rich and filling. It is traditionally served as part of a meze with marinated olives and pitta bread.

SERVES 6

INGREDIENTS
1 small cucumber
300ml/½ pint/1¼ cups thick natural (plain) yogurt
3 garlic cloves, crushed
30ml/2 tbsp chopped fresh mint
30ml/2 tbsp chopped fresh dill or parsley
salt and ground black pepper
mint or parsley and dill, to garnish
olive oil, olives and pitta bread, to serve

1 Finely chop the cucumber and layer in a colander with plenty of salt. Leave to drain for 30 minutes. Wash the cucumber in several changes of cold water and drain thoroughly. Pat dry on kitchen paper.

2 Mix together the yogurt, garlic and herbs and season with salt and black pepper. Stir in the cucumber. Garnish with herbs, drizzle over a little olive oil and serve with olives and pitta bread.

COOK'S TIP
Make sure you leave the salted cucumber for a full 30 minutes or the vegetable will retain too much moisture and the tzatziki will be too wet for dipping with the pitta bread.

Brandade de Morue

Salt cod is popular in Spain and France and it can be found cooked in a number of ways. This recipe is a purée, flavoured with garlic and olive oil.

Serves 6

Ingredients
675g/1½lb salt cod, soaked for 24 hours then drained
300ml/½ pint/1¼ cups olive oil
250ml/8fl oz/1 cup milk
1 garlic clove, crushed
grated nutmeg, lemon juice and ground white pepper, to taste
parsley sprigs, to garnish

For the croutes
50ml/2fl oz/¼ cup olive oil
6 slices white bread, crusts removed
1 garlic clove, halved

1 To make the croûtes, heat the oil in a frying pan. Cut the bread slices in half diagonally and fry in the oil until golden brown. Drain on kitchen paper, then rub on both sides with garlic.

2 Put the cod in a large pan, with enough cold water to cover. Cover the pan and bring to the boil. Simmer gently for 8–10 minutes, until just tender. Drain and cool. Flake the fish and discard any skin and bone.

3 Heat the oil in a pan until very hot. In a separate pan, scald the milk. Transfer the fish to a food processor and, with the motor running, slowly pour in the oil, followed by the milk, until the mixture is smooth. Transfer to a bowl and beat in the garlic. Season with nutmeg, lemon juice and pepper. Leave to cool, then chill.

4 Spoon the brandade into a shallow serving bowl and surround with the croûtes. Garnish with parsley sprigs and serve.

TARAMASALATA

This delicious Turkish and Greek speciality makes an excellent appetizer. It is traditionally made with tarama – pale orange smoked carp roe – but smoked mullet roe produces equally good results.

SERVES 4

INGREDIENTS
115g/4oz smoked mullet roe
2 garlic cloves, crushed
30ml/2 tbsp grated onion
60ml/4 tbsp olive oil
4 slices white bread, crusts removed
juice of 2 lemons
30ml/2 tbsp water or milk
paprika, to garnish (optional)

1 Place the smoked mullet roe, garlic, onion, olive oil, bread and lemon juice in a food processor or blender and process briefly until smooth.

2 Add the water or milk and process again for a few seconds. (This will give the taramasalata a creamier, more luxurious texture.)

3 Tip the taramasalata into a serving bowl, cover with clear film (plastic wrap) and chill for 1–2 hours before serving. When you are ready to serve, sprinkle with a little paprika, if liked.

COOK'S TIP
Since the roe of grey mullet tends to be rather expensive, smoked cod's roe is often used in its place for this dish. Smoked cod's roe is much paler than the burnt-orange colour of mullet roe but is still very good, producing a flavoursome dip.

Tapenade & Herb Aioli with Summer Vegetables

A beautiful platter of salad vegetables served with olive tapenade and creamy garlic aioli makes a thoroughly delicious and informal appetizer. This colourful French hors d'oeuvre is perfect for entertaining.

SERVES 6

INGREDIENTS
175g/6oz/1½ cups pitted black olives
50g/2oz can anchovy fillets, drained
30ml/2 tbsp capers
120ml/4fl oz/½ cup olive oil
finely grated rind of 1 lemon
15ml/1 tbsp brandy (optional)
ground black pepper
2 egg yolks
5ml/1 tsp Dijon mustard
10ml/2 tsp white wine vinegar
250ml/8fl oz/1 cup light olive oil
45ml/3 tbsp chopped mixed fresh herbs, such as chervil, parsley or tarragon
30ml/2 tbsp chopped watercress
5 garlic cloves, crushed
salt and ground black pepper

TO SERVE
2 red (bell) peppers, seeded and cut into wide strips
30ml/2 tbsp olive oil
225g/8oz new potatoes
115g/4oz green beans
225g/8oz baby carrots
225g/8oz young asparagus
12 quail's eggs (optional)
fresh herbs, to garnish
coarse salt, for sprinkling

1 To make the tapenade, finely chop the olives, anchovies and capers and beat together with the oil, lemon rind and brandy, if using. (Alternatively, lightly process the ingredients in a food processor or blender, scraping down the mixture from the sides of the bowl if necessary.) Season with pepper and blend in a little more oil if the mixture is very dry. Transfer to a serving dish.

2 To make the aioli, beat together the egg yolks, mustard and vinegar. Gradually blend in the oil, a trickle at a time, whisking well after each addition until thick and smooth. Season with salt and pepper to taste, adding a little more vinegar if the aioli tastes bland. Stir in the mixed herbs, watercress and garlic, then transfer to a serving dish. Cover and put in the refrigerator.

3 Put the peppers on a foil-lined grill (broiler) rack and brush with the oil. Grill (broil) under a high heat until just beginning to char.

4 Cook the new potatoes in a large pan of boiling, salted water until just tender. Add the beans and carrots and cook for 1 minute. Add the asparagus and cook for a further 30 seconds. Drain the vegetables. Cook the quail's eggs in boiling water for 2 minutes, if using. Drain and remove half of each shell.

5 Arrange all the vegetables, eggs and sauces on a serving platter. Garnish with fresh herbs and serve with coarse salt for sprinkling.

YOGURT CHEESE IN OLIVE OIL

Sheep's milk is widely used in cheese making in the eastern Mediterranean, particularly in Greece where sheep's yogurt is drained in muslin before patting into balls of soft cheese. Here it's bottled in olive oil with chilli and herbs.

FILLS TWO 450G/1LB JARS

INGREDIENTS
750g/1¾lb Greek (US strained plain) sheep's yogurt
2.5ml/½ tsp salt
10ml/2 tsp crushed dried chillies or chilli powder
15ml/1 tbsp chopped fresh rosemary
15ml/1 tbsp chopped fresh thyme or oregano
about 300ml/½ pint/1¼ cups olive oil, preferably garlic-flavoured
toasted bread to serve

1 Steep a 30cm/12in square of muslin (cheesecloth) in boiling water. Drain and lay over a large plate. Mix the yogurt with the salt and tip on to the centre of the muslin. Bring up the sides of the muslin and tie firmly with string. Hang the bag on a kitchen cupboard handle (where it is quite cool) and place a bowl underneath to catch the whey. Leave to drain for 2–3 days.

2 Sterilize two 450g/1lb glass preserving or jam jars by heating them in the oven at 150°C/300°F/Gas 2 for 15 minutes. Mix together the chilli and herbs.

3 Take teaspoonfuls of the cheese and roll into balls with your hands. Lower into the jars, sprinkling each layer with the herb mixture. Pour the oil over the cheese until completely covered. Store in the refrigerator for up to 3 weeks.

4 To serve the cheese, spoon out of the jars with a little of the flavoured olive oil and spread on to lightly toasted bread.

Marinated Pimientos

Pimientos are simply cooked, skinned peppers. You can buy them in cans or jars, but they are much tastier when home-made. Here they are marinated in their own juices, with added flavourings, to make a flavoursome appetizer.

SERVES 2–4

INGREDIENTS
3 red (bell) peppers
2 small garlic cloves, crushed
45ml/3 tbsp chopped fresh parsley
15ml/1 tbsp sherry vinegar
30ml/2 tbsp olive oil
salt

1 Preheat the grill (broiler) to high. Place the peppers on a baking sheet and grill (broil) for 8–12 minutes, turning occasionally, until the skins have blistered and blackened. Remove the peppers from the heat, cover with a clean dishtowel and leave for 5 minutes so that the steam softens the skin.

2 Make a small cut in the bottom of each pepper and squeeze out the juice into a small jug (pitcher). Peel away the skin and cut the peppers in half. Remove and discard the core, seeds and any pith.

3 Using a sharp knife, cut each pepper in half lengthways into 1cm/½in-wide strips and place them in a small bowl.

4 Add the crushed garlic, parsley, vinegar and olive oil to the pepper juices and whisk well to combine. Add salt to taste. Pour the dressing over the pepper strips and toss well. Cover and chill, but, if possible, bring the peppers back to room temperature before serving.

Tapas of Almonds, Olives & Cheese

These three simple ingredients are lightly flavoured with herbs and spices to create a delicious combination of Spanish tapas that's perfect for a casual appetizer served either with pre-dinner drinks or at the table.

SERVES 6–8

INGREDIENTS

FOR THE MARINATED OLIVES
2.5ml/½ tsp coriander seeds
2.5ml/½ tsp fennel seeds
5ml/1 tsp chopped fresh rosemary
10ml/2 tsp chopped fresh parsley
2 garlic cloves, crushed
15ml/1 tbsp sherry vinegar
30ml/2 tbsp olive oil
115g/4oz/⅔ cup black olives
115g/4oz/⅔ cup green olives

FOR THE MARINATED CHEESE
150g/5oz goat's cheese, preferably manchego
90ml/6 tbsp olive oil
15ml/1 tbsp white wine vinegar
5ml/1 tsp black peppercorns
1 garlic clove, sliced
3 fresh tarragon or thyme sprigs
tarragon sprigs, to garnish

FOR THE SALTED ALMONDS
1.5ml/¼ tsp cayenne pepper
30ml/2 tbsp sea salt
25g/1oz/2 tbsp butter
60ml/4 tbsp olive oil
200g/7oz/1¾ cups blanched almonds
extra salt for sprinkling (optional)

1 To make the marinated olives, crush the coriander and fennel seeds with a mortar and pestle. Mix together with the rosemary, parsley, garlic, vinegar and olive oil and pour over the olives in a small bowl. Cover with clear film (plastic wrap) and chill for up to 1 week.

2 To make the marinated cheese, cut the cheese into bitesize pieces, leaving the rind on. Mix together the olive oil, wine vinegar, peppercorns, garlic and tarragon or thyme sprigs and pour over the cheese in a small bowl. Cover with clear film (plastic wrap) and chill for up to 3 days.

3 To make the salted almonds, mix together the cayenne pepper and salt in a bowl. Melt the butter with the olive oil in a frying pan. Add the almonds to the pan and fry, stirring for about 5 minutes, until the almonds are golden.

4 Tip the almonds out of the frying pan, into the salt mixture and toss together until the almonds are well coated. Leave to cool, then store the nuts in a jar or airtight container for up to 1 week.

5 To serve the tapas, arrange the olives, cheese and nuts in small, shallow serving dishes. Use fresh sprigs of tarragon to garnish the marinated cheese and sprinkle the almonds with a little more salt, if liked.

COOK'S TIP
If you are serving the tapas with pre-dinner drinks, provide cocktail sticks (toothpicks) for spearing the black and green olives and the cheese, and provide a small dish for olive pits.

Roasted Pepper Antipasto with Sun-dried Tomatoes

Jars of Italian mixed peppers in olive oil are now commonly available in most supermarkets. None, however, can compete with this colourful, freshly made version, which makes a perfect appetizer.

Serves 6

Ingredients
3 red (bell) peppers
2 yellow or orange (bell) peppers
2 green (bell) peppers
50g/2oz/½ cup sun-dried tomatoes in oil, drained
1 garlic clove
30ml/2 tbsp balsamic vinegar
75ml/5 tbsp olive oil
a few drops of chilli sauce
4 canned artichoke hearts, drained and sliced
salt and ground black pepper
fresh basil leaves, to garnish

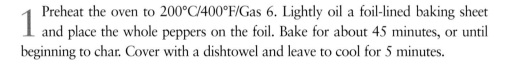

1 Preheat the oven to 200°C/400°F/Gas 6. Lightly oil a foil-lined baking sheet and place the whole peppers on the foil. Bake for about 45 minutes, or until beginning to char. Cover with a dishtowel and leave to cool for 5 minutes.

2 Meanwhile, slice the sun-dried tomatoes into thin strips. Thinly slice the garlic, and set it aside. In a small jug (pitcher) beat together the vinegar, oil and chilli sauce, then season with a little salt and ground black pepper.

3 Peel and slice the peppers. Mix with the artichoke hearts, tomatoes and garlic. Pour over the dressing. Serve scattered with the basil leaves.

Marinated Baby Aubergines with Raisins & Pine Nuts

Aubergines are popular in all the Mediterranean countries. This recipe has an Italian influence, using ingredients that have been used since Renaissance times. Prepare a day in advance, to allow the flavours to develop.

Serves 4

Ingredients

12 baby aubergines (eggplant), halved lengthways
250ml/8fl oz/1 cup extra virgin olive oil
juice of 1 lemon
30ml/2 tbsp balsamic vinegar
3 cloves
25g/1oz/⅓ cup pine nuts
25g/1oz/2 tbsp raisins
15ml/1 tbsp granulated sugar
1 bay leaf
large pinch of dried chilli flakes
salt and ground black pepper

1 Preheat the grill (broiler) to high. Place the aubergines, cut side up, in the grill pan and brush with a little of the olive oil. Grill (broil) for 10 minutes, or until slightly blackened, turning halfway through cooking.

2 Meanwhile, make the marinade. Put the remaining olive oil, the lemon juice, vinegar, cloves, pine nuts, raisins, sugar and bay leaf in a jug (pitcher). Add the chilli flakes and season with salt and pepper. Mix well.

3 Place the grilled aubergines in an earthenware or glass bowl, and pour over the marinade. Leave to cool, turning once or twice. Serve cold.

STUFFED VINE LEAVES WITH GARLIC YOGURT

This Greek recipe comes in many guises. This meatless version is highly flavoured with fresh herbs, lemon rind and a little dried chilli. The simple addition of garlic-flavoured yogurt turns this dish into a sophisticated appetizer.

SERVES 6

INGREDIENTS
225g/8oz packet preserved vine leaves
1 onion, finely chopped
½ bunch of spring onions (scallions), trimmed and finely chopped
60ml/4 tbsp chopped fresh parsley
10 large mint sprigs, chopped
finely grated rind of 1 lemon
2.5ml/½ tsp crushed dried chillies
7.5ml/1½ tsp fennel seeds, crushed
175g/6oz/scant 1 cup long grain rice
120ml/4fl oz/½ cup olive oil
150ml/¼ pint/⅔ cup thick natural (plain) yogurt
2 garlic cloves, crushed
salt
lemon wedges and mint leaves, to garnish (optional)

COOK'S TIP
To check that the rice is cooked, lift out one stuffed leaf and cut in half. The rice should have expanded and softened to make a firm parcel. If necessary, cook the stuffed leaves a little longer, adding a little more boiling water if needed.

1 Rinse the vine leaves in plenty of cold water. Put in a bowl, cover with boiling water and leave to stand for 10 minutes. Drain thoroughly.

2 Mix together the onion, spring onions, parsley, mint, lemon rind, chilli, fennel seeds, rice and 25ml/1½ tbsp of the oil. Mix well and season.

3 Place a vine leaf, veined side facing upwards, on a work surface and cut off any protruding stalk. Place a heaped teaspoonful of the rice mixture near the stalk end of the leaf. Fold the stalk end of the leaf over the rice filling, then fold over the sides and carefully roll up into a neat cigar shape.

4 Repeat this process with the remaining filling to make about 24 stuffed leaves. If some of the vine leaves are quite small, use two and patch them together to make parcels of about the same size.

5 Place any remaining leaves in the base of a large heavy pan. Pack the stuffed leaves in a single layer in the pan. Spoon over the remaining oil then add about 300ml/½ pint/1¼ cups boiling water.

6 Place a small heatproof plate over the leaves to keep them submerged in the water. Cover the pan and cook on a very low heat for 45 minutes.

7 Meanwhile, mix together the yogurt and crushed garlic and put in a small serving dish. Transfer the stuffed vine leaves to a serving plate and garnish with lemon wedges and mint, if you like. Serve hot or cold, with the garlic yogurt.

SPINACH EMPANADILLAS

These little pastry turnovers are quite delicious. The spinach and anchovy filling is given a strong Moorish accent by the inclusion of pine nuts and raisins. The sweetness of the raisins and the texture of the chopped pine nuts adds another dimension to the filling.

MAKES 20

INGREDIENTS
25g/1oz/2 tbsp raisins
25ml/1½ tbsp olive oil
450g/1lb fresh spinach, washed and chopped
6 canned anchovies, drained and chopped
2 garlic cloves, finely chopped
25g/1oz/⅓ cup pine nuts, chopped
350g/12oz ready-made puff pastry
1 egg, beaten
salt and ground black pepper

1 To make the filling, soak the raisins in a little warm water for 10 minutes. Drain, then chop roughly. Heat the oil in a large sauté pan or wok, add the spinach, stir, then cover and cook over a low heat for about 2 minutes. Uncover, turn up the heat and let any liquid evaporate.

2 Add the anchovies and garlic to the pan or wok and season with salt and pepper. Cook, stirring, for a further minute. Remove from the heat, add the raisins and pine nuts, and set aside to cool.

3 Preheat the oven to 180°C/350°F/Gas 4. Roll out the puff pastry to a 3mm/⅛in thickness. Using a 7.5cm/3in pastry cutter, cut out 20 rounds, re-rolling the dough if necessary.

4 Place about two teaspoonfuls of the filling in the middle of each round, then brush the edges with a little water. Bring up the sides of the pastry and seal well. Press the edges together with the back of a fork. Brush with egg. Place the turnovers on a lightly greased baking sheet and bake for about 15 minutes, until golden. Serve the empanadillas warm.

MEAT BRIOUATES

The Moroccans, who enjoy the taste of sweet and savoury together, traditionally sprinkle these little pastry snacks with ground cinnamon and icing sugar. It is an unusual but delicious combination.

MAKES ABOUT 24

INGREDIENTS
30ml/2 tbsp sunflower oil
1 onion, finely chopped
1 small bunch fresh coriander (cilantro), chopped
1 small bunch fresh parsley, chopped
375g/12oz lean minced (ground) beef or lamb
2.5ml/½ tsp paprika
5ml/1 tsp ground coriander
good pinch of ground ginger
2 eggs, beaten
175g/6oz filo pastry
40g/1½oz/3 tbsp butter, melted
sunflower oil, for frying
fresh flat leaf parsley, to garnish
ground cinnamon and icing sugar, to serve (optional)

1 Heat the sunflower oil in a frying pan and fry the onion and fresh coriander and parsley over a low heat for 4 minutes. Add the meat and cook for 5 minutes, stirring, until evenly browned and most of the moisture has evaporated. Stir in the paprika, coriander and ginger and cook for 1 minute. Remove from the heat and stir in the beaten eggs until they are lightly scrambled. Set aside.

2 Cut a sheet of filo pastry into 8.5cm/3½in strips. Cover the remaining pastry with clear film (plastic wrap). Brush the pastry with melted butter, then place a teaspoonful of the filling at a corner of the strip. Fold over a corner to make a triangular shape. Continue folding to the end of the strip. Repeat for the rest of the pastries.

3 Heat 1cm/½in oil in a heavy pan and fry the briouates in batches for about 2 minutes, or until golden, turning once. Drain on kitchen paper. Serve garnished with parsley and sprinkled with cinnamon and icing sugar, if liked.

Feta & Mozzarella Cheese Pasties

In Turkey, these little stuffed pasties, known as böreks, *are very popular. They are easy to make and are ideal as an appetizer. The feta and mozzarella cheese filling is delicately flavoured with fresh parsley, chives and mint.*

MAKES 35–40

INGREDIENTS
225g/8oz feta cheese, grated
225g/8oz mozzarella, grated
2 eggs, beaten
45ml/3 tbsp chopped fresh parsley
45ml/3 tbsp chopped fresh chives
45ml/3 tbsp chopped fresh mint
pinch of nutmeg
225g/8oz filo pastry
45–60ml/3–4 tbsp melted butter
ground black pepper

1 Preheat the oven to 180°C/350°F/Gas 4. In a bowl, blend the grated feta and mozzarella cheeses with the beaten eggs. Add the chopped herbs, season with nutmeg and black pepper, and stir well to combine.

2 Using a sharp knife, cut each sheet of pastry into four rectangular strips approximately 7.5cm/3in wide. Cover all but one or two strips of the pastry with a clean, damp dishtowel to prevent them from drying out. Brush one strip of pastry at a time with a little melted butter.

3 Place a teaspoonful of filling at the bottom edge. Fold one corner over the filling to make a triangular shape. Continue folding the pastry over itself until you get to the end of the strip. Keep making triangles until all the mixture is used up.

4 Place the pasties on a greased baking sheet and bake in the oven for about 30 minutes until golden brown and crisp. Serve warm or cold.

Deep-fried New Potatoes with Saffron Aioli

This is a delightfully simple appetizer. Aioli is a Spanish garlic mayonnaise, very similar to the French mayonnaise of the same name. In this recipe the inclusion of saffron adds colour and a subtle flavour.

SERVES 4

INGREDIENTS
1 egg yolk
2.5ml/½ tsp Dijon mustard
300ml/½ pint/1¼ cups extra virgin olive oil
15–30ml/1–2 tbsp lemon juice
1 garlic clove, crushed
2.5ml/½ tsp saffron strands
20 baby new potatoes
vegetable oil, for frying
salt and ground black pepper

1 To make the aioli, put the egg yolk in a bowl with the mustard and a pinch of salt. Beat together with a wooden spoon. Still beating, add the olive oil very slowly, drop by drop to begin with, then, as the aioli gradually thickens, in a thin stream. Add the lemon juice and salt and ground black pepper to taste, then beat in the crushed garlic.

2 Place the saffron in a small bowl, and add 10ml/2 tsp hot water. Press the saffron with the back of a teaspoon, to extract the colour and flavour, and leave to infuse for 5 minutes. Beat the saffron and the liquid into the mayonnaise.

3 Cook the potatoes in boiling salted water for 5 minutes, then turn off the heat. Cover the pan and leave for a further 15 minutes. Drain, then dry well.

4 Heat 1cm/½in oil in a deep pan. When the oil is very hot, add the potatoes, and fry quickly, turning, until crisp and golden. Drain on kitchen paper, and serve with the saffron aioli.

ARTICHOKE RICE CAKES

These delicious little appetizers are filled with Manchego cheese, which melts when the rice cakes are fried. They make an great tapas dish and are delicious served with aioli and salt-cured salmon.

SERVES 6

INGREDIENTS
1 globe artichoke
50g/2oz/¼ cup butter
1 small onion, finely chopped
1 garlic clove, finely chopped
115g/4oz/⅔ cup risotto rice
450ml/¾ pint/scant 2 cups hot chicken stock
50g/2oz/¼ cup freshly grated Parmesan cheese
150g/5oz Manchego cheese, very finely diced
45–60ml/3–4 tbsp fine cornmeal
olive oil, for frying
salt and ground black pepper

1 Remove and discard the stalk, leaves and choke from the artichoke. Finely chop the heart. Melt the butter in a pan and gently fry the chopped artichoke, onion and garlic for about 5 minutes until softened. Stir in the rice and cook for 1 minute.

2 Increase the heat and gradually pour the stock into the pan, stirring constantly, until all the liquid has been absorbed and the rice is cooked. This should take about 20 minutes. Season well and stir in the Parmesan cheese. Transfer to a bowl, leave to cool, then chill for at least 2 hours.

3 Put a tablespoonful of the chilled rice mixture into the palm of one hand and flatten slightly. Place a few pieces of diced cheese in the centre and shape the rice around it to make a ball. Flatten slightly, then roll in cornmeal. Repeat with the remaining mixture to make about twelve cakes.

4 Shallow-fry the cakes in olive oil for about 5 minutes until golden brown. Drain on kitchen paper and serve hot.

POLPETTES

These delicious little fried morsels of potato and Greek feta cheese are flavoured with fresh dill and lemon juice. The mixture is chilled before being shaped into polpettes to allow for easier handling.

SERVES 4

INGREDIENTS
500g/1¼lb potatoes, scrubbed
115g/4oz feta cheese
4 spring onions (scallions), chopped
45ml/3 tbsp chopped fresh dill
1 egg, beaten
15ml/1 tbsp lemon juice
45ml/3 tbsp olive oil
salt and ground black pepper
plain (all-purpose) flour, for dredging
lemon wedges, to serve

1 Boil the potatoes in their skins in a large pan of lightly salted water until soft. Drain, then peel while still warm. Place the potatoes in a bowl and mash.

2 Crumble the feta cheese into the potatoes and add the spring onions, dill, egg and lemon juice and season to taste. Cover and chill for about 1 hour until firm.

3 Divide the chilled potato mixture into walnut-size balls, then flatten them slightly. Place on a plate and dredge with flour.

4 Heat the olive oil in a frying pan and fry the polpettes in batches until golden brown all over, turning once. Drain on kitchen paper and serve immediately while still hot with lemon wedges for squeezing over.

COOK'S TIP
Feta cheese is very salty, so be sure to taste the mixture before adding extra salt.

DATES STUFFED WITH CHORIZO

This delicious dish from Spain combines sweet fresh dates with highly flavoured, spicy chorizo sausage. The flavours complement each other perfectly and the bacon wrapping secures them into bitesize parcels.

SERVES 4–6

INGREDIENTS
50g/2oz chorizo sausage
12 fresh dates, stoned (pitted)
6 streaky (fatty) bacon rashers (slices)
oil, for frying
plain (all-purpose) flour for dusting
1 egg, beaten
50g/2oz/1 cup fresh breadcrumbs

1 Trim the ends of the chorizo sausage and carefully peel away the skin. Cut into three 2cm/¾in slices. Cut these in half lengthways and then into quarters, giving 12 pieces.

2 Stuff each date with a piece of chorizo, closing the date around it. Stretch the bacon, by running the back of a knife along the rasher. Cut each rasher in half, widthways. Wrap a piece of bacon around each stuffed date and secure with a cocktail stick (toothpick).

3 In a deep pan, heat 1cm/½in of oil. Dust the dates with flour, dip them in the beaten egg, then coat in breadcrumbs. Fry the dates in the hot oil, turning them, until golden. Remove the dates with a slotted spoon, and drain well on kitchen paper. Serve immediately.

Chorizo in Olive Oil

Spanish chorizo sausage has a deliciously pungent taste; its robust seasoning of garlic, chilli and paprika flavours the ingredients it is cooked with. Frying chorizo with onions and olive oil makes a simple and delicious appetizer.

SERVES 4

INGREDIENTS
75ml/5 tbsp extra virgin olive oil
350g/12oz chorizo sausage, sliced
1 large onion, thinly sliced
roughly chopped fresh flat leaf parsley, to garnish
warm bread, to serve

1 Heat the olive oil in a large, heavy frying pan and fry the chorizo sausage over a high heat until beginning to colour. Remove the chorizo from the pan with a slotted spoon and set aside.

2 Add the onion to the pan and fry gently until coloured. Return the sausage slices to the pan and heat through for about 1 minute.

3 Tip the sausage and onion mixture into a shallow serving dish and scatter with the chopped parsley. Serve with warm bread.

VARIATION
Chorizo is usually available in large supermarkets or delicatessens. Other similarly rich, spicy sausages can be used as a substitute.

CHORIZO IN RED WINE

This simple dish is flamed with brandy just before serving. If you wish, use small chorizo sausages and leave them whole. Provide cocktail sticks (toothpicks) for your guests to spear the richly flavoured sausage.

SERVES 4

INGREDIENTS
225g/8oz cured chorizo sausage
90ml/6 tbsp red wine
30ml/2 tbsp brandy
chopped fresh parsley, to garnish

1 Prick the chorizo in several places using a fork, and place in a pan with the wine. Bring to the boil, lower the heat, then cover and simmer for 15 minutes. Remove from the heat and leave to cool, covered, for about 2 hours.

2 Remove the sausage from the pan and reserve the wine. Cut the sausage into 1cm/½in slices using a sharp knife, then heat in a heavy frying pan. Pour over the brandy and light with a match. When the flames have died down, add the reserved wine and cook for 2–3 minutes until hot. Serve garnished with parsley.

LAMB KEFTAS

This traditional Moroccan dish of spiced lamb skewers is very easy to prepare. Robustly flavoured lamb has a natural affinity with refreshing mint, so the cool mint and yogurt dressing complements the keftas beautifully.

MAKES 12–14

INGREDIENTS
675g/1½lb lamb
1 onion, quartered
3–4 fresh parsley sprigs
2–3 fresh coriander (cilantro) sprigs
1–2 fresh mint sprigs
2.5ml/½ tsp ground cumin
2.5ml/½ tsp mixed spice (apple pie spice)
5ml/1 tsp paprika
salt and ground black pepper
Moroccan bread, to serve

FOR THE DRESSING
30ml/2 tbsp finely chopped fresh mint
90ml/6 tbsp natural (plain) yogurt

1 Roughly chop the lamb, place in a food processor and process until smooth. Transfer the meat to a plate.

2 Place the onion and parsley, coriander and mint sprigs in the food processor and process until finely chopped. Add the lamb together with the cumin, mixed spice, paprika and salt and pepper and process again until very smooth. Transfer to a bowl and chill for about 1 hour.

3 To make the dressing, blend the chopped fresh mint with the natural yogurt in a food processor or blender and then chill in the refrigerator until required.

4 Mould the meat into small sausage shapes and skewer with wooden or metal kebab sticks. Preheat a grill (broiler) or barbecue. Cook the keftas for about 5 minutes, turning once. Serve immediately with the mint dressing. Moroccan bread makes a good accompaniment.

MARINATED ANCHOVIES

Make these at least 1 hour and up to 24 hours in advance to allow the flavours to develop fully. Fresh anchovies are tiny, so be prepared to spend time filleting them – the results will be well worth the effort.

SERVES 4

INGREDIENTS
225g/8oz fresh anchovies
juice of 3 lemons
30ml/2 tbsp extra virgin olive oil
2 garlic cloves, finely chopped
15ml/1 tbsp chopped fresh parsley
flaked sea salt

1 To fillet the anchovies, cut off the heads and tails, then split them open down one side. Open each one out flat and lift out the bone. Arrange the fish skin side down on a large plate. Sprinkle over two-thirds of the lemon juice and the salt.

2 Cover the anchovies with clear film (plastic wrap) and place in the refrigerator. Leave to marinate for 1–24 hours, basting the fish occasionally with the juices, until the flesh becomes white and no longer translucent.

3 Transfer the anchovies to a serving plate and drizzle over the extra virgin olive oil and the remaining lemon juice. Scatter over the chopped garlic and parsley, cover and chill until ready to serve.

COOK'S TIP
Since fresh anchovies can be hard to come by, freeze them when they are in plentiful supply. Fillet each fish, then pack them in a freezerproof container, separating the layers with clear film (plastic wrap).

FRIED WHITEBAIT
WITH HOT SHERRY SALSA

This Spanish dish is a wonderfully different way to serve whitebait. Make sure you use sweet sherry – an oloroso would be ideal – as a dry variety will not provide the richness of flavour required for the salsa.

SERVES 4

INGREDIENTS
225g/8oz whitebait, thawed if frozen
30ml/2 tbsp seasoned plain (all-purpose) flour
60ml/4 tbsp olive oil
60ml/4 tbsp vegetable oil

FOR THE SALSA
1 shallot, finely chopped
2 garlic cloves, finely chopped
4 ripe tomatoes, roughly chopped
1 small red chilli, seeded and finely chopped
30ml/2 tbsp olive oil
60ml/4 tbsp sweet sherry
30–45ml/2–3 tbsp chopped fresh herbs, such as basil, parsley or coriander (cilantro)
25g/1oz/½ cup fresh white breadcrumbs
salt and ground black pepper

1 To make the salsa, place the shallot, garlic, tomatoes, chilli and oil in a pan. Cover with a lid and cook gently for 10 minutes. Pour in the sherry and season to taste. Stir in the herbs and breadcrumbs, then cover and keep hot.

2 Wash the whitebait, drain well, then dust in the flour. Heat both oils together in a frying pan and fry the fish in batches until crisp and golden. Drain on kitchen paper and keep warm while you fry the rest. Serve at once with the salsa.

King Prawns in Sherry

These prawns are simply fried and flavoured with sherry. The addition of Tabasco sauce adds a fiery accent to the dish. Use whichever sherry you prefer – Fino, Amontillado and Oloroso work equally well, each imparting a subtly different taste.

SERVES 4

INGREDIENTS
12 raw king or tiger prawns (jumbo shrimp), peeled
30ml/2 tbsp olive oil
30ml/2 tbsp sherry
a few drops of Tabasco sauce
salt and ground black pepper

1 Make a shallow cut down the back of each prawn using a sharp knife, then pull out and discard the dark intestinal tract. Rinse under cold running water and pat dry on kitchen paper.

2 Heat the oil in a heavy frying pan and fry the prawns for 2–3 minutes until pink. Pour over the sherry and season with Tabasco sauce, salt and pepper. Tip into a dish and serve immediately.

ITALIAN PRAWN SKEWERS

These simple and delicious skewers are from the Amalfi coast in Italy. Prawns are coated in garlic-flavoured breadcrumbs then grilled until golden and deliciously crispy. They are served with lemon wedges for squeezing over.

SERVES 4

INGREDIENTS
900g/2lb raw tiger prawns (jumbo shrimp), peeled
60ml/4 tbsp olive oil
45ml/3 tbsp vegetable oil
75g/3oz/1¼ cups very fine dry breadcrumbs
1 garlic clove, crushed
15ml/1 tbsp chopped fresh parsley
salt and ground black pepper
lemon wedges, to serve

1 Make a shallow cut down the back of each prawn using a sharp knife, then pull out and discard the dark intestinal tract. Rinse under cold running water and pat dry on kitchen paper.

2 Put the olive oil and vegetable oil in a large bowl and add the prawns, mixing them to coat evenly. Add the breadcrumbs, crushed garlic and parsley and season with salt and ground black pepper. Toss the prawns thoroughly, to give them an even coating of breadcrumbs. Cover with clear film (plastic wrap) and leave to marinate for about 1 hour.

3 Thread the prawns on to four metal or previously soaked wooden skewers, curling them up as you do so, so that the tail is skewered in the middle.

4 Preheat the grill (broiler). Place the skewers in the grill pan and cook the prawns for about 2 minutes on each side, until the breadcrumbs are an even golden colour. Serve with lemon wedges.

GARLIC PRAWNS

For this simple Spanish tapas dish, you really need fresh raw prawns which absorb the flavours of the garlic and chilli as they are fried. Have everything ready for last-minute cooking so you can take it to the table still sizzling.

SERVES 4

INGREDIENTS
350–450g/12oz–1lb large raw prawns (shrimp)
2 fresh red chillies
75ml/5 tbsp olive oil
3 garlic cloves, crushed
salt and ground black pepper

1 Remove the heads and shells from the prawns, leaving the tails intact. Halve each chilli lengthways and discard the seeds.

2 Heat the olive oil in a flameproof pan, suitable for serving. (Alternatively, use a frying pan and have a warmed serving dish ready in the oven.)

3 Add all the prawns, chilli and garlic to the pan and cook over a high heat for about 3 minutes, stirring until the prawns turn pink. Season lightly with salt and pepper and serve immediately.

FRIED SQUID

The squid is simply dusted in flour and dipped in egg before being fried so the coating is light, and does not mask the delicate flavour. Be careful not to cook them for too long or their texture will become rubbery.

SERVES 4

INGREDIENTS
115g/4oz prepared squid, cut into rings
30ml/2 tbsp seasoned plain (all-purpose) flour
1 egg
30ml/2 tbsp milk
olive oil, for frying
sea salt
lemon wedges, to serve

1 Toss the squid rings in the seasoned flour in a bowl or strong plastic bag, until evenly coated. Beat the egg and milk together in a shallow bowl. Heat the olive oil in a heavy frying pan.

2 Dip the floured squid rings one at a time into the egg mixture, shaking off any excess liquid. Add to the hot oil, in batches if necessary, and fry for 2–3 minutes on each side until golden.

3 Lift the fried squid out of the pan with a slotted spoon and drain well on kitchen paper. Sprinkle with sea salt. Transfer the squid to a small warm serving plate and serve with the lemon wedges.

SOUPS

These dishes play an important part in the culinary heritage of the countries surrounding the Mediterranean. They are very versatile, making the best use of local produce, and may be served in many different ways – as an appetizer, a light lunch or a hearty main course. Chilled soups such as Spanish Gazpacho and Middle Eastern Yogurt and Cucumber Soup with Fresh Mint are perfect for warm Mediterranean evenings. Hearty, stew-like soups such as robust Moroccan Chickpea and Parsley Soup and Bouillabaisse, the traditional French fisherman's soup, are also popular throughout the region.

CHILLED ALMOND SOUP WITH GRAPES

This Spanish soup is very simple to make and wonderfully refreshing to eat on a hot day. Unless you have the time to spend pounding the ingredients for this dish by hand, a food processor or blender is essential.

SERVES 6

INGREDIENTS
115g/4oz fresh white bread
115g/4oz/1 cup blanched almonds
2 garlic cloves, sliced
75ml/5 tbsp olive oil
25ml/1½ tbsp sherry vinegar
seedless green and black grapes, halved and skinned
salt and ground black pepper
toasted flaked (slivered) almonds, to garnish

1 Break the white bread into a bowl and pour over 150ml/¼ pint/⅔ cup cold water. Leave to soak for 5 minutes.

2 Put the almonds and garlic in a food processor or blender and process until very finely ground. Add the soaked white bread and blend again. Gradually add the olive oil until the mixture forms a smooth paste. Then add the sherry vinegar along with 600ml/1 pint/2½ cups cold water and process until smooth.

3 Transfer the mixture to a large bowl and season with salt and pepper, adding a little more water if the soup is very thick. Chill for at least 2 hours.

4 When you are ready to serve, ladle the soup into individual bowls, add a few skinned grapes and scatter with the toasted almonds.

YOGURT & CUCUMBER SOUP WITH FRESH MINT

Yogurt is used extensively in Middle Eastern cookery, and is usually made at home. Sometimes it is added at the end of cooking a dish, to prevent it from curdling, but in this cold soup the yogurt is one of the main ingredients.

SERVES 4

INGREDIENTS
1 large cucumber, peeled
300ml/½ pint/1¼ cups single (light) cream
150ml/¼ pint/⅔ cup natural (plain) yogurt
2 garlic cloves, crushed
30ml/2 tbsp white wine vinegar
15ml/1 tbsp chopped fresh mint
salt and ground black pepper
sprigs of mint, to garnish

1 Grate the cucumber coarsely using either a hand grater or a food processor. Place in a large bowl with the cream, yogurt, garlic, white wine vinegar and chopped mint. Stir well and season with salt and pepper to taste.

2 Chill the soup for at least 2 hours before serving. Just before serving, stir again. Pour into individual bowls and garnish with mint sprigs.

CHILLED TOMATO & SWEET PEPPER SOUP

This delicious soup is inspired by Spanish gazpacho – the difference is that this soup is cooked first, and then chilled. The initial cooking creates a rich flavour, and the soup is served simply with croûtons which provide a contrast in texture.

SERVES 4

INGREDIENTS
2 red (bell) peppers, halved, cored and seeded
45ml/3 tbsp olive oil
1 onion, finely chopped
2 garlic cloves, crushed
675g/1½lb ripe well-flavoured tomatoes
150ml/¼ pint/⅔ cup red wine
600ml/1 pint/2½ cups chicken stock
salt and ground black pepper
chopped fresh chives, to garnish

FOR THE CROUTONS
2 slices white bread, crusts removed
60ml/4 tbsp olive oil

> COOK'S TIP
> *It is always best to use home-made stock when making soups. However, if you do not have time, choose freshly made stock from the supermarket chiller cabinet in preference to using a stock cube, which may contain too much salt.*

1 Cut each pepper half into quarters. Place skin side up on a grill (broiler) rack and cook until the skins have charred all over. Transfer to a bowl and cover.

2 Heat the oil in a large pan. Add the onion and garlic and cook until soft. Meanwhile, remove the skin from the peppers and roughly chop the flesh. Cut the tomatoes into chunks.

3 Add the chopped peppers and tomatoes to the pan, then cover and cook the
   mixture gently for 10 minutes. Add the red wine and cook for a further
5 minutes, then add the chicken stock and salt and ground black pepper to taste,
and continue to simmer for about 20 minutes.

4 To make the croûtons, cut the bread into cubes. Heat the oil in a small frying
   pan, add the bread and fry until golden on all sides. Drain on kitchen paper
then store in an airtight box.

5 Process the soup in a food processor or blender until smooth. Pour into a clean
   glass or ceramic bowl and leave to cool thoroughly before chilling in the
refrigerator for at least 3 hours.

6 When the soup is cold, check the seasoning and add more salt and pepper if
   necessary. Serve the soup in bowls, topped with the croûtons and garnished
with chopped fresh chives.

GAZPACHO

There are many versions of this refreshingly chilled, pungent soup from southern Spain. All contain an intense blend of tomatoes, peppers, cucumber and garlic. The soup is served with a range of accompaniments, as well as croûtons.

SERVES 6

INGREDIENTS
900g/2lb ripe tomatoes
1 cucumber
2 red (bell) peppers, seeded and roughly chopped
2 garlic cloves, crushed
175g/6oz/3 cups fresh white breadcrumbs
30ml/2 tbsp white wine vinegar
30ml/2 tbsp sun-dried tomato paste
90ml/6 tbsp olive oil
salt and ground black pepper

TO SERVE
1 slice white bread, crust removed and cut into cubes
30ml/2 tbsp olive oil
6–12 ice cubes
small bowl of mixed chopped garnishes, such as tomato, cucumber, red onion, hard-
   boiled (hard-cooked) egg and flat leaf parsley or tarragon leaves

1 Plunge the tomatoes into boiling water for 30 seconds, then refresh in cold water. Peel away the skins and quarter. Peel and roughly chop the cucumber. Mix the tomatoes and cucumber in a bowl with the peppers, garlic, breadcrumbs, vinegar, tomato paste and olive oil and season lightly with salt and pepper.

2 Process half the mixture in a food processor or blender until fairly smooth, then tip into a large bowl. Process the remaining mixture and mix with the first. Check the seasoning and adjust if necessary, and add a little cold water if the soup is too thick. Chill for several hours.

3 To serve, fry the bread in the oil until golden on all sides. Spoon the soup into bowls, adding one or two ice cubes to each. Serve accompanied by the croûtons and the mixed chopped garnishes.

FRESH TOMATO SOUP

Intensely flavoured sun-ripened tomatoes need little embellishment in this wonderful, fresh-tasting soup. Choose the ripest tomatoes and add sugar and vinegar according to taste. On a hot day this Italian soup is also delicious chilled.

SERVES 6

INGREDIENTS
1.5kg/3–3½lb ripe tomatoes
400ml/14fl oz/1⅔ cups chicken or vegetable stock
45ml/3 tbsp sun-dried tomato paste
30–45ml/2–3 tbsp balsamic vinegar
10–15ml/2–3 tsp caster (superfine) sugar
small handful of basil leaves
salt and ground black pepper
basil leaves, to garnish
toasted cheese croûtes and crème fraîche, to serve

1 Plunge the tomatoes into boiling water for 30 seconds, then refresh in cold water. Peel away the skins and quarter the tomatoes. Discard any tough core. Put the tomatoes in a large pan and pour over the stock. Bring to the boil, reduce the heat, cover and simmer gently for 10 minutes until the tomatoes are pulpy.

2 Stir in the tomato paste, vinegar and sugar according to taste, then add the basil. Season with salt and pepper, then cook gently, stirring, for 2 minutes. Process the soup in a food processor or blender, then return to the pan and reheat gently. Serve in bowls topped with one or two toasted cheese croûtes and a spoonful of crème fraîche, garnished with basil leaves.

COOK'S TIP
If you can, use tomatoes that have been ripened on the vine. They have a wonderful, rich flavour and really make all the difference in this simple Mediterranean soup. If you cannot find vine-ripened tomatoes, choose deep-red tomatoes with a firm, yielding flesh instead.

SPICY PUMPKIN SOUP

Pumpkin is popular all over the Mediterranean and is an important ingredient in Middle Eastern cookery. Ground ginger and cumin add subtle spicy flavour and complement the sweet taste of pumpkin.

SERVES 4

INGREDIENTS
900g/2lb pumpkin, peeled and seeds removed
30ml/2 tbsp olive oil
2 leeks, trimmed and sliced
1 garlic clove, crushed
5ml/1 tsp ground ginger
5ml/1 tsp ground cumin
900ml/1½ pints/3¾ cups chicken stock
salt and ground black pepper
coriander (cilantro) leaves, to garnish
60ml/4 tbsp natural (plain) yogurt, to serve

1 Cut the pumpkin into chunks then set aside until required. Heat the olive oil in a large pan and add the leeks and garlic. Cook gently over a low heat until softened but not browned.

2 Add the ginger and cumin and cook, stirring, for a further minute. Add the pumpkin and the chicken stock and season with salt and pepper. Bring to the boil and simmer for 30 minutes, until the pumpkin is tender.

3 Tip the soup, in batches if necessary, into a food processor or blender. Process until smooth. Return to the cleaned pan and reheat gently, then ladle into warmed individual bowls. To serve, add a swirl of natural yogurt to each bowl and garnish with coriander leaves.

AVGOLEMONO

This is the most popular of Greek soups. The name means egg and lemon, the two key ingredients, which produce a light, nourishing soup. The soup also contains orzo, which is a Greek, rice-shaped pasta, but any small shape can be used instead.

SERVES 4–6

INGREDIENTS
1.75 litres/3 pints/7½ cups chicken stock
115g/4oz/½ cup orzo pasta
3 eggs
juice of 1 large lemon
salt and ground black pepper
lemon slices, to garnish

1 Pour the chicken stock into a large pan, and bring to the boil. Add the pasta and return to the boil, then simmer for 5 minutes until the orzo is cooked.

2 Beat the eggs until frothy, then add the lemon juice and a tablespoon of cold water. Slowly stir in a ladleful of the hot chicken stock, then add one or two more. Return this mixture to the pan, off the heat and stir well. Season with salt and pepper and serve at once, garnished with lemon slices. (Do not let the soup boil once the eggs have been added or it will curdle.)

Spanish Garlic Soup

*Garlic is one of the most popular ingredients in the Mediterranean and makes a
wonderfully simple and satisfying soup. Beef stock has a fuller flavour than chicken
or vegetable stock, and works well with the pungent flavour of garlic.*

Serves 4

Ingredients
30ml/2 tbsp olive oil
4 large garlic cloves, peeled
4 slices French bread, 5mm/¼in thick
15ml/1 tbsp paprika
1 litre/1¾ pints/4 cups beef stock
1.5ml/¼ tsp ground cumin
pinch of saffron strands
4 eggs
salt and ground black pepper
chopped fresh parsley, to garnish

1 Preheat the oven to 230°C/450°F/Gas 8. Heat the oil in a large pan. Add the whole garlic cloves and cook until golden. Remove and set aside. Fry the bread in the oil until golden, then set aside.

2 Add the paprika to the pan, and fry for a few seconds. Stir in the beef stock, cumin and saffron, then add the reserved garlic, crushing the cloves with the back of a wooden spoon. Season, then cook for about 5 minutes.

3 Ladle the soup into four ovenproof bowls and break an egg into each one. Place the slices of fried bread on top of the egg and then bake in the oven for about 3–4 minutes, until the eggs are set. Sprinkle with parsley and serve at once.

GREEN LENTIL SOUP

Lentil soup is an eastern Mediterranean classic, varying in its spiciness according to the region it comes from. Red or Puy lentils make an equally good substitute for the green lentils used here. Serve with warm bread.

SERVES 4–6

INGREDIENTS
225g/8oz/1 cup green lentils
75ml/5 tbsp olive oil
3 onions, finely chopped
2 garlic cloves, thinly sliced
10ml/2 tsp cumin seeds, crushed
1.5ml/¼ tsp ground turmeric
600ml/1 pint/2½ cups chicken or vegetable stock
salt and ground black pepper
30ml/2 tbsp roughly chopped fresh coriander (cilantro), to finish

1 Put the lentils in a pan and cover with cold water. Bring to the boil and boil rapidly for 10 minutes, then drain well.

2 Heat 30ml/2 tbsp of the oil in a pan and fry two of the onions with the garlic, cumin and turmeric for 3 minutes, stirring constantly. Add the lentils, stock and 600ml/1 pint/2½ cups water. Bring to the boil, reduce the heat, then cover and simmer gently for 30 minutes, until the lentils are soft.

3 Fry the third onion in the remaining oil until golden then set aside. Use a potato masher to mash the lentils lightly and make the soup pulpy. Reheat gently and season with salt and pepper to taste. Pour the soup into bowls. Stir the fresh coriander into the fried onion and scatter over the soup. Serve at once.

CHICKPEA & PARSLEY SOUP

Chickpeas are widely used in many Mediterranean countries. They are put to good use in this simple soup, which comes from Morocco.

SERVES 6

INGREDIENTS
225g/8oz/1⅓ cups dried chickpeas, soaked overnight
1 small onion
40g1½oz fresh parsley
30ml/2 tbsp olive and sunflower oil, mixed
1.2 litres/2 pints/5 cups chicken stock
juice of ½ lemon
salt and ground black pepper
lemon wedges and finely pared strips of rind, to garnish
Moroccan bread, to serve

1 Drain the chickpeas and rinse under cold water. Cook them in boiling water for 1–1½ hours until tender. Drain and rub away the outer skins.

2 Place the onion and parsley in a food processor or blender and process until the mixture is finely chopped. Heat the olive oil and sunflower oil in a pan or flameproof casserole. Fry the onion mixture for about 4 minutes over a low heat until the onion is slightly softened. stirring occasionally to prevent the onion from browning.

3 Add the chickpeas, cook gently for 1–2 minutes and add the stock. Season well with salt and pepper. Bring to the boil, then cover and simmer for 20 minutes until the chickpeas are very tender.

4 Allow the soup to cool a little and then part-purée in a food processor or blender, or by mashing the chickpeas fairly roughly with a fork, so that the soup is thick but still quite chunky.

5 Return the soup to the cleaned pan or casserole, add the lemon juice and adjust the seasoning if necessary. Heat gently, then serve garnished with lemon wedges and finely pared rind, and accompanied by Moroccan bread.

RIBOLLITA

This soup is rather like minestrone, but includes beans instead of pasta. In Italy it is traditionally served ladled over bread and a rich green vegetable, although you could omit this for a lighter version.

SERVES 6–8

INGREDIENTS
45ml/3 tbsp olive oil
2 onions, chopped
2 carrots, sliced
4 garlic cloves, crushed
2 celery sticks, thinly sliced
1 fennel bulb, trimmed and chopped
2 large courgettes (zucchini), thinly sliced
400g/14oz can chopped tomatoes
30ml/2 tbsp home-made or ready-made pesto
900ml/1½ pints/3¾ cups vegetable stock
400g/14oz can haricot (navy) or borlotti beans, drained
salt and ground black pepper

TO SERVE
15ml/1 tbsp extra virgin olive oil, plus extra for drizzling
450g/1lb young spinach
6–8 slices white bread
Parmesan cheese shavings

1 Heat the oil in a large, heavy pan. Add the onions, carrots, garlic, celery and fennel and fry gently for about 10 minutes. Add the courgettes, then fry gently for a further 2 minutes.

2 Add the chopped tomatoes, pesto, stock and beans and bring to the boil. Reduce the heat, cover and simmer gently for 25–30 minutes, until the vegetables are completely tender. Season with salt and pepper to taste.

3 To serve, heat the oil in a pan and fry the spinach for 2 minutes. Spoon over the bread in soup bowls, then ladle the soup over the spinach. Serve with extra olive oil for drizzling and Parmesan cheese to sprinkle.

CHICKEN SOUP WITH VERMICELLI

In Morocco, a whole chicken would be used for this nourishing soup, which would be served to the large extended family. This is a slightly simplified version, using chicken portions.

SERVES 4–6

INGREDIENTS
30ml/2 tbsp sunflower oil
15g/½oz/1 tbsp butter
1 onion, chopped
2 chicken legs or breast pieces, halved or quartered
seasoned plain (all-purpose) flour, for dusting
2 carrots, cut into 4cm/1½in pieces
1 parsnip, cut into 4cm/1½in pieces
1.5 litres/2½ pints/6¼ cups chicken stock
1 cinnamon stick
good pinch of paprika
pinch of saffron
2 egg yolks
juice of ½ lemon
30ml/2 tbsp chopped fresh coriander (cilantro)
30ml/2 tbsp chopped fresh parsley
150g/5oz vermicelli
salt and ground black pepper
Moroccan bread, to serve

1 Heat the sunflower oil and butter in a heavy pan or flameproof casserole and fry the onion for 3–4 minutes until softened. Dust the chicken pieces in seasoned flour and fry gently until evenly browned.

2 Transfer the chicken to a plate and add the carrots and parsnip to the pan. Cook over a gentle heat for 3–4 minutes, stirring frequently, then return the chicken to the pan. Add the chicken stock, cinnamon stick and paprika and season well with salt and black pepper. Bring the soup to the boil, then cover and simmer for about 1 hour, or until the vegetables are very tender.

3 While the soup is cooking, put the saffron in a small bowl and pour over 30ml/ 2 tbsp boiling water and leave to stand. Beat the egg yolks with the lemon juice in a separate bowl and add the chopped coriander and parsley. When the saffron water has cooled, stir into the egg and lemon mixture.

4 When the vegetables are tender, transfer the chicken to a plate. Spoon away any excess fat from the surface of soup, then increase the heat a little and stir in the vermicelli. Cook for a further 5–6 minutes until the noodles are tender.

5 Meanwhile, remove the skin from the chicken and, if liked, remove the flesh from the bone and chop into bitesize pieces. If you prefer, simply skin the chicken and leave the pieces whole.

6 When the vermicelli is cooked, reduce the heat and stir in the chicken pieces and the egg, lemon and saffron mixture. Cook over a very low heat for 1–2 minutes, stirring all the time. (Do not allow the soup to boil as the eggs will curdle.) Adjust the seasoning and serve with Moroccan bread.

PISTOU

This variation of pistou, which is a delicious vegetable soup originally from Nice in the south of France, is served with a sun-dried tomato pesto and freshly grated Parmesan cheese for scattering over.

SERVES 4–6

INGREDIENTS
1 courgette (zucchini), diced
1 small potato, diced
1 shallot, chopped
1 carrot, diced
225g/8oz can chopped tomatoes
1.2 litres/2 pints/5 cups vegetable stock
50g/2oz green beans, cut into 1cm/½in lengths
50g/2oz/½ cup frozen petits pois (baby peas)
50g/2oz/½ cup small pasta shapes
60–90ml/4–6 tbsp pesto
15ml/1 tbsp sun-dried tomato paste
salt and ground black pepper
freshly grated Parmesan cheese, to serve

1 Place the courgette, potato, shallot, carrot and tomatoes in a large pan. Add the vegetable stock and season with salt and pepper. Bring to the boil, then cover and simmer for about 20 minutes.

2 Add the green beans, petits pois and pasta. Cook for a further 10 minutes, until the pasta is tender. Adjust the seasoning if necessary.

3 Ladle the soup into individual bowls. Mix together the pesto and sun-dried tomato paste, and stir a spoonful into each serving. Serve with grated Parmesan cheese to sprinkle into each bowl.

GALICIAN BROTH

This delicious, hearty soup is very similar to the warming, chunky meat and potato broths of cooler climates. For extra colour, a few onion skins can be added when cooking the gammon, but remember to remove them before serving.

SERVES 4

INGREDIENTS
450g/1lb gammon, in one piece
2 bay leaves
2 onions, sliced
10ml/2 tsp paprika
675g/1½lb potatoes, cut into large chunks
225g/8oz spring greens (collards)
425g/15oz can haricot (navy) or cannellini beans, drained
salt and ground black pepper

1 Soak the gammon overnight in cold water. The next day, drain and place in a large pan along with the bay leaves and sliced onions. Pour over 1.5 litres/2½ pints/6¼ cups cold water.

2 Bring the water to the boil then reduce the heat and simmer the gammon very gently for about 1½ hours until tender. Keep an eye on the pan during this time to make sure it doesn't boil over.

3 Drain the meat, reserving the cooking liquid and leave to cool slightly. Discard the skin and any excess fat and cut the meat into small chunks. Return to the pan with the paprika and potatoes. Cover and simmer gently for 20 minutes.

4 Cut away the cores from the greens. Roll up the leaves and cut into thin shreds. Add to the pan with the beans and simmer for about 10 minutes. Season with salt and pepper to taste and serve hot.

Moroccan Harira

This hearty meat and vegetable soup is eaten during the month of Ramadan, when the Muslim population fasts between sunrise and sunset. After sunset they gather together to share food among family and friends.

SERVES 4

INGREDIENTS
450g/1lb well-flavoured tomatoes
225g/8oz lamb, cut into 1cm/½in pieces
2.5ml/½ tsp ground turmeric
2.5ml/½ tsp ground cinnamon
25g/1oz/2 tbsp butter
60ml/4 tbsp chopped fresh coriander (cilantro)
30ml/2 tbsp chopped fresh parsley
1 onion, chopped
50g/2oz/¼ cup split red lentils
75g/3oz/½ cup dried chickpeas, soaked overnight
4 baby onions or small shallots, peeled
25g/1oz/¼ cup soup noodles
salt and ground black pepper
chopped fresh coriander (cilantro), lemon slices and ground cinnamon, to garnish

1 Plunge the tomatoes into boiling water for 30 seconds, then refresh in cold water. Peel away the skins. Cut into quarters and remove and discard the seeds and any tough core. Chop the flesh roughly.

2 Put the lamb, turmeric, cinnamon, butter, coriander, parsley and onion into a large pan, and cook over a medium heat, stirring, for 5 minutes. Add the chopped tomatoes and continue to cook for 10 minutes.

3 Rinse the lentils under running water and add to the pan with the drained chickpeas and 600ml/1 pint/2½ cups water. Season with salt and pepper. Bring to the boil, cover, and simmer gently for 1½ hours.

4 Add the baby onions or shallots and cook for a further 30 minutes. Add the noodles after 25 minutes. Ladle into serving bowls and garnish with the coriander, lemon slices and cinnamon.

SPICED MUSSEL SOUP

This Turkish potato and shellfish soup is chunky and colourful and is similar to a chowder in consistency. It is flavoured with spicy harissa sauce, which comes from Tunisia, giving it a peppery bite.

SERVES 6

INGREDIENTS
1.5kg/3–3½lb fresh mussels
150ml/¼ pint/⅔ cup white wine
3 tomatoes
30ml/2 tbsp olive oil
1 onion, finely chopped
2 garlic cloves, crushed
2 celery sticks, thinly sliced
1 bunch spring onions (scallions), thinly sliced
1 potato, diced
7.5ml/1½ tsp harissa sauce
45ml/3 tbsp chopped fresh parsley
ground black pepper
thick yogurt, to serve (optional)

1 Scrub the mussels, discarding any damaged ones or any open ones that do not close when tapped with a knife.

2 Pour the wine into a large pan and bring to the boil. Add the mussels and cover with a lid. Cook for 4–5 minutes until the mussels have opened wide. Discard any mussels that remain closed. Drain the mussels, reserving the cooking liquid. Reserve a few mussels in their shells for garnish and shell the rest.

3 Plunge the tomatoes into boiling water for 30 seconds, then refresh in cold water. Peel and dice the flesh. Heat the oil in a pan and fry the onion, garlic, celery and spring onions for 5 minutes. Add the shelled mussels, reserved liquid, potato, harissa sauce and tomatoes. Bring to the boil, then reduce the heat and cover. Simmer gently for 25 minutes, or until the potatoes are breaking up.

4 Stir in the parsley and pepper and add the reserved mussels. Heat through for about 1 minute. Serve hot with a spoonful of yogurt, if you like.

SEAFOOD SOUP WITH ROUILLE

This is a really chunky, aromatic mixed fish soup from France, flavoured with plenty of saffron and herbs. Rouille, a fiery hot paste, is served separately for everyone to swirl into their soup to flavour.

SERVES 6

INGREDIENTS
3 red mullet, scaled and gutted
12 large prawns (shrimp)
675g/1½lb white fish, such as cod, haddock, halibut or monkfish
225g/8oz fresh mussels
1 onion, quartered
5ml/1 tsp saffron strands
75ml/5 tbsp olive oil
1 fennel bulb, roughly chopped
4 garlic cloves, crushed
3 strips pared orange rind
4 thyme sprigs
675g/1½lb tomatoes or 400g/14oz can chopped tomatoes
30ml/2 tbsp sun-dried tomato paste
3 bay leaves
salt and ground black pepper

FOR THE ROUILLE
1 red (bell) pepper, seeded and roughly chopped
1 fresh red chilli, seeded and sliced
2 garlic cloves, chopped
75ml/5 tbsp olive oil
15g/½oz/¼ cup fresh breadcrumbs

1 To make the rouille, process the pepper, chilli, garlic, oil and breadcrumbs in a food processor or blender until smooth. Transfer to a serving dish and chill.

2 Fillet the mullet by cutting away the flesh from either side of the backbone, reserving the heads and bones. Cut the fillets into small chunks. Shell half the prawns and reserve the trimmings. Skin the white fish, discarding any bones, and cut into large chunks.

3 Scrub the mussels. Scrape off the beard and discard any damaged ones or any open ones that do not close when sharply tapped with the back of a knife.

4 Put the fish and prawn trimmings in a pan with the quartered onion and pour in 1.2 litres/2 pints/5 cups water. Bring to the boil, then simmer gently for 30 minutes. Cool slightly and strain.

5 Soak the saffron in 15ml/1 tbsp boiling water. Heat 30ml/2 tbsp of the olive oil in a large pan. Add the mullet and white fish and fry over a high heat for about 1 minute, then drain.

6 Heat the remaining oil in the pan and fry the fennel, garlic, orange rind and thyme until the mixture begins to colour. Make up the strained stock to about 1.2 litres/2 pints/5 cups with water.

7 If using fresh tomatoes, plunge them into boiling water for 30 seconds, then refresh in cold water. Peel and chop the flesh. Add the stock to the pan with the saffron, tomatoes, tomato paste and bay leaves. Season, bring almost to the boil, then simmer gently, covered, for 20 minutes.

8 Stir in the mullet, white fish and prawns and add the mussels. Cover the pan and cook for 3–4 minutes. Discard any mussels that do not open. Serve the soup hot with the rouille.

VARIATION
If you like, substitute the mussels for an equal weight of clams. Discard any clams that remain closed after cooking.

BOUILLABAISSE

Perhaps the most famous of all Mediterranean fish soups, this recipe, originating from Marseilles in the south of France, is a rich and colourful mixture of fish and shellfish, flavoured with tomatoes, saffron and orange.

SERVES 4–6

INGREDIENTS

1.5kg/3–3½lb mixed fish and raw shellfish, such as red mullet, John Dory, monkfish,
   red snapper, whiting, large prawns (shrimp) and clams
225g/8oz well-flavoured tomatoes
pinch of saffron strands
90ml/6 tbsp olive oil
1 onion, sliced
1 leek, sliced
1 celery stick, sliced
2 garlic cloves, crushed
1 bouquet garni
1 strip pared orange rind
2.5ml/½ tsp fennel seeds
15ml/1 tbsp tomato purée (paste)
10ml/2 tsp Pernod
4–6 thick slices French bread
45ml/3 tbsp chopped fresh parsley
salt and ground black pepper

COOK'S TIP
Pernod has a very strong aniseed flavour, which is not to everyone's liking. If you prefer add the same amount of cognac to the soup instead.

1 Remove the heads, tails and fins from the fish and put them and the shellfish in a large pan, with 1.2 litres/2 pints/5 cups water. Bring to the boil, and simmer for about 15 minutes. Strain, and reserve the liquid. Cut the fish into large chunks. Leave the shellfish in their shells. Plunge the tomatoes into boiling water for 30 seconds, then refresh in cold water. Peel and roughly chop the flesh. Soak the saffron in 15–30ml/1–2 tbsp hot water.

2 Heat the oil in a large pan, add the onion, leek and celery and cook until softened. Add the garlic, bouquet garni, orange rind, fennel seeds and tomatoes, then stir in the saffron and liquid and the fish stock. Season with salt and pepper, then bring to the boil and simmer for 30–40 minutes.

3 Add the shellfish and boil for about 6 minutes. Add the fish and cook for a further 6–8 minutes, until it flakes easily.

4 Using a slotted spoon, transfer the fish to a warmed serving platter. Keep the liquid boiling, to allow the oil to emulsify with the broth. Add the tomato purée and Pernod, then check the seasoning.

5 To serve, place a slice of French bread in each soup bowl, pour the broth over the top and serve the fish separately, sprinkled with chopped fresh parsley.

VEGETABLE DISHES

The climate around the Mediterranean is ideal for growing vegetables and there is always a wonderful range available at local markets. Throughout the region, vegetables form the basis of everyday meals and there are any number of ways of preparing them. They can be deep-fried, roasted, baked, stuffed, marinated, grilled (broiled), steamed, and used in pies, tarts, omelettes, stews and stuffings. The list of vegetable dishes is virtually endless and incredibly varied – from Spain come Marinated Mushrooms and Spinach with Raisins and Pine Nuts; from France Courgette Fritters with Pistou, a wonderful combination of basil and Parmesan cheese, and the classic Provençal dish Ratatouille; and from Turkey Baked Stuffed Aubergines and Spinach Pie.

Marinated Mushrooms

This Spanish recipe makes a nice change from the French classic, mushrooms à la Grecque. Make this dish the day before you eat it, as the flavours will develop and improve with a longer marinating time.

Serves 4

INGREDIENTS
30ml/2 tbsp olive oil
1 small onion, very finely chopped
1 garlic clove, crushed
15ml/1 tbsp tomato purée (paste)
50ml/2fl oz/¼ cup dry white wine
2 cloves
pinch of saffron strands
225g/8oz button (white) mushrooms, trimmed
salt and ground black pepper
chopped fresh parsley, to garnish

1 Heat the oil in a pan. Add the onion and garlic and cook until soft. Stir in the tomato purée, wine, 50ml/2fl oz/¼ cup water, the cloves and saffron and season with salt and ground black pepper. Bring to the boil, cover and simmer gently for 45 minutes, adding more water if the mixture becomes too dry.

2 Add the mushrooms to the pan, then cover and simmer for a further 5 minutes. Remove from the heat and, still covered, leave to cool. Chill in the refrigerator overnight. Serve cold, sprinkled with chopped parsley.

GARLIC MUSHROOMS

This flavoursome dish comes in many guises, from simple baked dishes to mushrooms in batter, deep-fried until crisp and golden. This version has a lovely creamy sauce, which is very garlicky, so serve with plenty of crusty bread.

SERVES 4

INGREDIENTS
25g/1oz/2 tbsp butter
225g/8oz large flat mushrooms, sliced
4 garlic cloves, thinly sliced
30ml/2 tbsp chopped fresh parsley
30ml/2 tbsp double (heavy) cream
salt and ground black pepper

1 Heat the butter in a large frying pan. Add the mushrooms and garlic and cook gently for about 5 minutes, or until the mushrooms are very tender and have released their juices.

2 Add the parsley and cream to the mushrooms, season to taste and cook for a further 1–2 minutes until piping hot. Serve immediately.

VARIATION
Use a mixture of different mushrooms, such as chestnut mushrooms, oyster mushrooms and tiny button (white) mushrooms.

CHARRED ARTICHOKES WITH LEMON OIL DIP

The delicate flavour of globe artichokes is perfectly enhanced by this citrus dressing. Lots of garlic gives this dish an extra kick.

SERVES 4

INGREDIENTS
15ml/1 tbsp lemon juice or white wine vinegar
2 globe artichokes, trimmed
12 garlic cloves, unpeeled
90ml/6 tbsp olive oil
1 lemon
sea salt
sprigs of flat leaf parsley, to garnish

1 Preheat the oven to 200°C/400°F/Gas 6. Add the lemon juice or vinegar to a bowl of cold water. Cut each artichoke lengthways into wedges. Pull the hairy choke out from the centre of each wedge, then drop them into the acidulated water.

2 Drain the artichoke wedges and place in a roasting pan with the garlic. Pour over 45ml/3 tbsp of the oil and toss well to coat. Sprinkle with salt and roast for 40 minutes, stirring once or twice, until they are tender and a little charred.

3 Meanwhile, using a small, sharp knife thinly pare away two strips of rind from the lemon. Lay the strips on a board and carefully scrape away any remaining pith. Place the rind in a small pan with cold water to cover. Bring to the boil, then simmer for about 5 minutes. Drain the rind, refresh it in cold water, then chop it roughly. Set it aside.

4 Arrange the cooked artichokes on a serving plate and set aside to cool for a few minutes. Using the back of a fork, gently flatten the garlic cloves so that the flesh squeezes out of the skins. Transfer the garlic flesh to a bowl, mash to a purée then add the lemon rind. Squeeze the juice from the lemon, then, using the fork, whisk the lemon juice and the remaining olive oil into the garlic mixture. Serve the artichokes warm, garnished with parsley, with the lemon dip.

SPINACH WITH RAISINS & PINE NUTS

Sweet raisins and toasted pine nuts are a classic Spanish combination. Here they are tossed with wilted young spinach leaves to make a delicious snack, light lunch dish or main meal accompaniment.

SERVES 4

INGREDIENTS
50g/2oz/⅓ cup raisins
1 thick slice crusty white bread
45ml/3 tbsp olive oil
25g/1oz/⅓ cup pine nuts
500g/1¼lb young spinach, stalks removed
2 garlic cloves, crushed
salt and ground black pepper

1 Put the raisins in a small bowl with boiling water and leave to soak for about 10 minutes until plump. Drain and set aside.

2 Remove the crusts, then cut the bread into cubes. Heat 30ml/2 tbsp of the oil in a frying pan and fry the bread until golden. Drain on kitchen paper.

3 Heat the remaining oil in the pan. Fry the pine nuts until beginning to colour. Add the spinach and crushed garlic and cook quickly, turning the spinach until it has just wilted.

4 Toss in the soaked raisins and season lightly with salt and pepper. Transfer to a warmed serving dish. Scatter with the croûtons and serve hot.

VARIATION
Use Swiss chard or spinach beet instead of the spinach, cooking them a little longer. You could prepare other leafy vegetables such as curly kale in this way, but shred them first so they cook quickly.

Fried Tomatoes & Spinach with Garlic

This is a versatile dish that can be served hot to accompany cooked meats and other vegetable dishes or, alternatively, chilled thoroughly and drizzled with a little freshly squeezed lemon juice just before serving.

SERVES 4

INGREDIENTS
2 tomatoes
450g/1lb spinach
2 garlic cloves, very thinly sliced
45ml/3 tbsp olive oil
salt and grated nutmeg

1 Spear each tomato in turn on a fork and hold in the flame of a gas burner for a few seconds on each side until the skin blisters. Alternatively, plunge the tomatoes in boiling water for 30 seconds, then refresh in cold water. Carefully peel off the skin, cut the tomatoes in half, scoop out the seeds and discard. Chop the flesh into 5mm/¼in pieces.

2 Wash the spinach well, then drain, squeezing out as much water as possible. Place it in a large pan with the chopped tomatoes and the garlic. Cover and steam for 5 minutes until dark green and wilted. Drain well.

3 Heat the olive oil in a large frying pan. Gently fry the spinach and tomato mixture, tossing and turning until it is glossy and hot. Do not let the garlic darken, or it will taste bitter. Season with salt and grated nutmeg and serve, sprinkled with a little more nutmeg.

BRAISED BUTTERY CABBAGE WITH CHORIZO

This dish is equally delicious without the inclusion of the chorizo sausage,
so can make a good vegetarian dish or accompaniment for a meat dish.

SERVES 4

INGREDIENTS
50g/2oz/¼ cup butter
5ml/1 tsp caraway seeds
225g/8oz green cabbage, shredded
2 garlic cloves, finely chopped
50g/2oz cured chorizo sausage, roughly chopped
60ml/4 tbsp dry sherry or white wine
salt and ground black pepper

1 Melt the butter in a frying pan, add the caraway seeds and cook for 1 minute. Add the cabbage to the pan with the chopped garlic and chorizo. Stir-fry for about 5 minutes until the cabbage is tender.

2 Add the sherry or wine to the cabbage and season well. Cover the pan and cook for 15–20 minutes until the cabbage is tender. Check the seasoning and serve.

VARIATION
Smoked bacon makes a good substitute for chorizo
sausage in this recipe. Add it to the pan after the
caraway seeds and cook for a few minutes before
adding the cabbage.

Broad Beans with Bacon

This is a classic combination that can be found throughout the Mediterranean. It is equally good made with sun-dried tomatoes. Simply replace the chopped bacon with the same quantity of drained sun-dried tomatoes in oil.

SERVES 4

INGREDIENTS
30ml/2 tbsp olive oil
1 small onion, finely chopped
1 garlic clove, finely chopped
50g/2oz rindless smoked streaky (fatty) bacon, roughly chopped
225g/8oz broad (fava) beans, thawed if frozen
5ml/1 tsp paprika
15ml/1 tbsp sweet sherry
salt and ground black pepper

1 Heat the oil in a pan and fry the onion, garlic and bacon over a high heat for about 5 minutes until softened and browned.

2 Add the beans and paprika to the pan and stir-fry for about 1 minute. Pour over the sherry, cover and cook for 5–10 minutes until the beans are tender. Add salt and ground black pepper to taste, then transfer to a warmed serving dish and serve immediately.

MOROCCAN BROAD BEANS

These beans are richly flavoured with a popular Mexican combination of spring onions, fresh herbs and cumin. Peeling the broad beans is a bit time-consuming, but gives wonderfully tender results and is well worth the effort.

SERVES 4

INGREDIENTS
375g/12oz frozen broad (fava) beans
15g/½oz/1 tbsp butter
4–5 spring onions (scallions), sliced
15ml/1 tbsp chopped fresh coriander (cilantro)
5ml/1 tsp chopped fresh mint
2.5–5ml/½–1 tsp ground cumin
10ml/2 tsp olive oil
salt

1 Bring a pan of lightly salted water to the boil, add the broad beans and simmer for 3–4 minutes until tender. Drain and, when cool enough to handle, peel away the outer skins, so you are left with the bright green beans beneath.

2 Melt the butter in a small pan and gently fry the spring onions for 2–3 minutes. Add the broad beans and then stir in the coriander, mint, cumin and a pinch of salt. Stir in the olive oil and serve immediately.

COURGETTE FRITTERS WITH PISTOU

The delicate flavour of courgette in these crispy fritters is complemented perfectly by the basil and garlic pistou. Other sauces will work equally well – try a rich garlic and tomato sauce or a light herb dressing.

SERVES 4

INGREDIENTS
450g/1lb courgettes (zucchini), grated
75g/3oz/⅔ cup plain (all-purpose) flour
1 egg, separated
15ml/1 tbsp olive oil
oil, for shallow-frying
salt and ground black pepper

FOR THE PISTOU
15g/½oz fresh basil leaves
4 garlic cloves, crushed
90g/3½oz/1 cup grated Parmesan cheese
finely grated rind of 1 lemon
150ml/¼ pint/⅔ cup olive oil

COOK'S TIP
When crushing garlic in a mortar, add a little salt as this will make the job much easier. Be careful not to add too much.

1 To make the pistou, crush the basil leaves and garlic with a mortar and pestle to make a fairly fine paste. Transfer the paste to a bowl and stir in the grated Parmesan cheese and lemon rind. Gradually blend in the oil, a little at a time, until combined, then transfer to a small serving dish.

2 To make the fritters, put the grated courgettes in a strainer over a bowl and sprinkle with salt. Leave for 1 hour, then rinse. Dry well on kitchen paper.

3 Sift the flour into a large mixing bowl and make a well in the centre, then add the egg yolk and olive oil. Measure 75ml/5 tbsp cold water and add a little to the egg and oil.

4 Whisk the egg yolk and oil, gradually incorporating the flour and enough water to make a smooth batter. Season with salt and ground black pepper and leave to stand for about 30 minutes.

5 Stir the grated courgettes into the batter. Whisk the egg white in a very clean bowl until stiff, then fold gently into the batter.

6 Heat 1cm/½in of oil in a frying pan. Add dessertspoonfuls of batter to the oil and fry for 2 minutes until golden. Drain the fritters on kitchen paper and keep warm while frying the rest. Serve warm with the pistou.

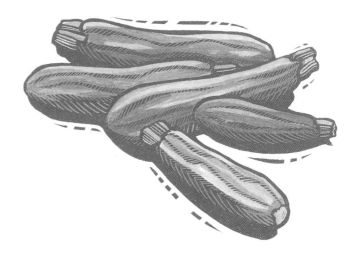

COURGETTE & TOMATO BAKE

This dish has been made for centuries in Provence. In the days before home kitchens had ovens, the assembled dish was carried to the baker's to make use of the heat remaining after the bread had been baked.

SERVES 4

INGREDIENTS
15ml/1 tbsp olive oil, plus more for drizzling
1 large onion (about 225g/8oz), sliced
1 garlic clove, finely chopped
450g/1lb tomatoes
450g/1lb courgettes (zucchini)
5ml/1 tsp dried herbes de Provence
30ml/2 tbsp grated Parmesan cheese
salt and ground black pepper

1 Preheat the oven to 180°C/350°F/Gas 4. Heat the oil in a heavy pan over a low heat and cook the onion and garlic for about 20 minutes until soft and golden. Spread over the base of a 30cm/12in shallow baking dish.

2 Cut the tomatoes crossways into 6mm/¼in thick slices. Cut the courgettes diagonally into slices about 1cm/½in thick. Arrange alternating rows of courgettes and tomatoes over the onion mixture and sprinkle with herbs, cheese and salt and pepper. Drizzle with olive oil, then bake for 25 minutes until the vegetables are tender. Serve hot or warm.

BAKED TOMATOES WITH GARLIC

These richly flavoured tomatoes are perfect with roast meat, particularly lamb, or poultry. You can prepare them a few hours ahead if you like. Cook them while you are carving the roast and bring them to the table sizzling hot.

SERVES 4

INGREDIENTS
2 large tomatoes
45ml/3 tbsp dry breadcrumbs
2 garlic cloves, very finely chopped
30ml/2 tbsp chopped fresh parsley
30–45ml/2–3 tbsp olive oil
salt and ground black pepper
flat leaf parsley sprigs, to garnish

1 Preheat the oven to 220°C/425°F/Gas 7. Cut the tomatoes in half crossways and arrange them cut side up on a foil-lined baking sheet.

2 In a bowl, mix together the breadcrumbs, garlic and parsley. Season with salt and freshly ground black pepper, then spoon over the prepared tomato halves, lightly pressing the breadcrumbs on to the tomatoes.

3 Drizzle the olive oil over the tomatoes and breadcrumbs and bake at the top of the oven for 8–10 minutes until lightly browned. Serve at once, garnished with a few flat leaf parsley sprigs.

BAKED PEPPERS & TOMATOES

Make sure there is a basket of warm bread on hand so that none of the delicious juices from this dish are wasted. This dish provides colour at the table and is good made with orange peppers as well.

SERVES 8

INGREDIENTS
2 red (bell) peppers
2 yellow (bell) peppers
1 red onion, sliced
2 garlic cloves, halved
6 plum tomatoes, quartered
50g/2oz/¼ cup black olives
5ml/1 tsp soft light brown sugar
45ml/3 tbsp sherry
3–4 rosemary sprigs
30ml/2 tbsp olive oil
salt and ground black pepper

1 Preheat the oven to 200°C/400°F/Gas 6. Seed the red and yellow peppers, then cut each into 12 strips. Place the peppers, onion, garlic, tomatoes and olives in a large roasting pan. Sprinkle over the sugar, then pour over the sherry. Season well, cover with foil and bake for 45 minutes.

2 Remove the foil from the tin and stir the mixture well. Add the rosemary sprigs. Drizzle over the olive oil. Return the pan to the oven for a further 30 minutes until the vegetables are tender. Serve hot.

COOK'S TIP
Use four or five well-flavoured beefsteak tomatoes instead of plum tomatoes if you prefer. Cut them into thick wedges instead of quarters.

RATATOUILLE

This highly versatile vegetable stew comes from Provence in the South of France.
Ratatouille is delicious hot or cold, on its own or with eggs, pasta, fish or meat –
particularly roast lamb. When served cold, the flavours have time to develop further.

SERVES 6

INGREDIENTS
900g/2lb ripe, well-flavoured tomatoes
120ml/4fl oz/½ cup olive oil
2 onions, thinly sliced
2 red (bell) peppers, seeded and cut into chunks
1 yellow or orange (bell) pepper, seeded and cut into chunks
1 large aubergine (eggplant), cut into chunks
2 courgettes (zucchini), cut into thick slices
4 garlic cloves, crushed
2 bay leaves
15ml/1 tbsp chopped young thyme
salt and ground black pepper

1 Plunge the tomatoes into boiling water for 30 seconds, then refresh in cold water. Peel away the skins and chop the flesh roughly.

2 Heat a little of the oil in a large, heavy pan; fry the onions for 5 minutes. Add the peppers and fry for a further 2 minutes. Drain. Add the aubergine and more oil and fry gently for 5 minutes. Add the remaining oil and courgettes and fry for 3 minutes. Then drain the vegetables.

3 Add the garlic and tomatoes to the pan with the herbs and seasoning. Cook gently until the tomatoes have softened and are turning pulpy.

4 Return all the vegetables to the pan and cook gently, stirring frequently, for about 15 minutes, until fairly pulpy but retaining a little texture. Season with more salt and pepper to taste.

Stewed Aubergines with Tomatoes & Garlic

Slow-cooked aubergines take on a luxurious, velvety texture yet hold their shape. They readily absorb the flavours of other ingredients with which they are cooked, giving a rich, sweet, juicy result.

SERVES 4

INGREDIENTS
60–90ml/4–6 tbsp olive oil
1 large aubergine (eggplant), sliced into 1cm/½in rounds
2 shallots, thinly sliced
4 tomatoes, quartered
2 garlic cloves, thinly sliced
60ml/4 tbsp red wine
30ml/2 tbsp chopped fresh parsley, plus extra to garnish
salt and ground black pepper

1 Heat 15ml/1 tbsp of the olive oil in a large frying pan. Cook the aubergine slices in batches (adding more oil as necessary, but reserving about 15ml/1 tbsp), until golden brown. Drain the slices on kitchen paper, cut them into strips about 1cm/½in wide, and set aside.

2 Heat the reserved oil in a pan and cook the shallots for 5 minutes until golden. Add the aubergine strips with the tomatoes, garlic and red wine. Season with salt and ground black pepper to taste. Cover and simmer over a gentle heat for about 30 minutes. Stir in the parsley, check the seasoning and adjust if necessary. Serve sprinkled with chopped fresh parsley.

VARIATION
To make a slightly more substantial dish, spoon the cooked aubergine mixture into a flameproof dish and sprinkle with grated cheese and breadcrumbs. Grill (broil) for about 5 minutes until the topping is bubbling and golden.

Spicy Chickpea
& Aubergine Stew

This subtly spiced dish is from Lebanon but similar recipes are found all over the Mediterranean region, varying slightly from country to country.

SERVES 4

INGREDIENTS
3 large aubergines (eggplant), cubed
200g/7oz/1 cup dried chickpeas, soaked overnight
60ml/4 tbsp olive oil
3 garlic cloves, chopped
2 large onions, chopped
2.5ml/½ tsp ground cumin
2.5ml/½ tsp ground cinnamon
2.5ml/½ tsp ground coriander
3 × 400g/14oz cans chopped tomatoes
salt and ground black pepper
cooked rice, to serve

FOR THE GARNISH
30ml/2 tbsp olive oil
1 onion, sliced
1 garlic clove, sliced
sprigs of coriander (cilantro)

1 Place the aubergines in a colander in a bowl and sprinkle with salt. Leave for 30 minutes then rinse with cold water and dry on kitchen paper. Drain the chickpeas and put in a pan with enough water to cover. Bring to the boil and simmer for about 30 minutes, or until tender, then drain well.

2 Heat the oil in a large pan. Cook the garlic and onion until soft. Add the spices and stir for a few seconds. Stir in the aubergine; cook for 5 minutes. Add the tomatoes, chickpeas and seasoning. Cover and simmer for 20 minutes.

3 To make the garnish, heat the oil and fry the onion and garlic until golden and crisp. Serve the stew with rice, topped with the onion, garlic and coriander.

OKRA WITH CORIANDER & TOMATOES

Okra is frequently combined with tomatoes and mild spices in various parts of the Mediterranean. Buy okra that is soft and velvety, not dry and shrivelled.

SERVES 4

INGREDIENTS
450g/1lb tomatoes or 400g/14oz can chopped tomatoes
450g/1lb fresh okra
45ml/3 tbsp olive oil
2 onions, thinly sliced
10ml/2 tsp coriander seeds, crushed
3 garlic cloves, crushed
2.5ml/½ tsp caster (superfine) sugar
finely grated rind and juice of 1 lemon
salt and ground black pepper

1 If using fresh tomatoes, plunge them into boiling water for 30 seconds, then refresh in cold water. Peel away the skins and chop the flesh.

2 Trim off any stalks from the okra and leave whole. Heat the oil in a sauté pan and fry the onions and coriander for 3–4 minutes until beginning to colour.

3 Add the okra and garlic and fry for 1 minute. Gently stir in the tomatoes and sugar and simmer gently for about 20 minutes, until the okra is tender, stirring once or twice during this time.

4 Stir in the lemon rind and juice and add salt and pepper to taste, adding a little more sugar if necessary. Serve warm or cold.

Spiced Turnips with Spinach & Tomatoes

Sweet baby turnips, tender spinach and ripe tomatoes make tempting partners in this simple eastern Mediterranean vegetable stew.

Serves 6

INGREDIENTS
450g/1lb plum or other well-flavoured tomatoes
60ml/4 tbsp olive oil
2 onions, sliced
450g/1lb baby turnips, peeled
5ml/1 tsp paprika
2.5ml/½ tsp caster (superfine) sugar
60ml/4 tbsp chopped fresh coriander (cilantro)
450g/1lb fresh young spinach, stalks removed
salt and ground black pepper

1 Plunge the tomatoes into a bowl of boiling water for 30 seconds, then refresh in a bowl of cold water. Peel the tomatoes and chop the flesh roughly. Heat the oil in a large frying pan or sauté pan and fry the onion for about 5 minutes until softened and golden.

2 Add the baby turnips, tomatoes and paprika to the pan with 60ml/4 tbsp water and cook until the tomatoes are pulpy. Cover with a lid and continue cooking until the baby turnips have softened.

3 Stir the sugar and coriander into the vegetables, then add the spinach along with a little salt and pepper. Cook for a further 2–3 minutes until the spinach has wilted but is still bright green. Serve warm or cold.

SPANISH POTATOES

This is an adaptation of a peppery potato dish, of which there are several versions. All of them are fried and mildly spiced with the added tang of wine vinegar. Serve with cold meats or as a tapas.

SERVES 4

INGREDIENTS
675g/1½lb small new potatoes
75ml/5 tbsp olive oil
2 garlic cloves, sliced
2.5ml/½ tsp crushed dried chillies
2.5ml/½ tsp ground cumin
10ml/2 tsp paprika
30ml/2 tbsp red or white wine vinegar
1 red or green (bell) pepper, seeded and sliced
coarse sea salt, to serve (optional)

1 Cook the potatoes in a large pan of boiling salted water until almost tender. Drain and, if preferred, peel them. Cut into even-size chunks.

2 Heat the olive oil in a large frying or sauté pan and fry the potatoes, turning them frequently until they are golden brown all over.

3 Meanwhile, crush together the garlic, chillies and cumin in a mortar using a pestle. Tip the crushed spices into a small bowl and mix in the paprika and wine vinegar.

4 Add the garlic mixture to the potatoes with the sliced pepper and cook, stirring, for 2 minutes. Serve warm, or leave until cold. Scatter with coarse sea salt, if you like, to serve.

STUFFED PEPPERS

Couscous is a form of semolina, and is used extensively throughout the Middle East. It makes an excellent stuffing in this recipe, combined with other ingredients whose flavours it absorbs very well.

SERVES 6

INGREDIENTS
6 (bell) peppers
25g/1oz/2 tbsp butter
1 onion, finely chopped
5ml/1 tsp olive oil
2.5ml/½ tsp salt
175g/6oz/1 cup couscous
25g/1oz/2 tbsp raisins
30ml/2 tbsp chopped fresh mint
1 egg yolk
salt and ground black pepper
mint leaves, to garnish

1 Preheat the oven to 200°C/400°F/Gas 6. Carefully slit (without halving) each pepper and remove the core and seeds. Melt the butter in a small pan and add the chopped onion. Cook until soft but not browned.

2 Bring 250ml/8fl oz/1 cup water to the boil. Add the oil and the salt, then remove the pan from the heat and add the couscous. Stir and leave to stand for 5 minutes. Stir in the onion, raisins and mint, then season. Stir in the egg yolk.

3 Using a teaspoon, fill the peppers with the couscous to about three-quarters full. Place in a lightly oiled ovenproof dish and bake, uncovered, for about 20 minutes until tender. Serve hot or cold, garnished with the mint leaves.

Baked Tomatoes & Peppers Stuffed with Rice

Colourful peppers and tomatoes make perfect containers for various meat and vegetable stuffings. This rice and herb version originated in Greece and makes a perfect vegetarian main course.

SERVES 4

INGREDIENTS

2 large ripe tomatoes
1 green (bell) pepper
1 yellow or orange (bell) pepper
60ml/4 tbsp olive oil, plus extra for sprinkling
2 onions, chopped
2 garlic cloves, crushed
50g/2oz/½ cup blanched almonds, chopped
75g/3oz/scant ½ cup long grain rice, boiled and drained
15g/½oz fresh mint, roughly chopped
15g/½oz fresh parsley, roughly chopped
25g/1oz/2 tbsp sultanas (golden raisins)
45ml/3 tbsp ground almonds
salt and ground black pepper
chopped fresh mixed herbs, to garnish

1 Preheat the oven to 190°C/ 375°F/Gas 5. Cut the tomatoes in half and scoop out the pulp and seeds using a teaspoon. Leave the tomatoes to drain on kitchen paper with cut sides down. Roughly chop the tomato pulp and seeds.

2 Halve the peppers, but leave the cores intact. Scoop out the seeds. Brush the peppers with 15ml/1 tbsp of the olive oil and bake on a baking sheet for about 15 minutes. Place the peppers and tomatoes in a shallow ovenproof dish, then season with salt and ground black pepper.

3 Heat the remaining olive oil in a heavy frying pan, then add the chopped onions and fry over a low heat for about 5 minutes, or until transparent. Add the garlic and chopped almonds and fry for a further minute.

4 Remove the pan from the heat and stir in the rice, chopped tomatoes, mint, parsley and sultanas. Season well with salt and black pepper and spoon the mixture into the tomatoes and peppers.

5 Pour 150ml/¼ pint/⅔ cup boiling water around the tomatoes and peppers and bake, uncovered, for 20 minutes. Scatter with the ground almonds and sprinkle with a little extra olive oil. Return to the oven and bake for a further 20 minutes, or until turning golden. Serve garnished with fresh herbs.

VARIATION
Small aubergines (eggplant) or large courgettes (zucchini) also make good vegetables for stuffing. Halve and scoop out the centres of the vegetables, then oil the vegetable cases and bake for about 15 minutes. Chop the centres, fry for 2–3 minutes to soften and add to the stuffing mixture. Fill the aubergine or courgette cases with the stuffing and bake as for the peppers and tomatoes.

BAKED STUFFED AUBERGINES

The name of this famous Turkish meze *dish,* Imam Bayaldi, *literally means the Imam fainted – perhaps with pleasure at the deliciousness of the dish.*

SERVES 6

INGREDIENTS
3 aubergines (eggplant)
60ml/4 tbsp olive oil
1 large onion, chopped
1 small red (bell) pepper, seeded and diced
1 small green (bell) pepper, seeded and diced
3 garlic cloves, crushed
5–6 tomatoes, skinned and chopped
30ml/2 tbsp chopped fresh parsley
about 250ml/8fl oz/1 cup boiling water
15ml/1 tbsp lemon juice
salt and ground black pepper
chopped fresh parsley, to garnish
bread, salad and yogurt dip, to serve

COOK'S TIP
These aubergines are also very good served cold. Allow to cool and then chill for at least an hour before serving. Drizzle a little olive oil over the top if you wish and serve with the same accompaniments as above.

1 Preheat the oven to 190°C/375°F/Gas 5. Cut the aubergines in half lengthways and scoop out the flesh, reserving the shells. Chop the flesh.

2 Heat 30ml/2 tbsp of the olive oil in a pan and fry the onion and peppers for 5–6 minutes until both are slightly softened but not too tender.

3 Add the garlic to the pan and continue to cook for a further 2 minutes, then stir in the tomatoes, parsley and aubergine flesh. Season with salt and pepper, then stir well and fry over a medium heat for 2–3 minutes.

4 Heat the remaining oil in a separate, large pan and fry the aubergine shells, two at a time, on both sides.

5 Stuff the aubergine shells with the sautéed vegetables. Arrange them closely together in an ovenproof dish and pour enough boiling water around the aubergines to come halfway up their sides.

6 Cover with foil and bake in the oven for 45–60 minutes, or until the aubergines are tender and most of the liquid has been absorbed.

7 Place a half aubergine on each serving plate and sprinkle with a little lemon juice. Serve hot, garnished with chopped fresh parsley and accompanied by bread, salad and a yogurt dip.

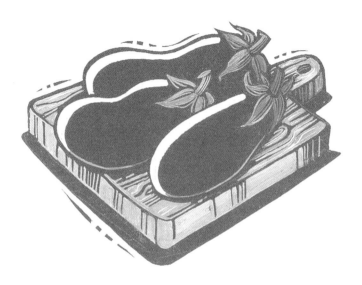

SPINACH PIE

This Turkish dish is called Fatayer. *It uses the classic combination of spinach and feta cheese, with pine nuts for added interest. The soft filling contrasts wonderfully with the crispy filo pastry case. This dish is an excellent choice for vegetarians but will be equally enjoyed by non-vegetarians too.*

SERVES 6

INGREDIENTS
450g/2lb fresh spinach, chopped
25g/1oz/2 tbsp butter or margarine
2 onions, chopped
2 garlic cloves, crushed
250g/10oz feta cheese, crumbled
100g/4oz/³⁄4 cup pine nuts
5 eggs, beaten
2 saffron strands, soaked in 10ml/²⁄3 tbsp boiling water
5ml/1 tsp paprika
1.5ml/¹⁄4 tsp ground cumin
1.5ml/¹⁄4 tsp ground cinnamon
14 sheets filo pastry
about 60ml/4 tbsp olive oil
salt and ground black pepper
lettuce, to serve

> VARIATION
> *Cheddar, Parmesan or any other hard cheese can be added to this dish along with the feta cheese for a deeper flavour.*

1 Place the spinach in a large colander, sprinkle with a little salt, mix into the leaves and leave for 30 minutes to drain the excess liquid.

2 Preheat the oven to 180°C/350°F/Gas 4. Melt the butter or margarine in a large pan and fry the onions until golden. Add the garlic, feta cheese and pine nuts. Remove from the heat and stir in the eggs, spinach, saffron and spices. Season with salt and pepper and mix well.

3 Grease a large rectangular baking dish. Take seven of the sheets of filo pastry and brush one side with a little olive oil. Use to line the base of the dish, leaving the pastry hanging over the sides.

4 Spoon all of the spinach mixture into the pastry case and carefully drizzle 30ml/2 tbsp of the remaining olive oil over the top.

5 Fold the overhanging pastry over the top of the filling. Cut the remaining pastry sheets to the dish size and brush each one with more olive oil. Arrange the pastry on top of the filling.

6 Brush the pastry with water to prevent curling, then bake in the oven for about 30 minutes, or until the pastry is golden brown. Serve with the lettuce.

VEGETABLES WITH BAKED EGGS

This is a Moroccan version of a dish from neighbouring Tunisia called chakcouka. *Include one or two red or orange peppers as their sweetness adds extra flavour.*

SERVES 4

INGREDIENTS
45ml/3 tbsp olive oil
1 Spanish onion, finely sliced
1 garlic clove, crushed
4 (bell) peppers, cored, seeded and sliced
4–5 tomatoes, peeled and chopped
250ml/8fl oz/1 cup puréed canned tomatoes or tomato juice
25ml/1½ tbsp chopped fresh parsley
5ml/1 tsp paprika (optional)
a little lemon juice (optional)
4 eggs
45ml/3 tbsp single (light) cream
salt and ground black pepper

1 Preheat the oven to 180°C/350°F/Gas 4. Heat the oil in a frying pan and gently fry the onion and garlic for about 5 minutes until softened, stirring occasionally.

2 Add the sliced peppers to the pan and fry over a gentle heat for about 10 minutes, stirring occasionally, until softened slightly.

3 Add the chopped tomatoes, puréed tomatoes or juice, 15ml/1 tbsp of the parsley, the paprika, if using, and seasoning to the pan and stir very gently. Cook over a gentle heat for about 10 minutes until the peppers are soft. Season to taste, and sharpen with lemon juice, if liked.

4 Spoon the mixture into four ovenproof dishes, preferably earthenware. Make a well in the centre and break an egg into each hole. Pour some of the cream over each egg and sprinkle with a little black pepper or paprika, as liked.

5 Bake the eggs for about 15 minutes or until the white of the egg is set. Sprinkle with the remaining chopped parsley before serving.

POTATO & ONION TORTILLA

This delicious thick potato and onion omelette is a classic Spanish dish that is eaten at all times of the day, hot or cold.

SERVES 4

INGREDIENTS
300ml/½ pint/1¼ cups olive oil
6 large potatoes, peeled and sliced
2 Spanish onions, sliced
6 eggs
salt and ground black pepper
cherry tomatoes, halved, to serve

1 Heat the oil in a large non-stick frying pan. Stir in the potato, onion and a little salt. Cover and cook gently for 20 minutes until soft.

2 Beat the eggs in a large bowl. Remove the onion and potato from the pan with a slotted spoon and add to the beaten eggs. Season with salt and pepper. Pour off some of the oil, leaving about 60ml/4 tbsp in the pan. (Reserve the leftover oil for other cooking.) Heat the pan again.

3 When the oil is very hot, pour in the egg mixture. Cook for 2–3 minutes. Cover the pan with a plate and invert the omelette on to it. Slide it back into the pan and cook for a further 5 minutes, until golden brown and moist in the middle. Serve in wedges, with the cherry tomatoes.

SALADS

The climate of the Mediterranean is perfect for growing salad vegetables. Market stalls throughout the region are piled high with vegetables, fruit and fresh herbs that can be made into delicious and varied salads. These salads can be as simple as lettuce dressed in vinaigrette or more complex, such as Sweet and Sour Onion Salad from France, Spanish Asparagus and Orange Salad, and Roasted Peppers with Tomatoes and Anchovies from the island of Sicily. Elsewhere in the region salads tend to be more robust, relying on ingredients other than salad greens. Some of these, such as Moroccan Cooked Salad or Fattoush from Syria and Lebanon, can be served as a main course.

GLOBE ARTICHOKES WITH GREEN BEANS & AIOLI

Just like the French aioli, there are many recipes for the Spanish equivalent. This one is exceptionally garlicky, a perfect partner to freshly cooked vegetables.

SERVES 4–6

INGREDIENTS
225g/8oz green beans
3 small globe artichokes
15ml/1 tbsp olive oil
pared rind of 1 lemon
coarse salt, for sprinkling
lemon wedges, to garnish

FOR THE AIOLI
6 large garlic cloves, sliced
10ml/2 tsp white wine vinegar
250ml/8fl oz/1 cup olive oil
salt and ground black pepper

COOK'S TIPS
• Mediterranean baby artichokes are perfect for this kind of salad as, unlike the larger ones, they can be eaten whole. Cook them until just tender, then cut in half to serve.
• Canned artichoke hearts, thoroughly drained and sliced, can be substituted when fresh ones are out of season or not available.

1 To make the aioli, put the garlic and vinegar in a mini food processor or blender. With the machine switched on, gradually pour in the olive oil until the mixture is thickened and smooth. (Alternatively, crush the garlic to a paste with the vinegar and gradually beat in the oil using a hand whisk.) Season with salt and ground black pepper to taste.

2 To make the salad, cook the green beans in boiling water for 1–2 minutes until slightly softened. Drain.

3 Trim the artichoke stalks close to the base. Cook the artichokes in a large pan of salted water for about 30 minutes, or until you can easily pull away a leaf from the base. Drain well. Using a sharp knife, halve the artichokes lengthways and ease out the choke using a teaspoon.

4 Arrange the artichokes and beans on individual serving plates and drizzle with the olive oil. Scatter with the lemon rind and season with coarse salt and a little ground black pepper.

5 Spoon the aioli into the artichoke hearts and serve warm, garnished with lemon wedges. To eat artichokes, pull the leaves from the base one at a time and use to scoop a little of the sauce. It is only the fleshy end of each leaf that is eaten as well as the base or heart of the artichoke.

Spanish Asparagus
& Orange Salad

Like most salad dressings found in Spain, this one relies simply on the wonderful flavour of a good quality olive oil.

Serves 4

Ingredients
225g/8oz asparagus, trimmed and cut into 5cm/2in pieces
2 large oranges
2 well-flavoured tomatoes, cut into eighths
50g/2oz romaine lettuce leaves, shredded
30ml/2 tbsp extra virgin olive oil
2.5ml/½ tsp sherry vinegar
salt and ground black pepper

1 Cook the asparagus in boiling salted water for 3–4 minutes, until just tender. Drain and refresh under cold water.

2 Grate the rind from half an orange and reserve. Peel all the oranges and cut into segments. Squeeze out the juice from the membrane and reserve the juice.

3 Put the asparagus, orange segments, tomatoes and lettuce into a salad bowl. Mix together the oil and vinegar and add 15ml/1 tbsp of the reserved orange juice and 5ml/1 tsp of the rind. Season with salt and pepper. Just before serving, pour the dressing over the salad and mix gently to coat.

Cook's Tip
If you prefer, Little Gem (Bibb) lettuce can be used in place of the romaine, or use a mixture of crisp lettuce leaves for a more varied effect.

ORANGE, TOMATO & AVOCADO SALAD

This Spanish salad provides a feast of flavours and textures. Garnished with almonds and olives, it creates a colourful dish for the table.

SERVES 4

INGREDIENTS
2 oranges
2 well-flavoured tomatoes
2 small avocados
60ml/4 tbsp extra virgin olive oil
30ml/2 tbsp lemon juice
15ml/1 tbsp chopped fresh parsley
1 small onion, sliced into rings
salt and ground black pepper
25g/1oz/¼ cup flaked (slivered) almonds and 10–12 black olives, to garnish

1 Peel the oranges and slice into thick rounds. Plunge the tomatoes into boiling water for 30 seconds, then refresh in cold water. Peel away the skins, cut into quarters, remove the seeds and chop the flesh roughly.

2 Cut the avocados in half, remove the stones (pits) and carefully peel away the skin. Cut the flesh into chunks.

3 In a small jug (pitcher), mix together the oil, lemon juice and parsley. Season with salt and pepper. Toss the avocados and tomatoes in half of the dressing.

4 Arrange the sliced oranges on a plate and scatter over the onion rings. Drizzle with the rest of the dressing. Spoon the avocados and tomatoes on top, then scatter over the flaked almonds and olives.

Moroccan Date, Carrot & Orange Salad

This is a colourful and unusual salad with exotic ingredients – fresh dates and orange flower water – combined with crisp leaves, carrots, oranges and toasted almonds.

SERVES 4

INGREDIENTS
1 Little Gem (Bibb) lettuce
2 carrots, finely grated
2 oranges
115g/4oz fresh dates, stoned (pitted) and cut into eighths, lengthways
25g/1oz/¼ cup toasted whole almonds, chopped
30ml/2 tbsp lemon juice
5ml/1 tsp caster (superfine) sugar
1.5ml/¼ tsp salt
15ml/1 tbsp orange flower water

1 Separate the lettuce leaves and arrange them in the base of a salad bowl or on individual serving plates. Place the grated carrot in a mound on top. Peel and segment the oranges and arrange them around the carrot. Pile the dates on top, then sprinkle with the toasted almonds.

2 Mix together the lemon juice, sugar, salt and orange flower water and sprinkle over the salad. Chill for about 30 minutes before serving to allow the flavours to blend and develop.

COOK'S TIP
For the best results, use really juicy, seedless oranges for this salad. Choose firm fruits that feel heavy for their size. Blood oranges, with their ruby-red flesh, make a pretty alternative.

FATTOUSH

This very simple peasant salad has become a popular dish all over Syria and the Lebanon. The generous addition of fresh herbs gives it a wonderfully aromatic flavour. If you prefer, make this salad in the traditional way. After toasting the pitta bread, crush it in your hand and sprinkle it over the salad before serving.

SERVES 4

INGREDIENTS
1 yellow or red (bell) pepper
1 large cucumber
4–5 tomatoes
a bunch spring onions (scallions)
30ml/2 tbsp finely chopped fresh parsley
30ml/2 tbsp finely chopped fresh mint
30ml/2 tbsp finely chopped fresh coriander (cilantro)
2 garlic cloves, crushed
75ml/5 tbsp olive oil
juice of 2 lemons
salt and ground black pepper
2 pitta breads

1 Slice the pepper, discarding the seeds and core, then roughly chop the cucumber and tomatoes. Place them in a large salad bowl.

2 Trim and slice the spring onions. Add to the cucumber, tomatoes and pepper with the finely chopped parsley, mint and coriander.

3 To make the dressing, blend the garlic with the olive oil and lemon juice in a small jug (pitcher), then season to taste with salt and black pepper. Pour the dressing over the salad and toss lightly to mix.

4 Toast the pitta breads in a toaster or under a hot grill (broiler) until crisp, then cut in half and serve with the salad.

Moroccan Cooked Salad

This salad is a version of a North African favourite. It is usually served as a side dish with a main course. If you have time, make this salad the day before to allow the flavours to develop fully.

SERVES 4

INGREDIENTS

2 well-flavoured tomatoes, quartered
2 onions, chopped
½ cucumber, halved lengthways, seeded and sliced
1 green (bell) pepper, halved, seeded and chopped
30ml/2 tbsp lemon juice
45ml/3 tbsp olive oil
2 garlic cloves, crushed
30ml/2 tbsp chopped fresh coriander (cilantro)
salt and ground black pepper
sprigs of coriander (cilantro), to garnish

1 Put the tomatoes, onions, cucumber and green pepper into a large pan, add 60ml/4 tbsp water and simmer for 5 minutes. Set aside and leave to cool.

2 To make the dressing, mix together the lemon juice, olive oil and garlic in a small jug (pitcher). Strain the cooked vegetables, then transfer to a serving bowl. Pour over the dressing, season with salt and pepper and stir in the chopped coriander. Serve at once, garnished with coriander sprigs.

WARM BROAD BEAN SALAD

This recipe is loosely based on a typical medley of fresh-tasting Greek salad ingredients – broad beans, tomatoes and feta cheese. The subtle flavour of the beans works well with the fresh tomatoes and sharp-tasting cheese.

SERVES 4–6

INGREDIENTS
900g/2lb broad (fava) beans, shelled, or 350g/12oz shelled frozen beans
60ml/4 tbsp olive oil
175g/6oz plum tomatoes, halved, or quartered if large
4 garlic cloves, crushed
115g/4oz firm feta cheese, cut into chunks
45ml/3 tbsp chopped fresh dill, plus extra to garnish
12 black olives
salt and ground black pepper

1 Cook the fresh or frozen broad beans in boiling salted water for about 5 minutes, or until just tender. Drain well and set aside.

2 Meanwhile, heat the olive oil in a heavy frying pan and add the tomatoes and garlic. Cook until the tomatoes are beginning to colour.

3 Add the feta cheese to the pan and toss the ingredients together for 1 minute. Mix with the drained beans, chopped dill, olives and salt and pepper. Serve garnished with extra chopped dill.

BROAD BEAN, MUSHROOM & CHORIZO SALAD

Broad beans are used in both their fresh and dried forms in various Mediterranean countries. This Spanish salad could be served as either an appetizer or lunch dish.

SERVES 4

INGREDIENTS
225g/8oz shelled broad (fava) beans
175g/6oz chorizo sausage
60ml/4 tbsp extra virgin olive oil
225g/8oz brown cap (cremini) mushrooms, sliced
a handful of fresh chives
salt and ground black pepper

1 Cook the broad beans in boiling salted water for about 7 minutes. Drain and refresh under cold water.

2 Remove and discard the skin from the chorizo sausage and cut the meat into small chunks. Heat the oil in a frying pan, add the chorizo and cook for 2–3 minutes. Tip the chorizo and oil into the mushrooms and mix well. Leave to cool.

3 Snip half the chives with a pair of kitchen scissors. If the beans are large, peel away the tough outer skins. Stir the beans and snipped chives into the mushroom mixture, and season with salt and ground black pepper to taste. Serve at room temperature, garnished with the remaining chives.

BROWN BEAN SALAD WITH EGGS

Brown beans, sometimes called ful medames, are widely used in Egyptian cookery. Dried broad beans, black or red kidney beans make a good substitute.

SERVES 6

INGREDIENTS
350g/12oz/1½ cups dried brown beans
3 thyme sprigs
2 bay leaves
1 onion, halved
4 garlic cloves, crushed
7.5ml/1½ tsp cumin seeds, crushed
3 spring onions (scallions), finely chopped
90ml/6 tbsp chopped fresh parsley
20ml/4 tsp lemon juice
90ml/6 tbsp olive oil
3 hard-boiled (hard-cooked) eggs, shelled and roughly chopped
1 pickled cucumber, roughly chopped
salt and ground black pepper

1 Put the brown beans in a large bowl and pour over cold water to cover. Leave to soak overnight.

2 Drain the beans and place in a large pan. Cover with fresh water, bring to the boil and boil rapidly for about 10 minutes. Reduce the heat and add the thyme, bay leaves and onion. Simmer very gently for about 1 hour until tender. Drain and discard the herbs and onion.

3 Meanwhile, mix together the garlic, cumin, spring onions, parsley, lemon juice, oil and add a little salt and pepper. Pour over the beans and toss the ingredients lightly together. Gently stir in the eggs and cucumber and serve at once.

HALLOUMI & GRAPE SALAD

Firm salty halloumi cheese from Cyprus is made from goat's, cow's or sheep's milk.
It is often served fried for breakfast or supper. In this recipe it is tossed with sweet,
juicy grapes, which really complement its distinctive flavour.

SERVES 4

INGREDIENTS
150g/5oz mixed green salad leaves
75g/3oz seedless green grapes
75g/3oz seedless black grapes
250g/9oz halloumi cheese
45ml/3 tbsp olive oil
fresh young thyme leaves or dill, to garnish

FOR THE DRESSING
60ml/4 tbsp olive oil
15ml/1 tbsp lemon juice
2.5ml/½ tsp caster (superfine) sugar
15ml/1 tbsp chopped fresh thyme or dill
salt and ground black pepper

1 To make the dressing, mix together the olive oil, lemon juice and sugar in a jug (pitcher). Season with salt and pepper. Stir in the thyme or dill and set aside.

2 In a large bowl, toss together the salad leaves and the green and black grapes, then arrange on a large serving plate.

3 Thinly slice the halloumi cheese. Heat the olive oil in a large frying pan. Add the cheese and fry briefly until turning golden brown on the underside. Turn the cheese with a fish slice (spatula) and cook the other side.

4 Arrange the fried cheese over the salad. Pour over the dressing and garnish with thyme or dill. Serve immediately.

GREEK SALAD

*Anyone who has spent a holiday in Greece will have eaten a version of this salad –
the Greeks' equivalent to a mixed salad. Its success relies on using the freshest of
ingredients, and a good quality olive oil.*

SERVES 6

INGREDIENTS
1 small cos (romaine) lettuce, sliced
450g/1lb well-flavoured tomatoes, cut into eighths
1 cucumber, seeded and chopped
200g/7oz feta cheese, crumbled
4 spring onions (scallions), sliced
50g/2oz/½ cup black olives, pitted and halved

FOR THE DRESSING
90ml/6 tbsp extra virgin olive oil
25ml/1½ tbsp lemon juice
salt and ground black pepper

1 Put the sliced lettuce, tomatoes and cucumber in a large serving bowl and toss gently to mix. Add the crumbled feta cheese, spring onions and olives, and toss again to combine.

2 To make the dressing, whisk together the olive oil and lemon juice in a small jug (pitcher), then season generously with salt and ground black pepper. Pour the dressing over the salad. Toss well and serve immediately.

SPICED AUBERGINE SALAD

Serve this flavoursome salad from the Middle East with warm pitta bread, either as an appetizer or to accompany a main course rice pilaff.

SERVES 4

INGREDIENTS
2 small aubergines (eggplant), sliced
75ml/5 tbsp olive oil
50ml/2fl oz/¼ cup red wine vinegar
2 garlic cloves, crushed
15ml/1 tbsp lemon juice
2.5ml/½ tsp ground cumin
2.5ml/½ tsp ground coriander
½ cucumber, thinly sliced
2 well-flavoured tomatoes, thinly sliced
30ml/2 tbsp natural (plain) yogurt
salt and ground black pepper
chopped flat leaf parsley, to garnish

1 Preheat the grill (broiler). Brush the aubergine slices lightly with some of the oil and grill (broil) under a high heat, turning once, until they are golden and tender. Cut the slices into quarters.

2 In a large bowl, mix together the remaining oil, vinegar, garlic, lemon juice, cumin and coriander. Season with salt and pepper and mix thoroughly. Add the warm aubergines, stir well and chill for at least 2 hours.

3 When ready to serve, add the sliced cucumber and tomatoes and toss lightly. Transfer to a serving dish and spoon the yogurt on top. Sprinkle with parsley and serve at once.

SWEET & SOUR ONION SALAD

This recipe is primarily from Provence in the south of France but there are influences from other Mediterranean countries, too.

SERVES 6

INGREDIENTS
450g/1lb baby (pearl) onions, peeled
50ml/2fl oz/¼ cup white wine vinegar
45ml/3 tbsp olive oil
40g/1½oz/3 tbsp caster (superfine) sugar
45ml/3 tbsp tomato purée (paste)
1 bay leaf
2 parsley sprigs
65g/2½oz/½ cup raisins
salt and ground black pepper

1 Put all the ingredients in a pan with 300ml/½ pint/1¼ cups water. Bring to the boil and simmer gently, uncovered, for about 45 minutes, or until the onions are tender and most of the liquid has evaporated.

2 Remove and discard the bay leaf and parsley and check the seasoning, adding more if necessary. Transfer to a serving dish and leave to cool. Serve at room temperature.

ROASTED PEPPERS
WITH TOMATOES & ANCHOVIES

This is a Sicilian-style salad, using classic ingredients from the Italian island. The flavour improves if the salad is made and dressed an hour or two before serving.

SERVES 4

INGREDIENTS
1 red (bell) pepper
1 yellow (bell) pepper
4 ripe plum tomatoes, sliced
2 canned anchovies, drained and chopped
4 sun-dried tomatoes in oil, drained and sliced
15ml/1 tbsp capers, drained
15ml/1 tbsp pine nuts
1 garlic clove, very thinly sliced

FOR THE DRESSING
75ml/5 tbsp extra virgin olive oil
15ml/1 tbsp balsamic vinegar
5ml/1 tsp lemon juice
chopped fresh mixed herbs
salt and ground black pepper

1 Cut the peppers in half, and remove the seeds and stalks. Cut into quarters and cook, skin side up, under a hot grill (broiler) until the skin chars. Transfer to a bowl, and cover with a plate. Leave to cool. Peel the peppers and cut into strips.

2 Arrange the peppers and fresh tomatoes on a serving dish. Scatter over the anchovies, sun-dried tomatoes, capers, pine nuts and garlic.

3 To make the dressing, mix together the olive oil, vinegar, lemon juice and chopped herbs in a small jug (pitcher) and season with plenty of salt and ground black pepper. Pour over the salad just before serving.

SALAD NIÇOISE

Made with good quality ingredients, this Provençal salad makes a simple yet unbeatable summer lunch or supper dish, which is always popular. Serve with country-style bread and chilled white wine.

SERVES 4

INGREDIENTS
115g/4oz green beans, trimmed
115g/4oz mixed salad leaves
½ small cucumber, thinly sliced
4 ripe tomatoes, quartered
200g/7oz can tuna in oil, drained
50g/2oz can anchovies, drained
4 eggs, hard-boiled (hard-cooked)
½ bunch radishes, trimmed
50g/2oz/½ cup small black olives
flat leaf parsley, to garnish

FOR THE DRESSING
90ml/6 tbsp extra virgin olive oil
2 garlic cloves, crushed
15ml/1 tbsp white wine vinegar
salt and ground black pepper

1 To make the dressing, whisk together the oil, garlic and vinegar in a small jug (pitcher) and season to taste with salt and ground black pepper.

2 Halve the green beans and cook in a pan of boiling water for 2 minutes until just tender, then drain and leave to cool. Place the salad leaves, cucumber, tomatoes and beans in a large, shallow salad bowl and toss lightly. Flake the tuna and halve the anchovies lengthways. Shell and quarter the hard-boiled eggs.

3 Scatter the radishes, tuna, anchovies, eggs and olives over the salad. Pour over the dressing and toss together lightly. Serve garnished with parsley.

ORANGE CHICKEN SALAD

With their tangy flavour, orange segments are the perfect partner for tender chicken in this rice salad. To appreciate all the flavours, serve at room temperature.

SERVES 4

INGREDIENTS
3 large seedless oranges
175g/6oz/scant 1 cup white long grain rice
10ml/2 tsp Dijon mustard
2.5ml/½ tsp caster (superfine) sugar
175ml/6fl oz/¾ cup vinaigrette dressing (see Cook's Tip)
450g/1lb cooked chicken, diced
45ml/3 tbsp chopped fresh chives
75g/3oz/¾ cup cashew nuts, toasted
salt and ground black pepper
mixed salad leaves, to serve

1 Pare one of the oranges thinly. Put the orange rind in a pan and add the rice. Pour in 475ml/16fl oz/2 cups cold water and add a pinch of salt. Bring to the boil, cover and cook gently for about 15 minutes, or until tender.

2 Meanwhile, peel all the oranges. Working over a bowl to catch the juices, cut them into segments. In a jug (pitcher), whisk together the orange juice, mustard and sugar to the vinaigrette dressing. Taste and add more salt and pepper if needed. Spoon the rice into a bowl, discarding the orange rind; let it cool slightly, then add half the dressing. Toss well and cool completely.

3 Add the chicken, chives, cashew nuts and orange segments to the rice. Add the remaining dressing and toss gently. Serve on a bed of mixed salad leaves.

COOK'S TIP
To make vinaigrette dressing, put 45ml/3 tbsp red wine vinegar in a small jug (pitcher) and whisk with salt and black pepper to taste. Whisk in 90ml/6 tbsp corn oil and 60ml/4 tbsp olive oil.

Roasted Pepper
& Red Rice Salad

Peppers, sun-dried tomatoes and garlic give a distinctly Mediterranean flavour to this salad dish, which uses the red rice of Camargue. It makes an excellent accompaniment to spicy sausages or fish.

SERVES 4

INGREDIENTS
225g/8oz/generous 1 cup Camargue red rice
vegetable or chicken stock or water
45ml/3 tbsp olive oil
3 red (bell) peppers, seeded and sliced into strips
4–5 sun-dried tomatoes
4–5 whole garlic cloves, unpeeled
1 onion, chopped
30ml/2 tbsp chopped fresh parsley, plus extra to garnish
15ml/1 tbsp chopped fresh coriander (cilantro)
10ml/2 tsp balsamic vinegar
salt and ground black pepper

1 Cook the rice in stock or water, following the instructions on the packet. Heat the oil in a frying pan and add the peppers. Cook over a medium heat for 4 minutes, shaking occasionally.

2 Lower the heat, add the sun-dried tomatoes, whole garlic cloves and onion, cover the pan and cook for a further 8–10 minutes, stirring occasionally. Uncover and cook for 3 minutes more.

3 Off the heat, remove the garlic cloves and set aside. Stir in the parsley, coriander and balsamic vinegar into the pepper mixture and season with salt and ground black pepper to taste.

4 Spread the rice out on a serving dish and spoon the pepper mixture on top. Peel the whole garlic cloves, cut the flesh into slices and scatter these over the salad. Serve at room temperature, garnished with more fresh parsley.

SPANISH RICE SALAD

This colourful dish from Spain combines long grain rice with a selection of chopped raw salad vegetables. The well-flavoured dressing enhances the fresh flavours of the vegetables.

SERVES 6

INGREDIENTS
275g/10oz/1½ cups long grain rice
1 bunch spring onions (scallions), finely sliced
1 green (bell) pepper, seeded and finely diced
1 yellow (bell) pepper, seeded and finely diced
225g/8oz tomatoes, peeled, seeded and chopped
30ml/2 tbsp chopped fresh coriander (cilantro)

FOR THE DRESSING
75ml/5 tbsp mixed sunflower and olive oil
15ml/1 tbsp rice vinegar
5ml/1 tsp Dijon mustard
salt and ground black pepper

1 Cook the rice in a large pan of boiling water for 10–12 minutes until tender but still *al dente*. Drain, rinse under cold water and drain again. Leave to cool, then place in a large serving bowl. Add the spring onions, green and yellow peppers, tomatoes and coriander.

2 Make the dressing. Mix all the ingredients in a screw-top jar and shake vigorously until well mixed. Season to taste, then stir 60–75ml/4–5 tbsp of the dressing into the rice. Cover and chill for about 1 hour before serving. Offer the remaining dressing separately for guests to help themselves.

VARIATION
For even more colour and flavour, add cooked garden peas, cooked diced carrot and drained, canned sweetcorn to the salad.

PRAWN & MELON SALAD

This rich and colourful salad tastes best when made with fresh prawns. The chorizo sausage adds a lovely, rich spiciness to the dish.

SERVES 4

INGREDIENTS
1 avocado
15ml/1 tbsp lemon juice
½ small melon, cut into wedges
15g/½oz/1 tbsp butter
½ garlic clove
115g/4oz raw prawns, peeled and deveined
25g/1oz chorizo sausages, finely sliced
450g/1lb/4 cups cooked long grain rice
flat leaf parsley sprigs, to garnish

FOR THE DRESSING
75ml/5 tbsp natural (plain) yogurt
45ml/3 tbsp mayonnaise
15ml/1 tbsp olive oil
3 fresh tarragon sprigs
ground black pepper

1 Peel the avocado, remove the stone (pit) and cut the flesh into chunks. Place in a mixing bowl and toss lightly with the lemon juice. Slice off the melon rind, cut the flesh into chunks and add to the avocado.

2 Melt the butter in a small pan and fry the garlic for 30 seconds. Add the prawns and cook for about 3 minutes until evenly pink. Add the chorizo and stir-fry for 1 minute more. Mix into the avocado and melon, then leave to cool.

3 Make the dressing. Mix together all the ingredients in a food processor or blender and season to taste. Put the rice in a large salad bowl. Stir half the dressing into the rice and the rest into the avocado mixture. Pile the salad on top of the rice. Chill for about 30 minutes before serving, garnished with parsley sprigs.

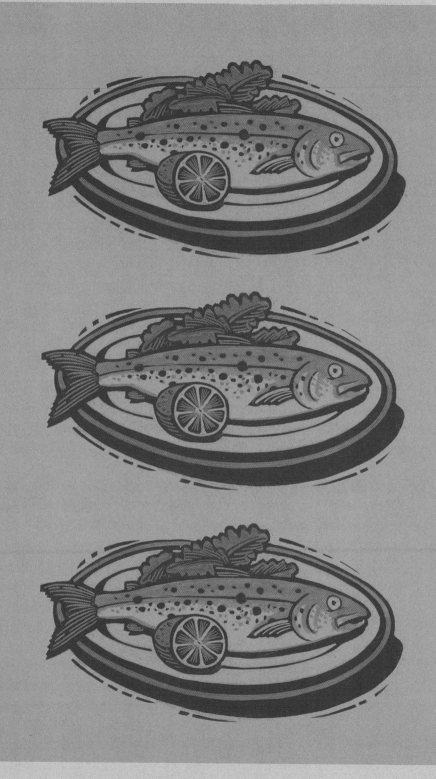

FISH & SHELLFISH

The Mediterranean is an abundant source of seafood and catches are brought to the markets in the region daily. Fish and shellfish are usually cooked simply – often pan-fried or grilled (broiled), or baked whole with herbs, spices and aromatics. Red mullet, sea bass, prawns (shrimp) and mussels are all excellent grilled. Oily fish such as sardines feature prominently in the region and Sardine Gratin is a favourite in Sicily. Local cooks also prepare delicious fish stews, using whatever combination of fish and shellfish is available in the market. The Spanish Zarzuela is a classic example of this.

TURKISH COLD FISH

Cold fish dishes are much appreciated in the Middle East and for good reason as they are delicious. This dish from Turkey can be made using mackerel if preferred.

SERVES 4

INGREDIENTS
60ml/4 tbsp olive oil
900g/2lb red mullet or snapper
2 onions, sliced
1 green (bell) pepper, seeded and sliced
1 red (bell) pepper, seeded and sliced
3 garlic cloves, crushed
15ml/1 tbsp tomato purée (paste)
50ml/2fl oz/¼ cup fish stock or water
5–6 tomatoes, peeled and sliced or 400g/14oz can tomatoes
30ml/2 tbsp chopped fresh parsley
30ml/2 tbsp lemon juice
5ml/1 tsp paprika
15–20 green and black olives
salt and ground black pepper
bread and salad, to serve

1 Heat half the oil in a large frying pan and fry the fish on both sides until golden brown. Remove from the pan and keep warm. Heat the remaining oil in the pan and fry the onion for 2–3 minutes. Add the peppers and cook for 3–4 minutes, stirring occasionally, then add the garlic and stir-fry for 1 minute.

2 In a jug (pitcher) blend the tomato purée with the fish stock or water, then stir into the peppers with the tomatoes, parsley, lemon juice, paprika and seasoning. Simmer very gently for 15 minutes, stirring occasionally. Return the fish to the pan and cover with the sauce. Cook for 10 minutes then add the green and black olives and cook for a further 5 minutes.

3 Transfer the fish to a serving dish and pour the sauce over. Allow to cool, then cover and chill. Serve cold with bread and salad.

PAN-FRIED RED MULLET WITH BASIL & CITRUS SAUCE

Red mullet is popular all over the Mediterranean. This Italian recipe combines it with oranges and lemons, which grow in abundance in the region.

SERVES 4

INGREDIENTS
4 red mullet, about 225g/8oz each, filleted
90ml/6 tbsp olive oil
10 peppercorns, crushed
2 oranges, one peeled and sliced and one squeezed
30ml/2 tbsp plain (all-purpose) flour
15g/½oz/1 tbsp butter
2 drained canned anchovies, chopped
1 lemon, ½ peeled and sliced and ½ squeezed
60ml/4 tbsp shredded fresh basil
salt and ground black pepper

1 Place the fish fillets in a shallow dish in a single layer. Pour over the olive oil and sprinkle with the crushed peppercorns. Lay the orange slices on top of the fish. Cover the dish, and leave to marinate in the refrigerator for at least 4 hours.

2 Lift the fish out of the marinade, and pat dry on kitchen paper. Reserve the marinade and orange slices. Season the fish with salt and ground black pepper and dust lightly with flour.

3 Heat 45ml/3 tbsp of the marinade in a frying pan. Add the fish and fry for 2 minutes on each side. Then remove from the pan and keep warm. Discard the marinade that is left in the pan.

4 Melt the butter in the pan with any of the remaining marinade. Add the anchovies and cook until softened. Stir in the orange and lemon juice, then check the seasoning and simmer until slightly reduced. Stir in the basil. Pour the sauce over the fish and garnish with the reserved orange slices and the lemon slices.

SAUTÉED SCALLOPS

Scallops go well with all sorts of sauces, but simple cooking is the best way to enjoy their sweet and delicate flavour. Here they are served with a delicate sauce flavoured with butter, dry vermouth and chopped fresh parsley.

SERVES 2

INGREDIENTS
450g/1lb shelled scallops
30g/1oz/2 tbsp butter
30ml/2 tbsp white dry vermouth
15ml/1 tbsp finely chopped fresh parsley
salt and ground black pepper

1 Rinse the scallops under cold running water to remove any sand or grit and pat dry using kitchen paper. Season them lightly with salt and pepper.

2 In a frying pan large enough to hold the scallops in one layer, heat half the butter until it begins to colour. Sauté the scallops for 3–5 minutes, turning, until golden brown on both sides and just firm to the touch. Remove to a serving platter and cover to keep warm.

3 Add the vermouth to the hot frying pan, swirl in the remaining butter, add the parsley and pour the sauce over the scallops. Serve immediately.

GRILLED MUSSELS WITH PARSLEY & PARMESAN

This is a wonderful way to serve mussels. As the mussels cook, they release an irresistible aroma and their delicate flavour is enhanced with the addition of good quality olive oil, Parmesan cheese and fresh garlic.

SERVES 4

INGREDIENTS
450g/1lb fresh mussels
45ml/3 tbsp water
15ml/1 tbsp melted butter
15ml/1 tbsp olive oil
45ml/3 tbsp freshly grated Parmesan cheese
30ml/2 tbsp chopped fresh parsley
2 garlic cloves, finely chopped
2.5ml/½ tsp coarsely ground black pepper

1 Scrub the mussels thoroughly, scraping off any barnacles with a round-bladed knife and pulling out the gritty beards. Discard any open mussels that fail to close when tapped sharply with the back of a knife.

2 Place the mussels and water in a large pan. Cover and steam for 5 minutes, or until the mussels have opened. Drain the mussels, discarding any that remain closed. Snap off and discard the top shell, leaving the mussel still attached to the bottom shell. Arrange the shells in a single layer in a flameproof dish, packing them closely together so they stay level.

3 Preheat the grill (broiler) to high. In a small bowl, mix together the melted butter, olive oil, Parmesan, parsley, garlic and black pepper. Using a teaspoon, place a small amount of this mixture on top of each mussel.

4 Grill (broil) the filled mussels for 2–3 minutes or until they are sizzling and golden. Serve the mussels immediately in their shells.

GRILLED KING PRAWNS WITH ROMESCO SAUCE

This tasty Spanish sauce is usually served with fish and shellfish. Its main ingredients are sweet pepper, tomatoes, garlic and almonds.

SERVES 4

INGREDIENTS
24 raw king prawns (jumbo shrimp)
30–45ml/2–3 tbsp olive oil
flat leaf parsley, to garnish
lemon wedges, to serve

FOR THE SAUCE
2 well-flavoured tomatoes
60ml/4 tbsp olive oil
1 onion, chopped
4 garlic cloves, chopped
1 canned pimiento, chopped
2.5ml/½ tsp dried chilli flakes or powder
75ml/5 tbsp fish stock
30ml/2 tbsp white wine
10 blanched almonds
15ml/1 tbsp red wine vinegar
salt

1 Make the sauce. Immerse the tomatoes in boiling water for 30 seconds, then refresh under cold water. Peel then roughly chop the flesh.

2 Heat 30ml/2 tbsp of the oil in a pan, add the onion and 3 of the garlic cloves and cook until soft. Add the pimiento, tomatoes, chilli, fish stock and white wine, then cover and simmer for 30 minutes.

3 Toast the almonds under the grill (broiler) until golden. Transfer to a food processor or blender and grind coarsely. Add the remaining 30ml/2 tbsp of oil, the vinegar and the last garlic clove and process until evenly combined. Add the tomato and pimiento sauce and process until smooth. Season with salt.

4 Remove the heads from the prawns leaving them otherwise unshelled and, with a sharp knife, slit each one down the back and remove the dark intestinal tract. Rinse under cold water and pat dry on kitchen paper. Toss the prawns in olive oil, then spread out in the grill (broiler) pan.

5 Grill (broil) the prawns for about 2–3 minutes on each side, until pink. Arrange on a serving platter with the lemon wedges. Serve at once, garnished with parsley, offering the sauce separately in a small bowl.

COOK'S TIP
If you would prefer a milder sauce, omit the chilli flakes or powder. Alternatively, substitute paprika, which will give the sauce a rich robust flavour without the heat of chilli.

GRILLED RED MULLET WITH HERBS

In Provence this fish is often charcoal-grilled with herbs from the region, or dried fennel branches which impart a light, sweet anise aroma.

SERVES 4

INGREDIENTS
olive oil, for brushing
4 red mullet (225–275g/8–10oz each), cleaned and scaled
fresh herb sprigs, such as parsley, dill, basil or thyme
30–45ml/2–3 tbsp pastis (anise liqueur)

1 About one hour before cooking, light a charcoal fire: when ready the coals should be grey with no flames. Generously brush a hinged grilling (broiling) rack with olive oil.

2 Brush each fish with a little olive oil and stuff the cavity with a few herb sprigs, breaking them to fit if necessary. Secure the fish in the grilling rack. Lay some dried fennel sticks, if you have them, over the coals and grill the fish for about 20 minutes, turning once during cooking.

3 Remove the fish to a warmed flameproof serving dish. Pour the pastis into a small pan and heat for a moment or two, then tilt the pan and carefully ignite with a long match. Pour over the fish and serve at once.

GRILLED SEA BASS WITH FENNEL & PERNOD

This dish is served in almost every fish restaurant on the French Mediterranean coast. The fennel is used in three different ways – the seeds for flavouring, the bulbs as a vegetable and the fronds to garnish.

SERVES 6–8

INGREDIENTS
1 sea bass, weighing 1.75kg/4–4½lb, cleaned
60–90ml/4–6 tbsp olive oil
10–15ml/2–3 tsp fennel seeds
2 large fennel bulbs, trimmed and thinly sliced (reserve any fronds)
60ml/4 tbsp Pernod
salt and ground black pepper

1 Using a sharp knife, make three or four deep cuts on both sides of the fish. Brush the fish with olive oil and season with salt and ground black pepper. Sprinkle the fennel seeds in the stomach cavity and in the cuts on both sides of the fish. Set aside while you cook the fennel.

2 Preheat the grill (broiler). Put the slices of fennel in a flameproof dish or on the grill rack and brush with oil. Grill (broil) for about 4 minutes on each side until tender. Transfer to a large platter.

3 Place the fish on the oiled grill rack and position about 10–13cm/4–5in away from the heat. Grill for about 10 minutes on each side, brushing with more olive oil occasionally.

4 Transfer the fish to the platter on top of the fennel. Garnish with fennel fronds. Heat the Pernod in a small pan, light it with a long match and pour it, still flaming, over the fish. Serve at once.

Monkfish with Tomatoes

Also known as angler fish, this fish was once scorned by fishermen because of its huge ugly head, yet now it is prized for its rich meaty texture. Here it is served in a rich tomato sauce flavoured with olives, capers and basil.

Serves 4

Ingredients
750g/1¾lb monkfish tail, skinned and filleted
plain (all-purpose) flour, for dusting
45–60ml/3–4 tbsp olive oil
125ml/4fl oz/½ cup dry white wine or fish stock
3 ripe tomatoes, peeled, seeded and chopped
2.5ml/½ tsp dried thyme
16 black olives (preferably Niçoise), pitted
15–30ml/1–2 tbsp capers, rinsed
15ml/1 tbsp chopped fresh basil
salt and ground black pepper
pine nuts, to garnish

1 Using a thin, sharp knife, remove any pinkish membrane from the monkfish tail. Holding the knife at a 45° angle, cut the fillets diagonally into 12 slices. Season the fish slices with salt and ground black pepper and dust lightly with flour, shaking off any excess.

2 Heat a large heavy frying pan over a high heat until very hot. Add 45ml/3 tbsp of the oil and swirl to coat. Add the monkfish slices and reduce the heat to medium-high. Cook the monkfish for 1–2 minutes on each side, adding a little more oil if necessary, until lightly browned and the flesh is opaque. Transfer the fish to a warmed plate and keep warm while you make the sauce.

3 Add the wine or fish stock to the pan and boil for 1–2 minutes, stirring constantly. Add the tomatoes and thyme and cook for 2 minutes, then stir in the olives, capers and basil and cook for a further minute to heat through. Arrange three pieces of fish on each of four warmed plates. Spoon over the sauce and serve immediately, garnished with pine nuts.

Tuna with Garlic, Tomatoes & Herbs

This classic dish comes from Provence in the South of France. Herbs, such as thyme, rosemary and oregano, grow wild on the nearby hillsides and feature in many of the recipes from this area.

SERVES 4

INGREDIENTS
4 tuna steaks, about 2.5cm/1in thick (175–200g/6–7oz each)
30–45ml/2–3 tbsp olive oil
3–4 garlic cloves, finely chopped
60ml/4 tbsp dry white wine
3 ripe plum tomatoes, peeled, seeded and chopped
5ml/1 tsp dried herbes de Provence
salt and ground black pepper
fresh basil leaves, to garnish

1 Season the tuna steaks with salt and pepper. Set a heavy frying pan over a high heat until very hot, add the oil and swirl to coat. Add the tuna steaks and press down gently, then reduce the heat to medium and cook for 6–8 minutes, turning once, until just slightly pink in the centre.

2 Transfer the steaks to a serving plate and cover to keep warm. Add the garlic to the pan and fry for 15–20 seconds, stirring all the time, then pour in the wine and boil until it is reduced by half. Add the tomatoes and dried herbs and cook for 2–3 minutes until the sauce is bubbly. Season with pepper and pour over the fish steaks. Serve, garnished with fresh basil leaves.

COOK'S TIP
Tuna is often served pink in the middle like beef. If you prefer it cooked through, reduce the heat and cook for an extra few minutes. However, be careful not to overcook it or it will become too dry.

BAKED FISH WITH TAHINI SAUCE

This North African dish evokes all the colour and rich flavours of Mediterranean cuisine. Choose any whole white fish, such as sea bass, hake, bream or snapper.

SERVES 4

INGREDIENTS
1 whole fish, about 1.1kg/2½lb, scaled and cleaned
10ml/2 tsp coriander seeds
4 garlic cloves, sliced
10ml/2 tsp harissa sauce
90ml/6 tbsp olive oil
6 plum tomatoes, sliced
1 mild onion, sliced
3 preserved lemons or 1 fresh lemon
plenty of fresh herbs, such as bay leaves, thyme and rosemary
salt and ground black pepper

FOR THE SAUCE
75ml/3fl oz/⅓ cup light tahini
juice of 1 lemon
1 garlic clove, crushed
45ml/3 tbsp finely chopped fresh parsley or coriander (cilantro)
extra herbs, to garnish

> COOK'S TIP
> *If you can't get a suitable large fish, use small whole fish such as red mullet or even substitute cod or haddock steaks. Remember to reduce the cooking time slightly.*

1 Preheat the oven to 200°C/400°F/Gas 6. Grease the base and sides of a large shallow ovenproof dish or roasting pan.

2 Slash the fish diagonally on both sides with a sharp knife. Finely crush the coriander seeds and garlic with a mortar and pestle. In a small bowl, combine the coriander seeds, garlic, harissa and about 60ml/4 tbsp of the olive oil.

3 Spread a little of the harissa, coriander and garlic paste inside the cavity of the fish. Spread the remainder over both sides of the fish and set aside.

4 Scatter the tomatoes, onion and preserved or fresh lemon into the dish or pan. (If using a fresh lemon, thinly slice.) Sprinkle with the remaining olive oil and season with salt and ground black pepper. Lay the fish on top and tuck plenty of herbs around it.

5 Bake the fish, uncovered, for about 25 minutes, or until the fish has turned opaque – test by piercing the thickest part with a knife.

6 Meanwhile, make the sauce. Put the tahini, lemon juice, garlic and parsley or coriander in a small pan with 120ml/4fl oz/½ cup water and add a little salt and black pepper. Cook gently until smooth and heated through. Serve the fish hot, handing the sauce separately for guests to help themselves.

MEDITERRANEAN BAKED FISH

This informal fish bake is said to have originated with the fishermen on the Côte d'Azur who would cook the remains of their catch for lunch in the still-warm baker's oven. Simply use the fish you have available.

SERVES 4

INGREDIENTS
3 potatoes
2 onions, halved and sliced
30ml/2 tbsp olive oil, plus extra for drizzling
2 garlic cloves, very finely chopped
675g/1½lb thick skinless fish fillets, such as turbot or sea bass
1 bay leaf
1 thyme sprig
3 tomatoes, peeled and thinly sliced
30ml/2 tbsp orange juice
60ml/4 tbsp dry white wine
2.5ml/½ tsp saffron threads soaked in 60ml/4 tbsp boiling water
salt and ground black pepper

1 Cook the potatoes in a pan of boiling salted water for 15 minutes, then drain. When the potatoes are cool enough to handle, peel and slice thinly.

2 Meanwhile, in a heavy frying pan, fry the onions in the oil over a medium-low heat for about 10 minutes, stirring frequently. Add the garlic and continue cooking for a few minutes until the onions are soft and golden.

3 Preheat the oven to 190°C/375°F/Gas 5. Layer half the slices of potato in a 2 litre/3⅓ pint/8 cup baking dish. Cover with half the onions. Season with salt and pepper. Place the fish on top of the vegetables and tuck in the herbs between them. Top with the tomato slices and then the remaining onions and potatoes.

4 Pour over the orange juice, wine and saffron liquid, season with salt and pepper and drizzle a little extra olive oil on top. Bake uncovered for about 30 minutes until the potatoes are tender and the fish is cooked. Serve hot or warm.

HAKE & CLAMS WITH SALSA VERDE

Hake is one of the most popular fish in Spain and here it is cooked in a sauce flavoured with parsley, lemon juice and garlic.

SERVES 4

INGREDIENTS
4 hake steaks, about 2cm/³⁄₄in thick
plain (all-purpose) flour for dusting, plus 30ml/2 tbsp
60ml/4 tbsp olive oil
15ml/1 tbsp lemon juice
1 small onion, finely chopped
4 garlic cloves, crushed
150ml/¼ pint/²⁄₃ cup fish stock
150ml/¼ pint/²⁄₃ cup white wine
90ml/6 tbsp chopped fresh parsley
75g/3oz/³⁄₄ cup frozen petits pois (baby peas)
16 fresh clams
salt and ground black pepper

1 Preheat the oven to 180°C/350°F/Gas 4. Season the fish with salt and pepper, then dust both sides with flour. Heat half the oil in a large sauté pan, add the fish and fry for about 1 minute on each side. Transfer to an ovenproof dish and sprinkle with lemon juice.

2 Clean the pan, then heat the remaining oil. Add the onion and garlic and cook until soft. Stir in the measured flour and cook for about 1 minute. Gradually add the stock and wine, stirring until thickened and smooth. Add 75ml/5 tbsp of the parsley and the petits pois and season with salt and pepper.

3 Pour the sauce over the fish, and bake in the oven for 15–20 minutes, adding the clams to the dish 3–4 minutes before the end of the cooking time. Discard any clams that do not open, then sprinkle with the remaining chopped parsley and serve immediately.

SEA BASS WITH CITRUS FRUIT

This delicious fish is enjoyed all along the Mediterranean coastline. The delicate flavour of sea bass is complemented perfectly by the zesty flavours of grapefruit, orange and lemon, and olive oil.

SERVES 6

INGREDIENTS
1 small grapefruit
1 orange
1 lemon
1 sea bass (about 1.35kg/3lb), cleaned and scaled
6 fresh basil sprigs
6 fresh dill sprigs
plain (all-purpose) flour, for dusting
45ml/3 tbsp olive oil
4–6 shallots, peeled and halved
60ml/4 tbsp dry white wine
15g/¹⁄₂oz/1 tbsp butter
salt and ground black pepper
fresh dill, to garnish

1 With a vegetable peeler, carefully remove the rind from the grapefruit, orange and lemon leaving any white pith behind. Cut into thin julienne strips, cover and set aside.

2 Peel off and discard the white pith from the fruits. Working over a bowl to catch the juices, cut out the segments from the grapefruit and orange and set aside for the garnish. Slice the lemon thickly.

3 Preheat the oven to 190°C/375°F/Gas 5. Wipe the fish dry inside and out and season the cavity with salt and ground black pepper. Using a sharp knife, make three diagonal slashes on each side.

4 Reserve a few basil sprigs for the garnish and fill the cavity with the remaining basil, the lemon slices and half the julienne strips of citrus rind.

5 Dust the fish lightly with flour. In a roasting pan or flameproof casserole large enough to hold the fish, heat 30ml/2 tbsp of the olive oil over a medium-high heat and cook the fish for about 1 minute until the skin just crisps and browns on one side. Add the shallots.

6 Bake the fish for about 15 minutes, then carefully turn the fish over and stir the shallots. Drizzle the fish with the remaining oil and bake for a further 10–15 minutes until the flesh is opaque throughout.

7 Using a fish slice (spatula), carefully transfer the fish to a heated serving dish and remove and discard the basil, lemon slices and citrus rind from the cavity. Pour off any excess oil from the pan or casserole and add the wine and 30–45ml/2–3 tbsp of the fruit juices.

8 Bring the mixture to the boil over a high heat, stirring. Stir in the remaining julienne strips of citrus rind and boil for 2–3 minutes, then whisk in the butter. Spoon the shallots and sauce around the fish and garnish with dill and the reserved basil and grapefruit and orange segments.

SARDINE GRATIN

In Sicily and other countries in the western Mediterranean, sardines are filled with a robust stuffing, flavoursome enough to compete with the rich oiliness of the fish itself. This dish is good served with a leafy green salad.

SERVES 4

INGREDIENTS
15ml/1 tbsp light olive oil
½ small onion, finely chopped
2 garlic cloves, crushed
40g/1½oz/6 tbsp blanched almonds, chopped
25g/1oz/2 tbsp sultanas (golden raisins), roughly chopped
10 black olives, pitted
30ml/2 tbsp capers, roughly chopped
30ml/2 tbsp roughly chopped fresh parsley
50g/2oz/1 cup breadcrumbs
16 large sardines, scaled and gutted
25g/1oz/⅓ cup grated Parmesan cheese
salt and ground black pepper
flat leaf parsley, to garnish

1 Preheat the oven to 200°C/400°F/Gas 6. Lightly oil a large shallow ovenproof dish large enough to accommodate the sardines in a single layer.

2 Heat the oil in a frying pan and fry the onion and garlic gently for 3 minutes. Stir in the almonds, sultanas, olives, capers, parsley and 25g/1oz/¼ cup of the breadcrumbs. Season lightly with salt and pepper.

3 Make two or three diagonal cuts on each side of the sardines. Pack the stuffing into the cavities and lay the sardines in the prepared dish.

4 Mix the remaining breadcrumbs with the cheese and scatter over the fish. Bake for 20 minutes until the fish are cooked through. Test by cutting one sardine through the thickest part. Garnish with parsley and serve immediately.

Cod Steaks with Tomato & Herb Sauce

This is a Greek dish called Plaki, *which is very popular all over the country. Generally, fish is treated very simply, but this recipe is a little more involved, baking the fish with onions and tomatoes. It is good served warm or cold.*

SERVES 6

INGREDIENTS
300ml/½ pint/1¼ cups olive oil
2 onions, thinly sliced
3 large well-flavoured tomatoes, roughly chopped
3 garlic cloves, thinly sliced
5ml/1 tsp sugar
5ml/1 tsp chopped fresh dill
5ml/1 tsp chopped fresh mint
5ml/1 tsp chopped fresh celery leaves
15ml/1 tbsp chopped fresh parsley
6 cod steaks
juice of 1 lemon
salt and ground black pepper
fresh dill, mint or parsley, to garnish

1 Heat the olive oil in a large sauté pan or flameproof dish. Add the onions and cook for about 5 minutes, or until pale golden. Add the tomatoes, garlic, sugar, dill, mint, celery leaves and parsley with 300ml/½ pint/1¼ cups water. Season with salt and ground black pepper, then simmer, uncovered, for 25 minutes, until the liquid has reduced by one-third.

2 Add the fish steaks to the sauce and cook gently for 10–12 minutes, until the fish is just cooked. Remove from the heat and add the lemon juice.

3 Cover the pan and leave to stand for 20 minutes before serving. Arrange the cod in a serving dish and spoon the sauce over. Garnish with herbs and serve.

Fresh Tuna & Tomato Stew

This is a deliciously simple dish that relies on good basic ingredients. For a real Italian flavour serve it with polenta or pasta and a salad of mixed leaves and herbs.

SERVES 4

INGREDIENTS
12 baby (pearl) onions, peeled
900g/2lb ripe tomatoes
675g/1½lb fresh tuna
45ml/3 tbsp olive oil
2 garlic cloves, crushed
45ml/3 tbsp chopped fresh herbs
2 bay leaves
2.5ml/½ tsp caster (superfine) sugar
30ml/2 tbsp sun-dried tomato paste
150ml/¼ pint/⅔ cup dry white wine
salt and ground black pepper
baby courgettes (zucchini) and fresh herbs, to garnish

1 Leave the onions whole and cook in a pan of boiling water for 4–5 minutes until softened. Drain thoroughly.

2 Plunge the tomatoes into boiling water for 30 seconds, then refresh in cold water. Peel away the skins and chop the flesh roughly.

3 Cut the tuna into 2.5cm/1in chunks. Heat the oil in a large frying pan or sauté pan and quickly fry the tuna until browned on all sides. Drain and remove the fish from the pan.

4 Add the onions, garlic, tomatoes, chopped herbs, bay leaves, sugar, tomato paste and white wine to the pan and bring the mixture to the boil, breaking up the tomatoes with a wooden spoon.

5 Reduce the heat and simmer gently for about 5 minutes. Return the fish to the pan and cook for a further 5 minutes. Season with salt and ground black pepper to taste, and serve hot, garnished with baby courgettes and fresh herbs.

SALT COD FISHCAKES

These bitesize fishcakes are irresistible. Start them in good time, as the salt cod needs long soaking. Serve with a rich garlic mayonnaise or aioli.

SERVES 6

INGREDIENTS
450g/1lb potatoes, peeled and cubed
115g/4oz salt cod, soaked in cold water for 48 hours
15ml/1 tbsp olive oil
1 small onion, finely chopped
2 garlic cloves, finely chopped
30ml/2 tbsp chopped fresh parsley
1 egg, beaten
Tabasco or chilli sauce
plain (all-purpose) flour, for dusting
vegetable oil, for frying
salt and ground black pepper
flat leaf parsley and lemon wedges, to garnish
garlic mayonnaise or aioli, to serve

1 Cook the cubed potatoes in a pan of boiling water for 10–12 minutes until tender. Drain well, then mash until smooth. Set aside.

2 Place the salt cod in a frying pan, add water to cover and bring to the boil. Drain, then remove the skin and bones. Using a fork, break up the flesh. Heat the olive oil in a small pan and cook the onion and garlic for about 5 minutes until softened but not browned.

3 In a large bowl, mix together the mashed potato, flaked fish, fried onion mixture and parsley. Mix in the egg, then add salt, pepper and Tabasco or chilli sauce to taste. With floured hands, shape the mixture into 18 balls. Flatten them slightly and place on a large floured plate. Chill for about 15 minutes.

4 Heat 1cm/½in vegetable oil in a large frying pan. Cook the fishcakes on each side for 3–4 minutes until golden. Drain on kitchen paper and serve hot, garnished with parsley and lemon wedges, with mayonnaise or aioli.

FISH BALLS IN SPICY TOMATO SAUCE

This is an unusual and tasty dish that is cooked in one pan. The fish balls are called boulettes *in their native France. It serves four people as a main course, but also makes a great appetizer for eight.*

SERVES 4

INGREDIENTS
675g/1½lb cod, haddock or sea bass fillets
pinch of saffron
½ bunch flat leaf parsley
1 egg
25g/1oz/½ cup fresh white breadcrumbs
25ml/1½ tbsp olive oil
15ml/1 tbsp lemon juice
salt and ground black pepper
fresh flat leaf parsley and lemon wedges, to garnish

FOR THE SAUCE
1 onion, very finely chopped
2 garlic cloves, crushed
6 tomatoes, peeled, seeded and chopped
1 green or red chilli, seeded and finely sliced
90ml/6 tbsp olive oil
150ml/¼ pint/⅔ cup water
15ml/1 tbsp lemon juice

> VARIATION
> *Children love fish balls, so this makes a great family dish. If you prefer a plain garlic and tomato sauce, simply omit the sliced chilli and season with ground black pepper instead.*

1 Skin the fish and, if necessary, remove any bones. Cut the flesh into large chunks and place in a food processor or a blender.

2 Put the saffron in a small bowl and pour over 30ml/2 tbsp boiling water. Leave to stand for 5 minutes, then pour into the food processor or blender with the parsley, egg, breadcrumbs, olive oil and lemon juice. Season well with salt and pepper and process for 10–20 seconds until the fish is finely chopped and all the ingredients are combined.

3 Wet your hands in cold water, then mould the mixture into small balls about the size of walnuts and place them in a single layer on a plate.

4 To make the sauce, place the onion, garlic, tomatoes, chilli, olive oil and water in a pan. Bring to the boil then simmer, partially covered, for 10–15 minutes until the tomatoes are pulpy and the sauce is slightly reduced.

5 Stir the lemon juice into the simmering sauce, then add the fish balls. Cover and simmer very gently for 12–15 minutes until the fish balls are cooked through, turning them over occasionally.

6 Serve the fish balls and sauce immediately, garnished with flat leaf parsley and lemon wedges for squeezing over.

Stuffed Squid in Tomato & White Wine Sauce

This Greek delicacy is best made with large squid as they are less fiddly to stuff. If you have to make do with small squid, buy about 450g/1lb. This recipe uses strongly flavoured halloumi cheese from Cyprus in the stuffing.

Serves 4

INGREDIENTS
30ml/2 tbsp olive oil
1 large onion, finely chopped
2 garlic cloves, crushed
50g/2oz/1 cup fresh white breadcrumbs
60ml/4 tbsp chopped fresh parsley
115g/4oz halloumi cheese, grated
4 squid tubes, each about 18cm/7in long
900g/2lb ripe tomatoes
45ml/3 tbsp olive oil
1 large onion, chopped
5ml/1 tsp caster (superfine) sugar
120ml/4fl oz/½ cup dry white wine
several rosemary sprigs
salt and ground black pepper
toasted pine nuts and flat leaf parsley, to garnish

> VARIATION
> *If you would prefer a less rich filling, halve the quantity of cheese and breadcrumbs in the stuffing and add 225g/8oz cooked spinach.*

1 To make the stuffing, heat the olive oil in a frying pan and fry the onion for about 3 minutes. Remove the pan from the heat and add the garlic, breadcrumbs, parsley, halloumi cheese and a little salt and ground black pepper. Stir until thoroughly blended.

2 Rinse the squid tubes in cold water and pat dry with kitchen paper. Using a teaspoon, fill the tubes with the prepared stuffing. Secure the ends of each stuffed tube with wooden cocktail sticks (toothpicks).

3 Plunge the tomatoes into boiling water for 30 seconds, then refresh in cold water. Peel away the skins and chop the flesh roughly.

4 Heat the olive oil in a frying pan or sauté pan. Add the stuffed squid and fry very briefly on all sides. Remove from the pan and set aside.

5 Add the onion to the pan and fry gently for 3 minutes. Stir in the tomatoes, sugar and wine and cook rapidly until the mixture becomes thick and pulpy.

6 Return the squid to the pan with the rosemary sprigs. Cover and cook gently for 30 minutes. Slice the squid and serve on individual plates with the sauce. Scatter over the pine nuts and garnish with parsley.

OCTOPUS & RED WINE STEW

Unless you're happy to clean and prepare octopus for this Greek dish, buy one that's ready for cooking. It will save a great deal of time.

SERVES 4

INGREDIENTS
900g/2lb prepared octopus
450g/1lb onions, sliced
2 bay leaves
450g/1lb ripe tomatoes
60ml/4 tbsp olive oil
4 garlic cloves, crushed
5ml/1 tsp caster (superfine) sugar
15ml/1 tbsp chopped fresh oregano or rosemary
30ml/2 tbsp chopped fresh parsley
150ml/¼ pint/⅔ cup red wine
30ml/2 tbsp red wine vinegar
chopped fresh herbs, to garnish
warm bread and pine nuts, to serve

1 Put the octopus in a large pan of gently simmering water with a quarter of the onions and the bay leaves. Cook gently for 1 hour, then drain.

2 Meanwhile, plunge the tomatoes into boiling water for 30 seconds, then refresh in cold water. Peel away the skins and chop the flesh roughly.

3 When the octopus is cool enough to handle, cut it into bitesize pieces, using a sharp knife. Discard the head.

4 Heat the olive oil in a pan and fry the octopus, the remaining onions and the garlic for about 3 minutes. Add the tomatoes, sugar, oregano or rosemary, parsley, wine and vinegar and cook, stirring, for 5 minutes, or until the tomatoes become pulpy.

5 Cover the pan and cook very gently over the lowest possible heat for about 1½ hours until the sauce is thickened and the octopus is tender. Garnish with fresh herbs and serve with plenty of warm bread, and pine nuts to scatter on top.

MOUCLADE OF MUSSELS

This recipe is similar to Moules Marinière but has the extra flavourings of fennel and mild curry. Traditionally the mussels are shelled and piled into scallop shells.

SERVES 6

INGREDIENTS
1.75kg/4½lb fresh mussels
250ml/8fl oz/1 cup dry white wine
good pinch of grated nutmeg
3 thyme sprigs
2 bay leaves
1 small onion, finely chopped
50g/2oz/¼ cup butter
1 fennel bulb, thinly sliced
4 garlic cloves, crushed
2.5ml/½ tsp curry paste or powder
30ml/2 tbsp plain (all-purpose) flour
150ml/¼ pint/⅔ cup double (heavy) cream
ground black pepper
chopped fresh dill, to garnish

1 Scrub the mussels, discarding any that are damaged or that do not close when tapped with a knife. Put the wine, nutmeg, thyme, bay leaves and onion in a large pan and bring to the boil. Tip in the mussels, cover and cook for 4–5 minutes. Drain, reserving the liquid. Discard any mussels that remain closed.

2 Melt the butter in a large pan; fry the fennel and garlic for 5 minutes until softened. Stir in the curry paste or powder and flour; cook for 1 minute. Remove from the heat and blend in the mussel liquid. Return to the heat and cook, stirring, for 2 minutes. Stir in the cream and a little pepper. Add the mussels and heat through for 2 minutes. Serve hot, garnished with dill.

COOK'S TIP
Saffron is a popular addition to a mouclade. Soak 2.5ml/½ tsp saffron strands in a little boiling water and add to the sauce with the stock.

ITALIAN FISH STEW

Each different region of Italy has its own variation of this dish but all require a good fish stock. Make sure you buy some of the fish whole so you can simply simmer them, remove the cooked flesh and strain the juices to make the stock.

SERVES 4–5

INGREDIENTS
900g/2lb mixture of fish fillets or steaks, such as monkfish, cod,
  haddock, halibut or hake
900g/2lb mixture of conger eel, red or grey mullet, red snapper
  or pompano, or small white fish
1 onion, halved
1 celery stick, roughly chopped
225g/8oz squid
225g/8oz fresh mussels
675g/1½lb ripe tomatoes
60ml/4 tbsp olive oil
1 large onion, thinly sliced
3 garlic cloves, crushed
5ml/1 tsp saffron strands
150ml/¼ pint/⅔ cup dry white wine
90ml/6 tbsp chopped fresh parsley
salt and ground black pepper
croûtons, to serve (see Cook's Tip)

COOK'S TIP
To make the croûtons, cut thin slices from a long
thin stick of bread and shallow-fry in a little butter
until golden all over. Drain on kitchen paper.

1 Remove any skin and bones from the fish fillets or steaks, cut the fish into large pieces and reserve. Place the bones in a pan with all the remaining fish.

2 Add the halved onion and the celery to the pan and cover with water. Bring almost to the boil, then reduce the heat and simmer gently for about 30 minutes. Lift out the fish and remove the flesh from the bones. Reserve the stock.

3 To prepare the squid, twist the head and tentacles away from the body. Cut the head from the tentacles. Discard the body contents and peel away the mottled skin. Wash the tentacles and bodies and pat dry with kitchen paper.

4 Scrub the mussels and scrape off the beards. Discard any that are damaged or open ones that do not close when tapped. Plunge the tomatoes into boiling water for 30 seconds, then refresh in cold water. Peel away the skins and chop the flesh roughly.

5 Heat the oil in a large pan or sauté pan. Add the sliced onion and the garlic and fry gently for 3 minutes. Add the squid and the reserved uncooked white fish, and fry quickly on all sides. Drain.

6 Add 475ml/16fl oz/2 cups strained reserved fish stock, the saffron and tomatoes to the pan. Pour in the wine. Bring to the boil, then reduce the heat and simmer for about 5 minutes. Add the mussels, cover, and cook for 3–4 minutes until the mussels have opened. Discard any that remain closed.

7 Season the sauce with salt and pepper and put all the fish in the pan. Cook gently for 5 minutes. Scatter with the parsley and serve with the croûtons.

SPANISH FISH STEW

This dish is called Zarzuela *in Spain, meaning light opera or musical comedy –
reflecting the liveliness and colour of the stew. This version includes lobster and
other shellfish, but any combination will work well.*

SERVES 6

INGREDIENTS
1 cooked lobster
24 fresh mussels
1 large monkfish tail
225g/8oz squid rings
15ml/1 tbsp plain (all-purpose) flour
90ml/6 tbsp olive oil
12 large raw prawns (shrimp)
450g/1lb ripe tomatoes
2 large mild onions, chopped
4 garlic cloves, crushed
30ml/2 tbsp brandy
2 bay leaves
5ml/1 tsp paprika
1 fresh red chilli, seeded and chopped
300ml/½ pint/1¼ cups fish stock
15g/½oz/2 tbsp ground almonds
30ml/2 tbsp chopped fresh parsley
salt and ground black pepper
green salad and bread, to serve

1 Using a large knife, cut the lobster in half lengthways. Remove the dark intestine that runs down the length of the tail. Crack the claws using a hammer.

2 Scrub the mussels, scrape off the beards, and discard any that are damaged or open ones that do not close when tapped with a knife. Cut the monkfish fillets away from the central cartilage and cut each fillet into three.

3 Toss the monkfish and squid in seasoned flour. Heat the oil in a large frying pan. Add the monkfish and squid and fry quickly; remove from the pan. Add the prawns and fry on both sides, then remove from the pan.

4 Plunge the tomatoes into boiling water for 30 seconds, then refresh in cold water. Peel away the skins and chop the flesh roughly.

5 Add the chopped onions and two-thirds of the garlic to the frying pan and fry for 3 minutes. Add the brandy and ignite with a taper. When the flames die down, add the tomatoes, bay leaves, paprika, chilli and stock.

6 Bring the mixture to the boil, reduce the heat and simmer gently for 5 minutes. Add the mussels, cover and cook for about 3 minutes, until the shells have opened. Remove the mussels from the sauce and discard any that remain closed.

7 Arrange all the fish, including the lobster, in a large flameproof serving dish. Blend the ground almonds to a paste with the remaining garlic and parsley and stir into the sauce. Season with salt and pepper.

8 Pour the sauce over the fish and lobster and cook gently for about 5 minutes until hot. Serve immediately with a green salad and plenty of warmed bread for mopping up the flavoursome sauce.

MEAT DISHES

Despite the rugged terrain of the Mediterranean countryside, cooks have always made the most of the meat available. The traditional cooking methods of braising, slow-roasting and grilling over charcoal or wood fires remain today, even though the quality of meat has improved tremendously. Other popular cooking techniques include marinating in yogurt or wine, or mincing and making into sausages, meatballs and patties. Classic Mediterranean meat dishes include Provençal Beef and Olive Daube, Moroccan-style Lamb Tagine with Spices, Beef Rolls with Garlic and Tomato Sauce, and Lebanese Meat Dumplings with Yogurt.

PROVENÇAL BEEF
& OLIVE DAUBE

A daube is a French method of braising meat with wine and herbs. This version from the south of France also includes black olives and tomatoes.

SERVES 6

INGREDIENTS
1.5kg/3¼lb topside (pot roast) beef
225g/8oz lardons or thick streaky (fatty) bacon, cut into strips
225g/8oz carrots, sliced
1 bay leaf
1 thyme sprig
2 parsley stalks
3 garlic cloves
225g/8oz/2 cups pitted black olives
400g/14oz can chopped tomatoes
crusty bread, flageolet (small cannellini) beans or pasta, to serve

FOR THE MARINADE
120ml/4fl oz/½ cup extra virgin olive oil
1 onion, sliced
4 shallots, sliced
1 celery stick, sliced
1 carrot, sliced
150ml/¼ pint/⅔ cup red wine
6 peppercorns
2 garlic cloves, sliced
1 bay leaf
1 thyme sprig
2 parsley stalks
salt

1 To make the marinade, heat the oil in a large shallow pan; add the onion, shallots, celery and carrot. Cook for 2 minutes, then lower the heat and add the red wine, peppercorns, garlic, bay leaf, thyme and parsley stalks. Season with salt, then cover and leave to simmer gently for 15–20 minutes. Set aside to cool.

2 Place the beef in a large glass or earthenware dish and pour over the cooled marinade. Cover the dish and leave to marinate in a cool place or in the refrigerator for 12 hours, turning the meat once or twice.

3 Preheat the oven to 160°C/325°F/Gas 3. Lift the meat out of the marinade and fit snugly into an ovenproof casserole. Add the lardons or bacon strips and carrots, along with the bay leaf, thyme, parsley and garlic. Strain in all the marinade. Cover the casserole with greaseproof (waxed) paper, then put the lid on and cook in the oven for 2½ hours.

4 Remove the casserole from the oven and stir in the olives and tomatoes. Re-cover the casserole, return to the oven and cook for a further 30 minutes. Serve the meat cut into thick slices, accompanied by crusty bread, beans or pasta.

Corsican Beef Stew with Macaroni

Pasta is eaten in many parts of the Mediterranean. In Corsica, it is often served with gravy rather than a sauce and, in this case, a rich beef stew. Dried mushrooms add an extra richness to this meaty stew.

Serves 4

INGREDIENTS
25g/1oz dried mushrooms (ceps or porcini)
6 garlic cloves
900g/2lb stewing beef, cut into 5cm/2in cubes
115g/4oz lardons or thick streaky (fatty) bacon, cut into strips
45ml/3 tbsp olive oil
2 onions, sliced
300ml/½ pint/1¼ cups dry white wine
30ml/2 tbsp passata (bottled strained tomatoes)
pinch of ground cinnamon
1 rosemary sprig
1 bay leaf
225g/8oz/2 cups large macaroni
50g/2oz/⅔ cup freshly grated Parmesan cheese
salt and ground black pepper

COOK'S TIP
If you do not have dried mushrooms use fresh ones instead. Slice or chop large ones but leave button (white) mushrooms whole. Add them to the pan for the final 30 minutes' cooking.

1 Soak the dried mushrooms in warm water for about 30 minutes. Drain, reserving the soaking liquid, and set the mushrooms aside. Cut three of the garlic cloves into thin strips and insert into the pieces of beef by making little slits with a sharp knife. Push the lardons or bacon strips into the beef with the garlic. Season the meat with salt and ground black pepper.

2 Heat the olive oil in a heavy pan, add half the beef and brown well on all sides. Transfer to a plate. Repeat with the remaining beef. Add the sliced onions to the pan and cook until lightly browned. Crush the remaining garlic and add to the onions with the meat.

3 Stir in the white wine, passata, mushrooms, cinnamon, rosemary and bay leaf and season with salt and ground black pepper. Cook gently for about 30 minutes, stirring often. Strain the mushroom liquid and add to the stew with enough water to cover. Stir to combine. Bring to the boil, cover and simmer very gently for 3 hours, or until the meat is very tender.

4 Cook the macaroni in a large pan of boiling salted water for 10 minutes, or until *al dente*. Lift the pieces of meat out of the gravy and transfer to a warmed serving platter. Drain the pasta and layer in a serving bowl with the gravy and cheese. Serve at once with the meat.

Beef Rolls with Garlic & Tomato Sauce

Italy has many regional variations of this technique of wrapping thin slices of beef around a richly flavoured stuffing. This recipe incorporates some of the classic ingredients of Italian cuisine.

Serves 4

Ingredients
4 thin slices of rump (round) steak (about 115g/4oz each)
4 slices smoked ham
150g/5oz Pecorino cheese, grated
2 garlic cloves, crushed
75ml/5 tbsp chopped fresh parsley
2 eggs, soft-boiled (soft-cooked), shelled and chopped
45ml/3 tbsp olive oil
1 large onion, finely chopped
150ml/¼ pint/⅔ cup passata (bottled strained tomatoes)
75ml/3fl oz/⅓ cup red wine
2 bay leaves
150ml/¼ pint/⅔ cup beef stock
salt and ground black pepper
flat leaf parsley, to garnish

Cook's Tip
Pecorino cheese is available from most supermarkets. It is made from sheep's milk and has a sharp, fruity tang. A good quality pecorino should feel moist, yet granular.

1 Preheat the oven to 160°C/325°F/Gas 3. Lay the beef slices on a sheet of baking parchment. Cover the beef with another sheet of baking parchment or clear film (plastic wrap) and beat with a mallet or rolling pin until very thin.

2 Lay a ham slice over each slice of beef. Mix the cheese in a bowl with the garlic, parsley, eggs and a little salt and ground black pepper. Stir well until all the ingredients are evenly mixed.

3 Spoon the stuffing on to the ham and beef slices. Fold two opposite sides of the meat over the stuffing, then carefully roll up the meat to form neat parcels. Secure with string.

4 Heat the olive oil in a frying pan. Add the parcels and fry quickly on all sides to brown. Transfer to an ovenproof dish.

5 Add the onion to the frying pan and fry for about 3 minutes. Stir in the passata, wine, bay leaves and stock and season with salt and pepper. Bring to the boil, then pour the sauce over the meat in the dish.

6 Cover the dish and bake in the oven for 1 hour. Drain the meat and remove the string. Spoon on to warmed serving plates. Taste the sauce, adding extra salt and ground black pepper if necessary, and spoon it over the meat. Serve garnished with flat leaf parsley.

VEAL STEW WITH TOMATOES

This is a very popular meat in Italy and is cooked in many different ways. Here it is cooked in a rich tomato sauce.

SERVES 6

INGREDIENTS
60ml/4 tbsp plain (all-purpose) flour
1.3kg/3lb boneless veal shoulder, cut into 4cm/1½in pieces
30–45ml/2–3 tbsp olive oil
4 or 5 shallots, finely chopped
2 garlic cloves, very finely chopped
300ml/½ pint/1¼ cups dry white wine
450g/1lb tomatoes, peeled, seeded and chopped
grated rind and juice of 1 orange
1 bouquet garni
15ml/1 tbsp tomato purée (paste)
15g/½oz/1 tbsp butter
350g/¾lb button (white) mushrooms, quartered if large
salt and ground black pepper
chopped fresh parsley, to garnish

1 Put the flour in a polythene bag and season with salt and pepper. Drop in the veal, shake to coat, then tap off any excess. Heat 30ml/2 tbsp of the oil in a flameproof casserole over a medium-high heat. Brown the veal on all sides in batches, then transfer to a plate.

2 In the same pan, cook the shallots and garlic over a medium heat, stirring, until softened. (Add more oil if needed.) Stir in the wine and bring to the boil. Return the veal to the pan and add the tomatoes, orange rind and juice, bouquet garni and tomato purée. Return to the boil, reduce the heat, cover and simmer for 1 hour.

3 Melt the butter in a frying pan over a medium heat and sauté the mushrooms until golden. Add the mushrooms to the casserole and cook, covered, for 20–30 minutes, or until the meat is very tender. Adjust the seasoning if needed and discard the bouquet garni before serving, garnished with parsley.

MEATBALLS IN TOMATO SAUCE

Serve this classic Spanish dish with crusty bread and a robust red wine or, for a light meal for two, with a bowl of steaming pasta tossed in olive oil.

SERVES 4

INGREDIENTS
225g/8oz minced (ground) beef or lamb
4 spring onions (scallions), thinly sliced
2 garlic cloves, finely chopped
30ml/2 tbsp freshly grated Parmesan
10ml/2 tsp fresh thyme leaves
15ml/1 tbsp olive oil
3 tomatoes, chopped
30ml/2 tbsp red or dry white wine
10ml/2 tsp chopped fresh rosemary
pinch of sugar
salt and ground black pepper
fresh thyme, to garnish

1 Place the minced beef or lamb in a bowl. Add the spring onions, garlic, Parmesan and thyme and plenty of salt and black pepper. Mix well, then shape the mixture into 12 small firm balls.

2 Heat the olive oil in a large frying pan, then add the meatballs and cook for about 5 minutes, turning frequently until evenly browned.

3 Add the chopped tomatoes, red or white wine, rosemary and sugar, and season with salt and ground black pepper to taste. Cover and cook gently for about 15 minutes until the tomatoes are pulpy and the meatballs are cooked. Serve hot, garnished with fresh thyme.

COOK'S TIP
Wet your hands before shaping the minced meat into balls. This will make the job much easier.

Sautéed Lamb with Yogurt

In the Middle East meat is normally stewed or barbecued. Here is a delicious exception from Turkey, in which the lamb is pan-fried instead.

Serves 4

Ingredients
450g/1lb lean lamb, preferably boned leg, cubed
40g/1½oz/3 tbsp butter
4 tomatoes, skinned and chopped
4 thick slices of bread, crusts removed
250ml/8fl oz/1 cup Greek (US strained plain) yogurt
2 garlic cloves, crushed
salt and ground black pepper
paprika and mint leaves, to garnish

For the marinade
120ml/4fl oz/½ cup Greek (US strained plain) yogurt
1 large onion, grated

1 Make the marinade. Blend together the yogurt, onion and a little seasoning in a large bowl. Add the cubed lamb, cover loosely with clear film (plastic wrap) and leave to marinate in a cool place for at least 1 hour.

2 Melt half the butter in a frying pan and fry the meat for 5–10 minutes, until tender but still moist. Transfer to a plate with a slotted spoon and keep warm while cooking the tomatoes.

3 Melt the remaining butter in the same pan and fry the tomatoes for 4–5 minutes until soft. Meanwhile, toast the bread and arrange in the base of a shallow serving dish. Season the tomatoes and then spread over the toasted bread.

4 Blend the yogurt and garlic and season with salt and ground black pepper. Spoon over the tomatoes in the serving dish.

5 Arrange the meat in a layer on top of the yogurt-covered tomatoes. Sprinkle with paprika and mint leaves and serve at once.

LAMB WITH RED PEPPERS

Plenty of garlic, peppers, herbs and red wine give this Spanish lamb stew a lovely rich flavour. Slice through the pepper stalks, rather than removing them.

SERVES 4

INGREDIENTS
900g/2lb lean lamb fillet
15ml/1 tbsp plain (all-purpose) flour
60ml/4 tbsp olive oil
2 red onions, sliced
4 garlic cloves, sliced
10ml/2 tsp paprika
1.5ml/¼ tsp ground cloves
400ml/14fl oz/1⅔ cups red Rioja
150ml/¼ pint/⅔ cup lamb stock
2 bay leaves
2 thyme sprigs
3 red (bell) peppers, halved and seeded
salt and ground black pepper
bay leaves and thyme sprigs, to garnish
green beans and saffron rice or boiled potatoes, to serve

1 Preheat the oven to 160°C/325°F/Gas 3. Cut the lamb into chunks. Put the flour in a bowl and season with salt and pepper. Add the lamb and toss lightly.

2 Heat the oil in a frying pan and fry the lamb, stirring, until browned. Transfer to an ovenproof dish. Add the onions, garlic, paprika and ground cloves to the pan and fry gently for a few minutes.

3 Add the Rioja, stock, bay leaves and thyme to the pan and bring to the boil. Pour over the browned lamb, cover and bake for 30 minutes.

4 Remove the dish from the oven. Stir the red peppers into the stew and season lightly with salt and pepper. Bake for a further 30 minutes until the meat is tender. Garnish with bay leaves and sprigs of thyme and serve with green beans and saffron rice or boiled potatoes.

LAMB CASSEROLE WITH GARLIC & BROAD BEANS

This recipe has a Spanish influence and makes a substantial meal, served with potatoes. Lamb is stewed with whole garlic cloves and dry sherry to create a deliciously aromatic stew. The addition of broad beans provides colour and counteracts the robust flavour of the hearty sauce.

SERVES 6

INGREDIENTS
45ml/3 tbsp olive oil
1.5kg/3¼lb lamb fillet, cut into 5cm/2in cubes
1 large onion, chopped
6 large garlic cloves, unpeeled
1 bay leaf
5ml/1 tsp paprika
120ml/4fl oz/½ cup dry sherry
115g/4oz shelled fresh or frozen broad (fava) beans
30ml/2 tbsp chopped fresh parsley
salt and ground black pepper

1 Heat 30ml/2 tbsp of the oil in a large flameproof casserole. Add half the meat and brown well on all sides. Transfer to a plate. Brown the rest of the meat in the same way and remove from the casserole.

2 Heat the remaining oil in the casserole, add the onion and cook for about 5 minutes, or until soft. Return the meat to the casserole.

3 Add the garlic cloves, bay leaf, paprika and sherry to the casserole. Season with salt and ground black pepper. Bring to the boil, then cover and simmer very gently for 1½–2 hours, or until the meat is tender.

4 Add the broad beans about 10 minutes before the end of the cooking time. Stir in the chopped parsley just before serving.

Lamb Tagine with Spices

This Moroccan-style tagine can be made with chops or cutlets. It can be left to marinate for a few hours or cooked immediately after seasoning.

Serves 4

Ingredients
4 lamb chump chops
2 garlic cloves, crushed
pinch of saffron strands
2.5ml/½ tsp ground cinnamon, plus for sprinkling
2.5ml/½ tsp ground ginger
15ml/1 tbsp chopped fresh coriander (cilantro)
15ml/1 tbsp chopped fresh parsley
1 onion, finely chopped
45ml/3 tbsp olive oil
300ml/½ pint/1¼ cups lamb stock
5ml/1 tsp sugar
salt and ground black pepper
50g/2oz/½ cup blanched almonds, to garnish

1 On a large plate, season the lamb with the garlic, saffron, cinnamon, ginger and a little salt and black pepper. Sprinkle with the coriander, parsley and onion. Cover loosely and set aside in the refrigerator for a few hours to marinate.

2 Heat the oil in a large frying pan over a medium heat. Add the lamb and fry for 1–2 minutes, turning once, then add the stock, bring to the boil and simmer gently for 30 minutes, turning the chops once.

3 Meanwhile prepare the garnish. Heat a small frying pan over a medium heat, add the almonds and dry-fry until golden all over.

4 Transfer the chops to a serving plate and keep warm. Boil the sauce until reduced by about half. Stir in the sugar. Pour the sauce over the chops and sprinkle with the fried almonds and a little extra ground cinnamon.

Turkish Lamb with Apricot & Cashew Nut Rice

The traditional way of cooking meat in Turkey is over hot charcoal or in a wood-burning stove. This produces a crusty, almost charred exterior enclosing beautifully moist, tender meat. In this recipe, the meat juices flavour the rice beneath.

Serves 6

Ingredients
half leg of lamb, about 1.5kg/3¼lb, boned
1 bunch of fresh parsley
1 small bunch of fresh coriander (cilantro)
50g/2oz/½ cup cashew nuts
2 garlic cloves
15ml/1 tbsp sunflower oil
1 small onion, finely chopped
200g/7oz/1¾ cups cooked white long grain rice
75g/3oz/scant ½ cup ready-to-eat dried apricots, finely chopped
salt and ground black pepper
fresh parsley or coriander sprigs, to garnish
tzatziki, black olives and pitta bread, to serve (optional)

Cook's Tip
In Turkey, the meat would be cooked until very well done, but it can also be served slightly pink, in the French style. For a doner kebab, split warmed pitta breads and stuff with meat, yogurt and a spicy tomato sauce. Alternatively, serve with the rice and a broad (fava) bean salad.

1 Preheat the oven to 200°C/400°F/Gas 6. Remove the excess fat from the lamb, then trim the joint, if necessary, so that it lies flat. (If the leg has been tunnel boned, you will need to cut the meat before it will lie flat.)

2 Put the parsley and coriander in a food processor or blender and process until finely chopped. Add the cashew nuts and pulse until roughly chopped.

3 Crush one of the garlic cloves. Heat the oil in a frying pan and fry the onion and crushed garlic for 3–4 minutes until softened but not browned.

4 Put the rice in a bowl. Using a spatula, scrape all the parsley and cashew nut mixture into the rice. Add the fried onion mixture and the chopped apricots. Season with salt and pepper, stir well, then spoon into the base of a roasting pan, which is just large enough to hold the lamb.

5 Cut the remaining garlic clove in half and rub the cut sides over the meat. Season with black pepper, then lay the meat on top of the rice, tucking all the rice under the meat, so that no rice is visible.

6 Roast the lamb on the middle shelf of the oven for 30 minutes, then lower the temperature to 180°C/350°F/Gas 4. Cook for 35–45 minutes more or until the meat is cooked to your taste.

7 Cover the lamb and rice with foil and leave to rest for 5 minutes, then lift the lamb on to a board and slice it thickly. Spoon the rice mixture on to a platter, arrange the meat slices on top and garnish with fresh parsley or coriander. Serve at once, with a bowl of tzatziki, black olives and pitta bread, if liked.

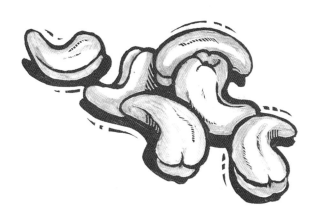

MOUSSAKA

Like many popular classics, a real moussaka bears little resemblance to the imitations experienced in many Greek tourist resorts. This one is mildly spiced, moist but not dripping in grease, and encased in a golden baked crust.

SERVES 6

INGREDIENTS
900g/2lb aubergines (eggplant)
120ml/4fl oz/½ cup olive oil
2 large tomatoes
2 large onions, sliced
450g/1lb minced (ground) lamb
1.5ml/¼ tsp ground cinnamon
1.5ml/¼ tsp ground allspice
30ml/2 tbsp tomato purée (paste)
45ml/3 tbsp chopped fresh parsley
120ml/4fl oz/½ cup dry white wine
45ml/3 tbsp toasted breadcrumbs
salt and ground black pepper

FOR THE SAUCE
50g/2oz/4 tbsp butter
50g/2oz/½ cup plain (all-purpose) flour
600ml/1 pint/2½ cups milk
1.5ml/¼ tsp grated nutmeg
25g/1oz/⅓ cup grated Parmesan cheese

1 Cut the aubergines into 5mm/¼in thick slices. Layer the slices in a colander, sprinkling each layer with plenty of salt. Leave to drain for 30 minutes.

2 Rinse the aubergines in several changes of cold water. Squeeze gently with your fingers to remove the excess water, then pat dry on kitchen paper.

3 Heat some of the oil in a large frying pan. Fry the aubergine slices in batches until golden on both sides, adding more oil when necessary. Leave the fried aubergine slices to drain on kitchen paper.

4 Plunge the tomatoes into boiling water for 30 seconds, then refresh in cold water. Peel away the skins and chop the flesh roughly.

5 Preheat the oven to 180°C/350°F/Gas 4. Heat 30ml/2 tbsp oil in a pan. Add the onions and lamb and fry gently for 5 minutes, stirring and breaking up the lamb with a wooden spoon.

6 Add the tomatoes, cinnamon, allspice, tomato purée, parsley, wine and black pepper and bring to the boil. Reduce the heat, cover with a lid and simmer gently for about 15 minutes.

7 Spoon alternate layers of the aubergines and meat mixture into a shallow ovenproof dish, finishing with a layer of aubergines.

8 To make the sauce, melt the butter in a small pan and stir in the flour. Cook, stirring, for 1 minute. Remove from the heat and gradually blend in the milk. Return to the heat and cook, stirring, for about 2 minutes, until thickened. Add the nutmeg, cheese and salt and pepper. Pour the sauce over the aubergines and sprinkle with the breadcrumbs. Bake for 45 minutes until golden. Serve hot, sprinkled with extra black pepper, if you like.

VARIATION
Sliced and sautéed courgettes (zucchini) or potatoes can be used instead of the aubergines in this dish. Or use a mixture of aubergines and courgettes.

MARINATED GREEK LAMB

In Greece, this dish is known as kleftiko. *Marinated lamb steaks or chops are slow-cooked to develop an unbeatable, meltingly tender flavour. The dish is sealed, like a pie, with a flour dough lid to trap succulence and flavour.*

SERVES 4

INGREDIENTS
juice of 1 lemon
15ml/1 tbsp chopped fresh oregano
4 lamb leg steaks or chump chops with bones
30ml/2 tbsp olive oil
2 large onions, thinly sliced
2 bay leaves
150ml/¼ pint/⅔ cup dry white wine
225g/8oz/2 cups plain (all-purpose) flour
salt and ground black pepper
boiled potatoes, to serve

1 Mix together the lemon juice, oregano and salt and pepper, and brush over both sides of the lamb steaks or chops. Leave to marinate in a cool place for at least 4 hours or preferably overnight.

2 Preheat the oven to 160°C/325°F/Gas 3. Drain the lamb steaks or chops, reserving the marinade, and dry the lamb with kitchen paper. Heat the olive oil in a large frying pan or sauté pan and fry the lamb over a high heat until browned on both sides.

3 Transfer the lamb to a shallow pie dish. Scatter the sliced onions and bay leaves around the lamb, then pour over the white wine and the reserved marinade.

4 Mix the flour with sufficient water to make a firm dough. Moisten the rim of the pie dish. Roll out the dough on a floured surface and use to cover the dish so that it is tightly sealed. Bake for 2 hours, then break away the dough crust and serve the lamb hot with boiled potatoes.

GREEK LAMB SAUSAGES

These sausages are known as Soudzoukakia *in Greece. They are more like elongated meatballs than the normal type of sausage. Here they are simmered in a rich tomato sauce so serve with rice or have plenty of crusty bread to hand round to your guests.*

SERVES 4

INGREDIENTS
50g/2oz/1 cup fresh white breadcrumbs
150ml/¼ pint/⅔ cup milk
675g/1½lb minced (ground) lamb
30ml/2 tbsp grated onion
3 garlic cloves, crushed
10ml/2 tsp ground cumin
30ml/2 tbsp chopped fresh parsley
flour, for dusting
olive oil, for frying
600ml/1 pint/2½ cups passata (bottled strained tomatoes)
5ml/1 tsp sugar
2 bay leaves
1 small onion, peeled
salt and ground black pepper
flat leaf parsley, to garnish

1 Mix together the breadcrumbs and milk. Add the lamb, onion, garlic, cumin and parsley and season with salt and pepper. Shape the mixture with your hands into little fat sausages, about 5cm/2in long and roll them in flour. Heat about 60ml/4 tbsp olive oil in a frying pan.

2 Fry the sausages for about 8 minutes, turning them until evenly browned. Remove and place on kitchen paper to drain.

3 Put the passata, sugar, bay leaves and whole onion in a pan and simmer for about 20 minutes. Add the sausages and cook for 10 minutes more. Remove the bay leaves and onion from the sauce before serving garnished with parsley.

LEBANESE MEAT DUMPLINGS WITH YOGURT

These delicious meat dumplings are a speciality in the Lebanon and are known as
Shish Barak. A lamb and nut filling is wrapped in a simple flour dough, then braised
in yogurt and drizzled with an aromatic garlic- and mint-flavoured butter. The fresh
mint garnish cuts through the richness of the dumplings.

SERVES 4

INGREDIENTS
5ml/1 tsp salt
225g/8oz/2 cups plain (all-purpose) flour
30ml/2 tbsp oil
1 large onion, chopped
60ml/4 tbsp pine nuts or chopped walnuts
450g/1lb minced (ground) lamb
25g/1oz/2 tbsp butter
3 garlic cloves, crushed
15ml/1 tbsp chopped fresh mint
salt and ground black pepper
mint leaves, to garnish
rice and green salad, to serve

FOR THE YOGURT SAUCE
2 litres/3½ pints/8 cups natural (plain) yogurt
1 egg, beaten
15ml/1 tbsp cornflour (cornstarch), blended with 15ml/1 tbsp cold water
salt and ground white pepper

1 Make the dough. Mix the salt and the flour together in a bowl, then stir in enough water to make a soft, pliable dough. Leave to rest for 1 hour.

2 Heat the oil in a large frying pan and fry the chopped onion for 3–4 minutes until soft and translucent. Add the pine nuts or walnuts and fry until golden. Stir in the minced lamb and cook until brown. Season with salt and ground black pepper, then remove the pan from the heat.

3 Roll out the dough thinly on a floured work surface. Cut into small rounds 5–6cm/2–2½in in diameter. Place 5ml/1 tsp of filling on each one, fold the pastry over and press the edges firmly together. Bring the two ends of the dough together to form a handle.

4 Meanwhile, make the yogurt sauce. Pour the yogurt into a pan and beat in the egg and cornflour mixture. Season with salt and white pepper and slowly bring to the boil, stirring constantly. Cook over a gentle heat until the sauce thickens and then carefully drop in the dumplings and simmer gently for about 20 minutes.

5 Spoon the dumplings and sauce on to warmed serving plates. Melt the butter in a small frying pan and fry the garlic until golden. Stir in the mint, cook briefly, then pour over the dumplings. Garnish with fresh mint leaves and serve with rice and a green salad.

SKEWERED LAMB WITH HERB YOGURT

Although lamb is the most commonly used meat for Turkish kebabs, lean beef or pork work equally well. For colour you can alternate pieces of pepper, lemon or onions, although this is not traditional.

SERVES 4

INGREDIENTS
900g/2lb lean boneless lamb
1 large onion, grated
3 bay leaves
5 thyme or rosemary sprigs
grated rind and juice of 1 lemon
2.5ml/½ tsp caster (superfine) sugar
75ml/3fl oz/⅓ cup olive oil
salt and ground black pepper
sprigs of rosemary, to garnish
grilled (broiled) lemon wedges, to serve

FOR THE YOGURT
150ml/¼ pint/⅔ cup thick natural (plain) yogurt
15ml/1 tbsp chopped fresh mint
15ml/1 tbsp chopped fresh coriander (cilantro)
10ml/2 tsp grated onion

1 To make the herb yogurt, mix together the yogurt, mint, coriander and grated onion and transfer to a small serving dish. Cover and chill.

2 Cut the lamb into small chunks and put in a bowl. Mix together the grated onion, herbs, lemon rind and juice, sugar, oil and salt and pepper. Pour over the lamb, stir to combine, then chill for several hours or overnight.

3 Drain the meat and thread on to skewers. Arrange on a grill (broiler) rack and cook under a preheated grill for about 10 minutes until the meat browns, turning occasionally. Transfer to a plate and garnish with rosemary. Serve with the grilled lemon wedges and the herb yogurt.

SKEWERED LAMB WITH RED ONION SALSA

This summery Spanish dish is ideal for outdoor eating, although, if the weather fails, the skewers can be cooked under a conventional grill. The simple red onion and tomato salsa makes a refreshing accompaniment.

SERVES 4

INGREDIENTS
225g/8oz lean lamb, cubed
2.5ml/½ tsp ground cumin
5ml/1 tsp paprika
15ml/1 tbsp olive oil
salt and ground black pepper

FOR THE SALSA
1 red onion, very thinly sliced
1 large well-flavoured tomato, seeded and chopped
15ml/1 tbsp red wine vinegar
3–4 fresh basil or mint leaves, roughly torn
small mint leaves, to garnish

1 Place the lamb in a bowl with the cumin, paprika, olive oil and plenty of salt and pepper. Toss well until the lamb is coated with spices. Cover the bowl with clear film (plastic wrap) and leave in a cool place for several hours, or in the refrigerator overnight, so that the lamb absorbs the spicy flavours.

2 Spear the lamb cubes on four small skewers – if using wooden skewers, soak them first in cold water for at least 30 minutes to prevent them burning.

3 To make the salsa, put the sliced onion, tomato, vinegar and basil or mint leaves in a small bowl and stir together until thoroughly blended. Season with salt to taste, garnish with mint, then set aside while you cook the lamb.

4 Cook the skewered lamb over hot coals or under a preheated grill (broiler) for about 5–10 minutes, turning the skewers frequently, until the lamb is well browned but still slightly pink in the centre. Serve hot, with the salsa.

STUFFED ROAST PORK

*This wonderful dish comes from Spain. Boned loin of pork is stuffed with figs,
olives and almonds, producing a contrast of sweet and savoury flavours.*

SERVES 4

INGREDIENTS
60ml/4 tbsp olive oil
1 onion, finely chopped
2 garlic cloves, chopped
75g/3oz/1½ cups fresh white breadcrumbs
4 ready-to-eat dried figs, chopped
8 pitted green olives, chopped
25g/1oz/¼ cup flaked (slivered) almonds
15ml/1 tbsp lemon juice
15ml/1 tbsp chopped fresh parsley
1 egg yolk
900g/2lb boned loin of pork
salt and ground black pepper

1 Preheat the oven to 200°C/400°F/Gas 6. Heat 45ml/3 tbsp of the oil in a pan,
add the onion and garlic, and cook gently until softened. Remove the pan from
the heat and stir in the breadcrumbs, figs, olives, almonds, lemon juice, parsley and
egg yolk. Season with salt and pepper to taste.

2 Remove any string from the pork and unroll the belly flap, cutting away any
excess fat or meat. Spread half the stuffing over the flat piece and roll up,
starting from the thick side. Tie at intervals with string.

3 Pour the remaining oil into a small roasting pan and put in the pork. Roast for
1¼ hours. Shape the remaining stuffing into balls and add to the roasting pan
after an hour.

4 Remove the pork from the oven and let it rest for 10 minutes. Carve into thick
slices and serve with the stuffing balls and any juices from the pan.

PORK WITH MARSALA & JUNIPER

Although most frequently used in desserts, Sicilian Marsala gives savoury dishes a rich, fruity and alcoholic tang. Use good quality butcher's pork.

SERVES 4

INGREDIENTS
25g/1oz dried mushrooms (ceps or porcini)
4 pork escalopes (scallops)
10ml/2 tsp balsamic vinegar
8 garlic cloves
15g/½oz/1 tbsp butter
45ml/3 tbsp Marsala
several rosemary sprigs
10 juniper berries, crushed
salt and ground black pepper
noodles and green vegetables, to serve

1 Put the dried mushrooms in a small bowl and pour over hot water to cover. Leave to stand for at least 30 minutes, then drain and strain and reserve the soaking liquid.

2 Brush the pork with 5ml/1 tsp of the vinegar and season with salt and pepper. Put the garlic cloves in a small pan of boiling water and cook for 10 minutes until soft. Drain and set aside.

3 Melt the butter in a large, heavy frying pan. Add the pork escalopes and fry quickly until browned on the underside. Turn the meat over, using tongs or a spatula, and cook for another minute.

4 Add the Marsala, rosemary, mushrooms, 60ml/4 tbsp of the soaking liquid, the garlic cloves, juniper berries and remaining vinegar.

5 Simmer gently for about 3 minutes until the pork is cooked through. Season lightly and serve hot with noodles and green vegetables.

CYPRIOT PORK STEW

This lightly-spiced pork stew is known as Afelia *in Cyprus. It makes a really delicious supper dish served simply with warmed bread, a leafy salad and a few olives.*

SERVES 4

INGREDIENTS
675g/1½lb pork fillet, boneless leg or chump steaks
20ml/4 tsp coriander seeds
2.5ml/½ tsp caster (superfine) sugar
45ml/3 tbsp olive oil
2 large onions, sliced
300ml/½ pint/1¼ cups red wine
salt and ground black pepper
fresh coriander (cilantro), to garnish

1 Cut the pork into small chunks, discarding any excess fat. Crush the coriander seeds in a mortar with a pestle until fairly finely ground. Mix the ground coriander seeds with the sugar and salt and black pepper and rub all over the meat. Leave to marinate in a cool place for up to 4 hours.

2 Preheat the oven to 160°C/325°F/Gas 3. Heat 30ml/2 tbsp of the oil in a frying pan over a high heat. Brown the meat quickly on all sides, then transfer to an ovenproof dish.

3 Add the remaining oil to the pan and fry the onions until beginning to colour. Stir in the wine and a little salt and pepper and bring just to the boil.

4 Pour the onion and wine mixture over the meat and cover with a lid. Bake for 1 hour, or until the meat is very tender. Serve scattered with fresh coriander.

COOK'S TIP
A coffee grinder can also be used to grind the coriander seeds. If you do not have a mortar and pestle or a coffee grinder, use 15ml/1 tbsp ground coriander.

BLACK BEAN STEW

This simple Spanish stew uses a few robust ingredients to create a deliciously intense flavour, rather like a French cassoulet.

SERVES 5–6

INGREDIENTS
275g/10oz/1⅓ cups dried black beans
675g/1½lb boneless belly pork rashers (strips)
60ml/4 tbsp olive oil
350g/12oz baby (pearl) onions
2 celery sticks, thickly sliced
10ml/2 tsp paprika
150g/5oz chorizo sausage, cut into chunks
600ml/1 pint/2½ cups light chicken or vegetable stock
2 green (bell) peppers, seeded and cut into large pieces
salt and ground black pepper

1 Put the beans in a bowl and cover with plenty of cold water. Leave to soak overnight. Drain the beans, place in a pan and cover with fresh water. Bring to the boil and boil rapidly for 10 minutes, then drain again.

2 Preheat the oven to 160°C/325°F/Gas 3. Cut away any rind from the pork and cut the meat into large chunks.

3 Heat the oil in a large frying pan and fry the onions and celery for 3 minutes. Add the pork and fry for 5–10 minutes until the pork is browned.

4 Add the paprika and chorizo sausage and fry for a further 2 minutes. Transfer to an ovenproof dish with the beans and mix together.

5 Add the stock to the pan and bring to the boil. Season lightly, then pour over the meat and beans. Cover and bake for 1 hour.

6 Stir the green peppers into the stew, re-cover, and return to the oven for a further 15 minutes. Serve hot.

SPANISH PORK & SAUSAGE CASSEROLE

This pork dish from Spain uses the spicy butifarra sausage. If you cannot find these sausages, sweet Italian varieties will do instead.

SERVES 4

INGREDIENTS
30ml/2 tbsp olive oil
4 boneless pork chops, about 175g/6oz
4 butifarra or sweet Italian sausages
1 onion, chopped
2 garlic cloves, chopped
120ml/4fl oz/½ cup dry white wine
4 plum tomatoes, chopped
1 bay leaf
30ml/2 tbsp chopped fresh parsley
salt and ground black pepper
green salad and baked potatoes, to serve

1 Heat the olive oil in a large deep frying pan. Cook the pork chops over a high heat until browned on both sides, then transfer to a plate.

2 Add the sausages, onion and garlic to the pan and cook over a medium heat, turning the sausages occasionally until browned all over.

3 Return the chops to the pan. Stir in the white wine, tomatoes, bay leaf and seasoning. Add the parsley. Cover the pan and cook for about 30 minutes.

4 Remove the sausages from the pan and cut into thick slices. Return them to the pan and heat through. Serve with a green salad and baked potatoes.

SPICY SAUSAGE STEW

This robust Spanish dish is very good served with a glass of chilled beer. Choose very well-spiced sausages as they will lend their flavour to the rich tomato sauce.

SERVES 4

INGREDIENTS
15ml/1 tbsp olive oil
1 onion, chopped
2 garlic cloves, finely chopped
1 carrot, chopped
4 fresh spicy sausages
150ml/¼ pint/⅔ cup tomato juice
15ml/1 tbsp brandy
1.5ml/¼ tsp Tabasco sauce
5ml/1 tsp sugar
salt and ground black pepper
30ml/2 tbsp chopped fresh coriander (cilantro), to garnish

1 Heat the oil in a large pan. Add the chopped onion, garlic, carrot and sausages and cook for 10 minutes, stirring occasionally until evenly browned.

2 Add the tomato juice, brandy, Tabasco and sugar to the pan and season to taste. Cover and simmer for about 25 minutes, or until the sausages are cooked through and the sauce has thickened. Serve at once, garnished with coriander.

COOK'S TIP
Spicy sausages are popular throughout the Mediterranean and every region produces its own varieties. Good sausages for this dish include luganeghe, colechino or salchichas.

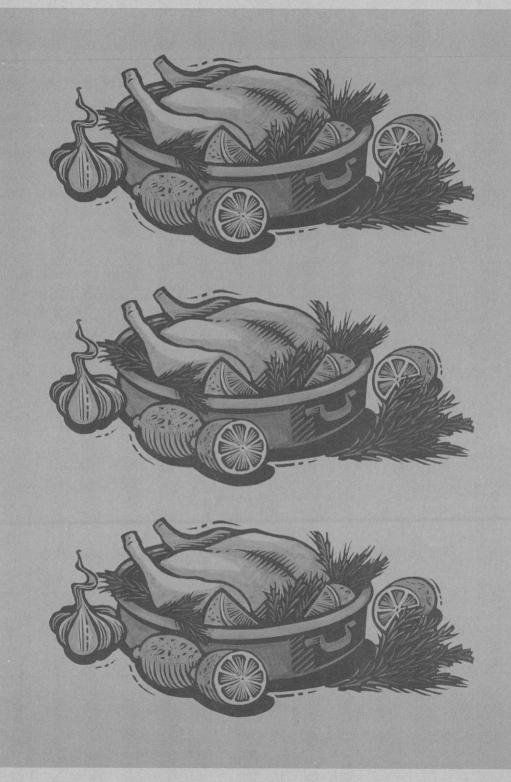

POULTRY & GAME

Throughout the Mediterranean region, people raise chickens and ducks on their own land, and rabbits and small game birds are hunted for the pot. Spices, herbs and local wines are all put to good use in a wide range of delicious dishes. This chapter includes a great selection of classic recipes such as Olive Oil Roasted Chicken and Mediterranean Vegetables, Cassoulet, and Chicken Casserole with Figs. Also included are slightly more unusual dishes such as Moroccan Pigeon Pie, where pigeon and eggs are mixed with spices and nuts and enclosed in filo pastry, and Cinnamon-spiced Duck with Pears.

Olive Oil Roasted Chicken & Mediterranean Vegetables

This is a delicious French alternative to a traditional roast chicken. Use a corn-fed or free-range bird, if available. This recipe also works well with guinea fowl.

SERVES 4

INGREDIENTS

1.75kg/4–4½lb roasting chicken
150ml/¼ pint/⅔ cup extra virgin olive oil
½ lemon
a few sprigs of fresh thyme
450g/1lb small new potatoes
1 aubergine (eggplant), cut into 2.5cm/1in cubes
1 red (bell) pepper, seeded and quartered
1 fennel bulb, trimmed and quartered
8 large garlic cloves, unpeeled
coarse salt and ground black pepper

1 Preheat the oven to 200°C/400°F/Gas 6. Rub the chicken all over with olive oil and season with pepper. Place the lemon half inside the bird with some thyme. Put the bird breast side down in a large roasting pan. Roast for 30 minutes.

2 Remove the chicken from the oven and season with salt. Turn the chicken right side up and baste with the pan juices. Surround the bird with the potatoes, roll them in the pan juices, and return the roasting pan to the oven.

3 After 30 minutes, add the aubergine, red pepper, fennel and garlic cloves to the pan. Drizzle with the remaining oil, and season with salt and pepper. Add any remaining thyme to the vegetables. Return to the oven, and cook for 30–50 minutes more, basting and turning the vegetables occasionally.

4 Check the chicken is cooked. Push the tip of a sharp knife between the thigh and breast. If the juices run clear, it is done. The vegetables should be tender and just beginning to brown. Serve the chicken and vegetables from the pan, handing around the skimmed juices in a gravy boat separately.

Chicken with Lemons & Olives

Preserved lemons and limes are frequently used in Mediterranean cookery, particularly in North Africa where their gentle flavour enhances all kinds of dishes.

SERVES 4

INGREDIENTS
2.5ml/½ tsp ground cinnamon
2.5ml/½ tsp ground turmeric
1.5kg/3¼lb chicken
30ml/2 tbsp olive oil
1 large onion, thinly sliced
5cm/2in piece fresh root ginger, grated
600ml/1 pint/2½ cups chicken stock
2 preserved lemons or limes, or fresh ones, cut into wedges
75g/3oz/½ cup pitted brown olives
15ml/1 tbsp clear honey
60ml/4 tbsp chopped fresh coriander (cilantro)
salt and ground black pepper
coriander (cilantro) sprigs, to garnish

1 Preheat the oven to 190°C/375°F/Gas 5. Mix the cinnamon and turmeric in a bowl with a little salt and black pepper and rub all over the chicken skin.

2 Heat the oil in a large sauté or shallow frying pan and fry the chicken on all sides until it turns golden. Transfer the chicken to an ovenproof dish.

3 Add the onion to the pan and fry for 3 minutes. Add the ginger and stock and bring just to the boil. Pour over the chicken, cover and bake for 30 minutes.

4 Remove the chicken from the oven and add the preserved lemons or limes and pitted brown olives. Drizzle over the honey, then bake, uncovered, for a further 45 minutes, or until tender. Sprinkle the chopped coriander over the chicken and season with salt and freshly ground black pepper. Garnish with coriander sprigs and serve at once.

CHICKEN IN A SALT CRUST WITH TOMATOES & PEPPERS

Cooking food in a casing of salt gives a deliciously moist, tender flavour that, surprisingly, is not too salty. The technique is used in both Italy and France for chicken and whole fish, although chicken tends to be easier to deal with.

SERVES 6

INGREDIENTS
1.75kg/4lb chicken
about 2.25kg/5lb coarse sea salt
450g/1lb onions, quartered
2 large garlic heads
120ml/4fl oz/½ cup olive oil
salt and ground black pepper
450g/1lb plum tomatoes
3 red (bell) peppers, seeded and quartered
1 fresh red chilli, seeded and finely chopped
90ml/6 tbsp olive oil
flat leaf parsley, to garnish

1 Preheat the oven to 220°C/425°F/Gas 7. Choose a deep ovenproof dish into which the whole chicken will fit snugly. Line the dish with a double thickness of heavy foil, allowing plenty of excess foil to overhang the top edge of the dish.

2 Truss the chicken very tightly with string so that the salt cannot fall into the cavity. Sprinkle a thin, even layer of salt in the foil-lined dish, then place the trussed chicken on top.

3 Pour the remaining salt all around and over the top of the chicken until it is completely encased. Sprinkle the top with a little water. Cover the chicken tightly with the foil and bake on the lower shelf of the oven for 1¾ hours.

4 Meanwhile, put the onions in a small heavy pan. Break up the garlic heads into separate cloves, but leave the skins on. Add to the pan with the olive oil and a little salt and ground black pepper.

5 Cover the pan and cook over the lowest possible heat for about 1 hour or until the garlic is completely soft.

6 Plunge the tomatoes into boiling water for 30 seconds, then refresh in cold water. Peel away the skins and quarter the flesh. Put the red peppers, tomatoes and chilli in a shallow ovenproof dish and sprinkle with the oil. Bake on the shelf above the chicken for 45 minutes or until the peppers are slightly charred.

7 When the garlic is cool enough to handle, squeeze the flesh out of the papery skins. Process the onions, garlic and pan juices in a food processor or blender until smooth. Return the onion and garlic purée to the cleaned pan.

8 To serve the chicken, open out the foil and ease it out of the dish. Place on a large serving platter. Transfer the roasted pepper mixture to a serving dish and garnish with parsley. Reheat the onion and garlic purée. Crack open the salt crust on the chicken and brush away the salt before carving and serving with the purée and tomatoes and peppers.

COOK'S TIP
When you want to serve something a little different, this recipe makes a really stunning main course. Take the salt-crusted chicken to the table garnished with plenty of fresh mixed herbs. Once you've scraped away the salt, transfer the chicken to a clean plate to carve it.

CHICKEN WITH TOMATOES & HONEY

This rich Moroccan dish is flavoured with aromatic spices and sweetened with clear honey. The garnish of dry-fried almonds and sesame seeds adds a lovely crunch.

SERVES 4

INGREDIENTS
30ml/2 tbsp sunflower oil
25g/1oz/2 tbsp butter
4 chicken quarters or 1 whole chicken, quartered
1 onion, grated or very finely chopped
1 garlic clove, crushed
5ml/1 tsp ground cinnamon
a good pinch of ground ginger
1.5kg/3¼lb tomatoes, peeled, cored and roughly chopped
30ml/2 tbsp clear honey
50g/2oz/⅓ cup blanched almonds
15ml/1 tbsp sesame seeds
salt and ground black pepper
Moroccan corn bread, to serve

1 Heat the oil and butter in a large casserole. Add the chicken and cook over a medium heat for 3 minutes until lightly browned. Add the onion, garlic, cinnamon, ginger, tomatoes and seasoning, and heat gently until beginning to bubble. Lower the heat, cover and simmer for 1 hour, stirring and turning occasionally.

2 Transfer the chicken to a plate, then increase the heat and cook the tomatoes until the sauce is reduced to a thick purée, stirring frequently. Stir in the honey, cook for 1 minute, then return the chicken to the pan and cook for 2–3 minutes to heat through. Dry-fry the almonds and sesame seeds until golden.

3 Transfer the chicken and sauce to a warmed serving dish and sprinkle with the almonds and sesame seeds. Serve hot with Moroccan corn bread.

CHICKEN WITH SPICY CHORIZO & SHERRY

Adding chorizo sausage and sherry gives this simple Spanish casserole a warm, interesting flavour. Serve simply with rice or boiled potatoes.

SERVES 4

INGREDIENTS
1 chicken, jointed, or 4 chicken legs, halved
10ml/2 tsp paprika
60ml/4 tbsp olive oil
2 small onions, sliced
6 garlic cloves, thinly sliced
150g/5oz chorizo sausage, sliced
400g/14oz can chopped tomatoes
12–16 bay leaves
75ml/5 tbsp medium sherry
salt and ground black pepper
rice or potatoes, to serve

1 Preheat the oven to 190°C/375°F/Gas 5. Coat the pieces of chicken in the paprika, making sure they are evenly covered, then season with salt. Heat the olive oil in a frying pan and fry the chicken until brown on all sides.

2 Transfer the chicken pieces to an ovenproof dish. Add the onions to the pan and fry quickly for about 3 minutes. Add the garlic and sliced chorizo sausage and fry for a further 2 minutes.

3 Add the tomatoes, two of the bay leaves and the sherry to the pan. Bring the mixture to the boil, then pour over the chicken and cover. Bake for 45 minutes.

4 Uncover the dish and season the stew with salt and black pepper. Cook for a further 20 minutes until the chicken is tender and golden. Serve with rice or potatoes, garnished with bay leaves.

Chicken Tagine with Almonds

The almonds in this Moroccan dish are precooked until soft, adding an interesting texture and flavour to the tender, slow-cooked chicken.

SERVES 4

INGREDIENTS

75g/3oz/½ cup blanched almonds
75g/3oz/½ cup dried chickpeas, soaked overnight
4 skinless part-boned chicken breast portions
50g/2oz/4 tbsp butter
2.5ml/½ tsp saffron
2 Spanish onions, finely sliced
900ml/1½ pints/3¾ cups chicken stock
1 small cinnamon stick
60ml/4 tbsp chopped fresh flat leaf parsley, plus extra to garnish
lemon juice, to taste
salt and ground black pepper

1 Place the almonds in a pan of water and simmer for 1½–2 hours until fairly soft, then drain. Meanwhile, cook the chickpeas in fresh water for 1–1½ hours until soft. Drain the chickpeas, then place in a bowl of cold water and rub with your fingers to remove the skins. Discard the skins and drain.

2 Place the chicken pieces in a pan, together with the butter, half of the saffron, salt and plenty of black pepper. Heat gently, stirring, until the butter has melted.

3 Add the onions and stock to the pan, bring to the boil, then add the chickpeas and cinnamon stick. Cover and cook very gently for 45–60 minutes, or until the chicken is very tender.

4 Transfer the chicken to a serving plate and keep warm. Bring the sauce to the boil and simmer until well reduced, stirring frequently. Add the almonds, parsley and remaining saffron and cook for 2–3 minutes. Add lemon juice to taste, then pour over the chicken and serve, garnished with extra flat leaf parsley.

CHICKEN CASSEROLE WITH FIGS

In Spain, meat is often cooked with fruit. This delicious dish makes the most of the luscious figs that are grown all over the Mediterranean.

SERVES 4

INGREDIENTS
150g/5oz/⅔ cup granulated sugar
120ml/4fl oz/½ cup white wine vinegar
1 lemon slice
1 cinnamon stick
450g/1lb fresh figs
120ml/4fl oz/½ cup medium-sweet white wine
pared rind of ½ lemon
1.5kg/3¼lb chicken, jointed into eight pieces
50g/2oz lardons or thick streaky (fatty) bacon rashers (strips)
15ml/1 tbsp olive oil
50ml/2fl oz/¼ cup chicken stock
salt and ground black pepper

1 Prepare the figs. Put the sugar, vinegar, lemon slice and cinnamon stick in a pan with 120ml/4fl oz/½ cup water. Bring to the boil, then simmer for about 5 minutes. Wipe the figs with a damp cloth, then add to the syrup, cover, and simmer for about 10 minutes. Then drain, place in a bowl and add the wine and lemon rind. Set aside for 3 hours.

2 Preheat the oven to 180°C/ 350°F/Gas 4. Season the chicken with salt and ground black pepper. In a large frying pan cook the lardons or bacon until golden. Transfer to a shallow ovenproof dish, leaving any fat in the pan. Add the olive oil and chicken to the pan and brown the chicken.

3 Drain the figs, adding the wine to the pan with the chicken. Boil until the sauce becomes syrupy. Transfer to the ovenproof dish and cook in the oven, uncovered, for about 20 minutes. Add the figs and stock, cover and return to the oven for a further 10 minutes.

CASSOULET

This is a classic French dish in which a feast of various meats is baked slowly with beans under a golden crumb crust. It is hearty and rich – perfect for winter.

SERVES 6–8

INGREDIENTS
675g/1½lb/3½ cups dried haricot (navy) beans
900g/2lb salt belly pork
4 large duck breast portions
60ml/4 tbsp olive oil
2 onions, chopped
6 garlic cloves, crushed
2 bay leaves
1.5ml/¼ tsp ground cloves
60ml/4 tbsp tomato purée (paste)
8 good quality sausages
4 tomatoes
75g/3oz/1½ cups stale white breadcrumbs
salt and ground black pepper

> VARIATION
> *You can easily alter the proportions and types of meat and vegetables in a cassoulet. Turnips, carrots and celeriac make suitable vegetable substitutes while cubed lamb and goose can replace the belly pork and duck breast portions.*

1 Put the beans in a large bowl and cover with plenty of cold water. Leave to soak overnight. Soak the salt belly pork overnight in a separate bowl.

2 Drain the beans and place in a large pan with fresh water to cover. Bring to the boil and boil rapidly for 10 minutes. Drain and set the beans aside.

3 Cut the soaked pork belly into large pieces and discard the rind. Halve the duck breast portions. Heat 30ml/2 tbsp of the olive oil in a frying pan and fry the pork in batches, until browned.

4 Put the beans in a large, heavy pan with the onions, garlic, bay leaves, ground cloves and tomato purée. Stir in the browned pork and pour over water to cover. Bring to the boil, then reduce the heat to the lowest setting and simmer, covered, for about 1½ hours until the beans are tender.

5 Preheat the oven to 180°C/350°F/Gas 4. Heat the remaining olive oil in a frying pan and fry the duck breast pieces and sausages until browned. Using a sharp knife, cut the sausages into smaller pieces.

6 Plunge the tomatoes into boiling water for 30 seconds, then refresh in cold water. Peel away the skins and cut the flesh into quarters.

7 Transfer the bean mixture to a large earthenware pot or ovenproof dish and stir in the fried sausages, duck breast pieces and chopped tomatoes. Season with salt and ground black pepper to taste.

8 Sprinkle the stew with an even layer of breadcrumbs and bake in the oven for about 50 minutes, until the crust is golden. Serve hot.

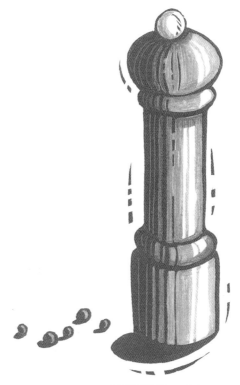

CHICKEN THIGHS WITH LEMON & GARLIC

Versions of this classic dish can be found in Spain and Italy. This particular recipe, however, is of French origin. Long, slow cooking mellows the flavour of the twenty cloves of garlic.

SERVES 4

INGREDIENTS
600ml/1 pint/2½ cups chicken stock
20 large garlic cloves
25g/1oz/2 tbsp butter
15ml/1 tbsp olive oil
8 chicken thighs
1 lemon, peeled, pith removed and sliced thinly
30ml/2 tbsp plain (all-purpose) flour
150ml/¼ pint/⅔ cup dry white wine
salt and ground black pepper
chopped fresh parsley or basil, to garnish
new potatoes or rice, to serve

1 Put the stock into a pan and bring to the boil. Add the garlic cloves, cover and simmer gently for 40 minutes. Heat the butter and oil in a sauté pan or frying pan, add the chicken thighs and cook gently on all sides until golden. Transfer to an ovenproof dish. Preheat the oven to 190°C/375°F/Gas 5.

2 Strain the stock and reserve it. Distribute the garlic and lemon slices among the chicken pieces. Add the flour to the fat in the pan in which the chicken was browned, and cook, stirring, for 1 minute. Add the wine, stirring constantly and scraping the base of the pan, then add the stock. Cook, stirring, until the sauce has thickened and is smooth. Season with salt and pepper.

3 Pour the sauce over the chicken, cover, and cook in the oven for about 45 minutes. If a thicker sauce is required, lift out the chicken pieces, and reduce the sauce by boiling rapidly on the stove top, until it reaches the desired consistency. Scatter over the chopped parsley or basil and serve with boiled new potatoes or rice.

TURKISH CHICKEN WITH WALNUT SAUCE

Although this is a Turkish dish, it is popular all over the Middle East. The chicken is poached and served cold with a flavoursome walnut sauce.

SERVES 6

INGREDIENTS
1.5kg/3¼lb chicken
2 onions, quartered
1 carrot, sliced
1 celery stick, trimmed and sliced
6 peppercorns
3 slices of bread, crusts removed
2 garlic cloves, roughly chopped
400g/14oz/3½ cups chopped walnuts, plus extra to garnish
15ml/1 tbsp walnut oil
salt and ground black pepper
paprika, to garnish

1 Place the chicken in a large, heavy pan, with the onions, carrot, celery and peppercorns. Add enough water to cover, and bring to the boil. Simmer for about 1 hour, uncovered, until the chicken is tender. Leave to cool in the stock. Drain the chicken, reserving the stock.

2 Tear up the bread and soak in 90ml/6 tbsp of the chicken stock. Transfer to a food processor or blender, with the chopped garlic and walnuts, then add 250ml/8fl oz/1 cup of the remaining stock. Process until smooth; transfer to a pan.

3 Over a low heat, gradually add more chicken stock to the sauce, stirring constantly, until it is of a thick pouring consistency. Season, remove from the heat and leave to cool. Skin and bone the chicken, and cut into bitesize chunks.

4 Place the chicken in a bowl and add a little sauce. Stir to coat, then arrange on a serving dish. Spoon the remaining sauce over the chicken, and drizzle with the walnut oil. Sprinkle with walnuts and paprika and serve.

CHICKEN & APRICOT PIE WITH FILO PASTRY

The filling for this pie has a Middle Eastern flavour. Chicken is combined with apricots, bulgur wheat, almonds and spices and fresh herbs, then encased in filo pastry with extra pastry crumpled on top for an attractive crisp finish.

SERVES 6

INGREDIENTS
75g/3oz/½ cup bulgur wheat
75g/3oz/6 tbsp butter
1 onion, chopped
450g/1lb minced (ground) chicken
50g/2oz/¼ cup ready-to-eat dried apricots, finely chopped
25g/1oz/¼ cup blanched almonds, chopped
5ml/1 tsp ground cinnamon
2.5ml/½ tsp ground allspice
50ml/2fl oz/¼ cup Greek (US strained plain) yogurt
15ml/1 tbsp chopped fresh chives
30ml/2 tbsp chopped fresh parsley
6 large sheets filo pastry
salt and ground black pepper
fresh chives, to garnish

> VARIATION
> *Prunes make a delicious alternative in this dish. Simply substitute the apricots with the same weight of pitted prunes.*

1 Preheat the oven to 200°C/ 400°F/Gas 6. Put the bulgur wheat in a bowl with 120ml/4fl oz/½ cup boiling water. Leave to soak for about 10 minutes.

2 Heat 25g/1oz/2 tbsp of the butter in a pan, and gently fry the onion and chicken until pale golden. Stir in the apricots, almonds and bulgur wheat and cook the mixture for a further 2 minutes. Remove from the heat and stir in the cinnamon, allspice, yogurt, chives and parsley. Season to taste with salt and pepper.

3 Melt the remaining butter. Carefully unroll the filo pastry and cut into 25cm/ 10in rounds. Keep the pastry rounds covered with a clean, damp dishtowel to prevent them from drying out.

4 Line a 23cm/9in loose-based flan tin (quiche pan) with three of the pastry rounds, brushing each one with melted butter as you layer them. Spoon in the chicken and apricot mixture, levelling the surface with the back of the spoon, and cover with three more pastry rounds, brushed with melted butter as before.

5 Crumple the remaining rounds and place them on top of the pie, then brush over any remaining melted butter. Bake the pie for about 30 minutes, or until the pastry is golden brown and crisp. Serve the pie hot or cold, cut into wedges and garnished with fresh chives.

CHICKEN LIVERS WITH SHERRY & CREAM

The rich flavours of this Spanish dish work together very well and the lightly pan-fried livers have a wonderful texture that literally melts in the mouth. Serve with plenty of crusty bread to mop up the sauces.

SERVES 4

INGREDIENTS
225g/8oz chicken livers, thawed if frozen
1 small onion
2 small garlic cloves
15ml/1 tbsp olive oil
5ml/1 tsp fresh thyme leaves
30ml/2 tbsp sweet sherry
30ml/2 tbsp sour or double (heavy) cream
salt and ground black pepper
fresh thyme, to garnish

1 Carefully trim any spots and sinews from the chicken livers. Finely chop the onion and garlic using a sharp knife.

2 Heat the olive oil in a frying pan and fry the onion, garlic, chicken livers and thyme for about 3 minutes, stirring occasionally.

3 Stir in the sherry and cook gently for 1 minute. Add the sour or double cream and cook over a low heat for 1–2 minutes more. Stir in salt and pepper to taste and serve at once, garnished with thyme.

COOK'S TIP
This dish is very quick and easy to prepare, and even quicker if you buy the chicken livers ready-trimmed. You may find it easier to use a pair of kitchen scissors when trimming away the sinews.

GRILLED POUSSINS WITH CITRUS GLAZE

This recipe is suitable for many kinds of small birds, including pigeons, snipe and partridges. It would also work with quail, but decrease the cooking time and spread the citrus mixture over, rather than under, the fragile skin.

SERVES 4

INGREDIENTS
50g/2oz/4 tbsp butter, softened
30ml/2 tbsp olive oil
2 garlic cloves, crushed
2.5ml/½ tsp dried thyme
1.5ml/¼ tsp cayenne pepper
grated rind and juice of 1 lemon
grated rind and juice of 1 lime
2 poussins (about 750g/1½lb each)
30ml/2 tbsp clear honey
salt and ground black pepper
fresh dill, to garnish
tomato salad, to serve

1 Beat the butter in a small bowl, then beat in 15ml/1 tbsp of the olive oil, the garlic, thyme, cayenne, salt and pepper, half the lemon and lime rind and 15ml/1 tbsp each of the lemon and lime juice.

2 Use a pair of scissors to cut out the birds' backbones. Cut the bird in half along the breastbone, then flatten with a rolling pin. Loosen the skin of each poussin breast. Spread the butter mixture between the skin and flesh.

3 Preheat the grill (broiler) and line a grill pan with foil. Mix together the remaining oil, citrus juices and honey. Place the bird halves, skin side up, on the grill pan and brush with the juice mixture. Grill (broil) for 10–12 minutes, basting once or twice. Turn over and grill for 7–10 minutes, basting once, or until cooked. Garnish with dill and serve with a tomato salad.

QUAIL WITH FRESH FIGS

*The fig trees in the South of France are laden with ripe purple fruit in early autumn,
coinciding with the quail shooting season to facilitate this sophisticated dish.*

SERVES 4

INGREDIENTS
8 oven-ready quail (150g/5oz each)
6 firm ripe figs, quartered
15g/½oz/1 tbsp butter
90ml/6 tbsp dry sherry
300ml/½ pint/1¼ cups chicken stock
1 garlic clove, finely chopped
2–3 thyme sprigs
1 bay leaf
7.5ml/1½ tsp cornflour (cornstarch) blended with 15ml/1 tbsp water
salt and ground black pepper

1 Season the quail inside and out with salt and pepper. Put a fig quarter in the cavity of each quail and tie the legs with string.

2 Melt the butter in a deep frying pan or heavy flameproof casserole over a medium-high heat. Cook the quail for 5–6 minutes, turning to brown all sides evenly. Pour the sherry over the quail and boil for 1 minute, then add the chicken stock, garlic, thyme and bay leaf. Bring to the boil, reduce the heat and simmer, covered, for 20 minutes.

3 Add the remaining fig quarters to the pan or casserole and continue cooking for a further 5 minutes, or until the juices run clear when the thigh of a quail is pierced with a knife. Transfer the quail and figs to a warmed serving dish, and cut off the trussing string. Cover to keep warm.

4 Bring the sauce to the boil, then stir in the blended cornflour. Cook gently for 3 minutes, stirring frequently, until the sauce is thickened, then strain into a gravy boat. Serve the quail and figs with the sauce.

SWEET & SOUR DUCK

This exotic dish originally came from Persia. Pan-fried duck breast portions are served with a delicious and decorative walnut and pomegranate sauce.

SERVES 6

INGREDIENTS
60ml/4 tbsp olive oil
2 onions, very thinly sliced
2.5ml/½ tsp ground turmeric
400g/14oz/3½ cups walnuts, roughly chopped
1 litre/1¾ pints/4 cups duck or chicken stock
6 pomegranates
30ml/2 tbsp caster (superfine) sugar
60ml/4 tbsp lemon juice
4 duck breast portions (about 225g/8oz each)
salt and ground black pepper

1 Heat half the oil in a frying pan. Add the onions and turmeric, and cook gently until soft. Transfer to a large pan, add the walnuts and stock, then season. Stir, then bring to the boil and simmer the mixture, uncovered, for 20 minutes.

2 Cut the pomegranates in half and scoop out the seeds into a bowl. Reserve the seeds of one pomegranate. Transfer the remaining seeds to a food processor or blender, and process. Strain through a sieve; stir in the sugar and lemon juice.

3 Score the skin of the duck breast portions in a lattice pattern. Heat the remaining oil in a frying pan and place the pieces of duck in it, skin side down. Cook gently for 10 minutes, pouring off the fat from time to time, until the skin is golden and crisp. Turn over and cook for 3–4 minutes more. Set aside on a plate.

4 Deglaze the frying pan with the pomegranate juice mixture, then add the walnut and stock mixture. Simmer for 15 minutes until thickened slightly. Serve the duck breasts sliced, drizzled with a little sauce, and garnished with the reserved pomegranate seeds. Serve the remaining sauce separately.

CINNAMON-SPICED DUCK WITH PEARS

This delicious casserole is based on a Spanish dish that uses goose or duck. The sautéed pears are added towards the end of cooking, along with picarda sauce – a pounded pine nut and garlic paste which both flavours and thickens.

SERVES 6

INGREDIENTS
6 duck portions, either breast or leg pieces
15ml/1 tbsp olive oil
1 large onion, thinly sliced
1 cinnamon stick, halved
2 thyme sprigs
475ml/16fl oz/2 cups duck or chicken stock

TO SERVE
3 firm ripe pears
30ml/2 tbsp olive oil
2 garlic cloves, sliced
25g/1oz/⅓ cup pine nuts
2.5ml/½ tsp saffron strands
25g/1oz/2 tbsp raisins
salt and ground black pepper
young thyme sprigs or parsley, to garnish
mashed potato and green vegetables, to serve (optional)

> COOK'S TIP
> A good stock is essential for this dish. Buy a large duck and joint it yourself, using the giblets and carcass for stock. Alternatively, buy duck portions and a carton of fresh chicken stock.

1 Preheat the oven to 180°C/350°F/Gas 4. In a large frying pan, fry the duck portions in the oil for 5 minutes until the skin is golden. Transfer the duck to an ovenproof dish and drain off all but 15ml/1 tbsp of the fat left in the pan.

2 Add the sliced onion to the pan and fry for about 5 minutes. Add the cinnamon stick, thyme sprigs and duck or chicken stock and bring to the boil. Pour over the duck, then bake in the oven for 1¼ hours.

3 Meanwhile, peel, core and halve the pears and fry quickly in the olive oil until beginning to turn golden on the cut sides. Pound the garlic, pine nuts and saffron in a mortar, using a pestle, to make a thick, smooth paste.

4 Add the garlic and pine nut paste to the casserole along with the raisins and pears. Bake for a further 15 minutes until the pears are tender.

5 Season the casserole to taste with salt and ground black pepper and garnish with fresh thyme or parsley sprigs. Serve with mashed potatoes and a green vegetable, if liked.

ROAST WILD DUCK WITH JUNIPER

Wild duck should be served slightly underdone or the meat will be very tough. There is little meat on the leg, so one duck will serve only two people.

SERVES 2

INGREDIENTS
15ml/1 tbsp juniper berries, fresh if possible
1 oven-ready wild duck (preferably a mallard)
30g/1oz/2 tbsp butter, softened
45ml/3 tbsp gin
125ml/4fl oz/½ cup duck or chicken stock
125ml/4fl oz/½ cup whipping cream
salt and ground black pepper
watercress, to garnish

1 Preheat the oven to 230°C/450°F/Gas 8. Reserve a few juniper berries for garnish and put the rest in a plastic bag. Crush with a rolling pin.

2 Wipe the duck with damp kitchen paper and remove any excess fat or skin. Tie the legs with string, then spread the butter over the duck. Sprinkle with salt and pepper and press the crushed juniper berries on to the skin.

3 Place the duck in a roasting pan and roast for about 20 minutes, basting occasionally; the juices should run slightly pink when the thigh is pierced with a knife. Pour the juices from the cavity into the roasting tin and transfer the duck to a carving board. Cover loosely with foil and leave to stand for 10–15 minutes.

4 Meanwhile, skim off the fat from the roasting pan, leaving the juniper berries in the pan, and place the pan over a medium-high heat. Add the gin and stir, scraping the base, and bring to the boil. Cook until the liquid has almost evaporated, then add the stock and boil to reduce by half. Add the cream and boil for 2 minutes, or until the sauce thickens. Strain into a small pan and keep warm.

5 Carve the legs from the duck and separate the thigh from the drumstick. Remove the breasts and arrange the duck in a warmed serving dish. Pour a little sauce over, sprinkle with the reserved juniper berries and garnish with watercress.

DUCK STEW WITH OLIVES

This method of preparing duck has its roots in Provence. The sweetness of the onions, which are not typical in all regional versions, balances the salty olives.

SERVES 6–8

INGREDIENTS
2 ducks (about 1.4kg/3¼lb each), quartered, or 8 duck leg quarters
225g/½lb baby (pearl) onions
30ml/2 tbsp plain (all-purpose) flour
350ml/12fl oz/1½ cups dry red wine
500ml/16fl oz/2 cups duck or chicken stock
bouquet garni
100g/3½oz/1 cup pitted green or black olives, or a combination
salt and ground black pepper

1 Put the duck pieces, skin side down, in a large frying pan over a medium heat and cook for 10–12 minutes until well browned, turning to colour evenly. You will need to cook in batches. Pour off the fat from the pan.

2 Heat 15ml/1 tbsp of the duck fat in a large flameproof casserole and cook the baby onions, covered, over a medium-low heat until evenly browned, stirring frequently. Sprinkle with flour and continue cooking, uncovered, for 2 minutes, stirring frequently.

3 Stir in the wine and bring to the boil, then add the duck pieces, stock and bouquet garni. Bring to the boil, then reduce the heat to very low and simmer, covered, for about 40 minutes, stirring occasionally.

4 Rinse the olives in cold water. If they are very salty, put in a small pan, cover with water and bring to the boil, then drain and rinse. Add the olives to the casserole and continue cooking for 20 minutes until the duck is very tender.

5 Transfer the duck pieces, onions and olives to a plate. Strain the cooking liquid, skim off all the fat and return the liquid to the pan. Boil to reduce by about one-third, then season to taste and return the duck and vegetables to the casserole. Simmer gently for a few minutes to heat through before serving.

PIGEON BREASTS WITH PANCETTA

Mild succulent pigeon breasts are easy to cook and make an impressive main course for a special dinner. Serve this Italian-style dish with polenta and green vegetables.

SERVES 4

INGREDIENTS

4 whole pigeons
2 large onions
2 carrots, roughly chopped
1 celery stick, trimmed and roughly chopped
25g/1oz dried porcini mushrooms
50g/2oz pancetta
25g/1oz/2 tbsp butter
30ml/2 tbsp olive oil
2 garlic cloves, crushed
150ml/¼ pint/⅔ cup red wine
salt and ground black pepper
flat leaf parsley sprigs, to garnish
cooked oyster mushrooms, to serve

COOK'S TIP
If buying pigeons from a butcher, order them in advance and ask him to remove the breast portions for you. You can joint the legs and fry these with the breasts, although there is little meat on them and you might prefer to let them flavour the stock.

1 To prepare a pigeon, cut down the length of the bird, just to one side of the breastbone with a sharp knife. Gradually lift away the meat from the breastbone until the breast comes away completely. Repeat on the other side.

2 Put the pigeon carcasses in a large pan. Halve one of the onions, leaving the skin on. Add to the pan with the carrots and celery and pour over water to cover. Bring to the boil, reduce the heat and simmer very gently, uncovered, for about 1½ hours to make a dark, rich stock. Leave to cool slightly, then strain the stock through a large sieve into a bowl.

3 Meanwhile, place the dried porcini mushrooms in a bowl and pour over 150ml/¼ pint/⅔ cup hot water. Leave to soak for 30 minutes. Strain the soaking liquid and set the strained liquid and mushrooms aside.

4 Cut the pancetta into small dice. Peel and finely chop the remaining onion. Melt half the butter with the oil in a large frying pan. Add the onion and pancetta and fry very gently for 3 minutes. Add the pigeon breast pieces, skin sides down, and fry for 2 minutes. Turn over and fry for a further 2 minutes.

5 Add the porcini mushrooms, with the strained soaking liquid, garlic, red wine and 250ml/8fl oz/1 cup of the stock. Bring just to the boil, then reduce the heat and simmer gently for about 5 minutes until the pigeon breast pieces are tender, but still a little pink in the centre.

6 Lift the pigeon pieces out of the pan and keep them hot. Return the sauce to the boil and boil rapidly to reduce slightly. Gradually whisk in all the remaining butter and season with salt and black pepper to taste.

7 Transfer the pigeon breast pieces to warmed serving plates and pour over the sauce. Serve at once, garnished with sprigs of flat leaf parsley and accompanied by oyster mushrooms.

MOROCCAN PIGEON PIE

This recipe is based upon a classic Moroccan dish called Pastilla, *which is a filo pastry pie, filled with an unusual but delicious mixture of pigeon, eggs, spices and nuts. If pigeon is unavailable, chicken makes a good substitute, although the meat will not be so strongly flavoured.*

SERVES 6

INGREDIENTS
3 pigeons
50g/2oz/4 tbsp butter
1 onion, chopped
1 cinnamon stick
2.5ml/½ tsp ground ginger
30ml/2 tbsp chopped fresh coriander (cilantro)
45ml/3 tbsp chopped fresh parsley
pinch of ground turmeric
15ml/1 tbsp caster (superfine) sugar
1.5ml/¼ tsp ground cinnamon
115g/4oz/1 cup toasted almonds, finely chopped
6 eggs, beaten
salt and ground black pepper
cinnamon and icing (confectioners') sugar, to garnish

FOR THE PASTRY
175g/6oz/¾ cup butter, melted
16 sheets filo pastry
1 egg yolk

1 Wash the pigeons and place in a large pan with the butter, onion, cinnamon stick, ginger, coriander, parsley and turmeric. Season with salt and pepper. Add just enough water to cover and bring to the boil. Cover, then simmer gently for about 1 hour, or until the pigeon flesh is very tender.

2 Strain off the stock and reserve. Skin and bone the pigeons, and shred the flesh into bitesize pieces. Preheat the oven to 180°C/350°F/Gas 4. Mix together the sugar, cinnamon and almonds, and set aside.

3 Measure 150ml/¼ pint/⅔ cup of the reserved stock into a small pan. Add the beaten eggs and mix well. Stir over a low heat until creamy and very thick and almost set. Season with salt and ground black pepper to taste.

4 Brush a 30cm/12in diameter ovenproof dish with some of the melted butter and lay the first sheet of filo pastry in the dish. Brush this with butter and continue with five more sheets of pastry. Cover with the almond mixture, then half the egg mixture. Moisten with a little stock.

5 Layer four more sheets of filo pastry on top of the egg mixture, brushing with butter as before. Lay the pigeon meat on top, then add the remaining egg mixture and more stock. Cover with all the remaining pastry, brushing each sheet with butter, and tuck in any overlap.

6 Brush the pie with egg yolk and bake for about 40 minutes. Increase the oven temperature to 200°C/400°F/Gas 6, and bake for 15 minutes more, until the pastry is crisp and golden. Garnish with a lattice design of cinnamon and icing sugar and serve hot.

Spanish Rabbit Sauté

This light, spicy dish is very tasty and is typical of Mediterranean cooking. Rabbit tastes very like chicken and convenient packs of jointed meat can be bought at supermarkets. Serve with a simple dressed salad.

Serves 4

Ingredients

675g/1½lb rabbit portions
300ml/½ pint/1¼ cups dry white wine
15ml/1 tbsp sherry vinegar
several oregano sprigs
2 bay leaves
90ml/6 tbsp olive oil
175g/6oz baby (pearl) onions, peeled and left whole
1 fresh red chilli, seeded and finely chopped
4 garlic cloves, sliced
10ml/2 tsp paprika
150ml/¼ pint/⅔ cup chicken stock
salt and ground black pepper
flat leaf parsley sprigs, to garnish

1 Put the rabbit in a bowl. Add the wine, vinegar, oregano and bay leaves and toss together lightly. Cover and leave to marinate for several hours or overnight.

2 Drain the rabbit, reserving the marinade, and pat dry on kitchen paper. Heat the oil in a large sauté pan or frying pan. Add the rabbit, fry on all sides until golden, then remove with a slotted spoon. Fry the onions until beginning to colour.

3 Remove the onions from the pan and add the chilli, garlic and paprika. Cook, stirring for about 1 minute. Add the reserved marinade, with the stock. Season lightly with salt and ground black pepper.

4 Return the rabbit to the pan with the onions. Bring to the boil, then reduce the heat and cover with a lid. Simmer very gently for about 45 minutes until the rabbit is tender. Alternatively, bake in the oven at 180°C/350°F/Gas 4 for about 50 minutes. Serve garnished with flat leaf parsley sprigs.

CASEROLED RABBIT WITH THYME

This is the sort of satisfying home cooking found in farmhouse kitchens and cosy neighbourhood restaurants in France, where rabbit is treated in much the same way as chicken and is enjoyed frequently.

SERVES 4

INGREDIENTS
1.2kg/2½lb rabbit
40g/1½oz/¼ cup plain (all-purpose) flour
15g/½oz/1 tbsp butter
15ml/1 tbsp olive oil
250ml/8fl oz/1 cup red wine
350–500ml/12–16fl oz/1½–2 cups chicken stock
15ml/1 tbsp fresh thyme leaves or 10ml/2 tsp dried thyme
1 bay leaf
2 garlic cloves, finely chopped
10–15ml/2–3 tsp Dijon mustard
salt and ground black pepper

1 Cut the rabbit into eight serving pieces: chop the saddle in half and separate the back legs into two pieces each; leave the front legs whole.

2 Put the flour in a plastic bag and season with salt and pepper. One at a time, drop the rabbit pieces into the bag and shake to coat them with flour. Tap off the excess, then discard any remaining flour.

3 Melt the butter with the oil over a medium-high heat in a large flameproof casserole. Add the rabbit pieces and cook until golden, turning to colour evenly.

4 Add the wine and boil for 1 minute, then add enough stock to cover the meat. Add the herbs and garlic, then simmer, covered, for 1 hour or until the rabbit is tender and the juices run clear when the thickest part of the meat is pierced.

5 Stir the mustard into the casserole, adjust the seasoning and strain the sauce. Arrange the rabbit pieces on a warmed serving platter with some sauce and serve the rest separately for guests to help themselves.

GRAINS, PULSES & PASTA

These staples of the Mediterranean diet are used in many inspired ways. Every area has its own favourites – in Spain rice is made into wonderful paellas, in North Africa couscous and chickpeas play a key role in many dishes, throughout the Middle East bulgur wheat and lentils are very popular, and in Italy wheat is ground and made into pasta. This chapter is filled with delicious recipes from simple pasta dishes such as Spaghetti with Tomatoes and Pancetta, and Linguine with Ham and Mascarpone, to more exotic and unusual dishes such as Egyptian Rice with Lentils and Turkish Lamb Pilau.

Pilaff with Saffron & Pickled Walnuts

This eastern Mediterranean rice pilaff is warmly spiced with saffron, garlic, allspice and fresh root ginger. The tangy flavour of pickled walnuts contrasts wonderfully with the sweet, juicy raisins and slightly earthy taste of pine nuts.

SERVES 4

INGREDIENTS
5ml/1 tsp saffron strands
40g/1½oz/½ cup pine nuts
45ml/3 tbsp olive oil
1 large onion, chopped
3 garlic cloves, crushed
1.5ml/¼ tsp ground allspice
4cm/1½in piece fresh root ginger, grated
225g/8oz/generous 1 cup long grain rice
300ml/½ pint/1¼ cups vegetable stock
50g/2oz/½ cup pickled walnuts, drained and roughly chopped
40g/1½oz/¼ cup raisins
45ml/3 tbsp roughly chopped fresh parsley or coriander (cilantro)
salt and ground black pepper
parsley or coriander (cilantro), to garnish
natural (plain) yogurt, to serve

1 Put the saffron in a bowl with 15ml/1 tbsp boiling water and leave to stand. Heat a large frying pan and dry-fry the pine nuts until golden. Set aside.

2 Heat the oil in the pan and fry the onion, garlic and allspice for 3 minutes. Stir in the ginger and rice and cook for 1 minute. Add the stock and bring to the boil. Reduce the heat, cover and simmer for 15 minutes until the rice is tender.

3 Stir the saffron and liquid, the pine nuts, pickled walnuts, raisins and herbs into the rice. Season to taste with salt and pepper, then heat through gently for 2 minutes. Garnish with parsley or coriander and serve with yogurt.

Bulgur Wheat
& Pine Nut Pilaff

Pilaff is a popular staple throughout the Middle East. This is a North African version using bulgur wheat instead of rice. The pine nuts provide a delightful bite to the dish and cinnamon and green chilli adds a subtle spiciness.

SERVES 4

INGREDIENTS
30ml/2 tbsp olive oil
1 onion, chopped
1 garlic clove, crushed
5ml/1 tsp ground saffron or turmeric
2.5ml/½ tsp ground cinnamon
1 fresh green chilli, seeded and chopped
600ml/1 pint/2½ cups vegetable stock
150ml/¼ pint/⅔ cups dry white wine
225g/8oz/1⅓ cups bulgur wheat
15g/½oz/1 tbsp butter or margarine
30–45ml/2–3 tbsp pine nuts
30ml/2 tbsp chopped fresh parsley
vegetable or meat stew, to serve

1 Heat the oil in a large pan and fry the onion until soft. Then add the garlic, saffron or turmeric, ground cinnamon and chilli, and fry for a few seconds. Add the stock and wine, bring to the boil and simmer for about 8 minutes.

2 Place the bulgur wheat in a large strainer and rinse under cold water, drain and add to the pan. Stir to combine, cover and simmer gently for about 15 minutes until the stock is absorbed.

3 Melt the butter in a small pan, add the pine nuts and fry gently for a few minutes until golden. Add to the bulgur wheat with the chopped parsley and stir with a fork to mix together. Spoon into a warmed serving dish and serve the pilaff with a vegetable or meat stew.

PESTO RISOTTO

This dish is incredibly simple to make, particularly if you use ready-made pesto. Try to buy fresh pesto, which is available from most supermarkets, or make your own.

SERVES 3–4

INGREDIENTS
30ml/2 tbsp olive oil
2 shallots, finely chopped
1 garlic clove, crushed
275g/10oz/1½ cups risotto rice
175ml/6fl oz/¾ cup dry white wine
1 litre/1¾ pints/4 cups simmering vegetable stock
45ml/3 tbsp pesto
25g/1oz/⅓ cup grated Parmesan cheese, plus extra to serve (optional)
salt and ground black pepper

1 Heat the olive oil in a pan and fry the shallots and garlic for 4–5 minutes until the shallots are soft but not browned.

2 Add the rice to the pan and cook over a medium heat, stirring all the time, until the grains are coated in oil and the outer part of the grain is translucent and the inner part opaque.

3 Pour the white wine into the pan. Cook, stirring continuously, until all of the wine has been absorbed, then start adding the hot vegetable stock, a ladleful at a time, stirring constantly and waiting until each addition of stock has been absorbed before adding the next.

4 After about 20 minutes, when all the stock has been absorbed and the rice is creamy and tender, stir in the pesto and grated Parmesan cheese. Check the seasoning, adding more salt and ground black pepper if necessary. Remove the pan from the heat, cover and leave to rest for 3–4 minutes. Spoon into a bowl and serve, with extra Parmesan, if you like.

JERUSALEM ARTICHOKE RISOTTO

This is a simple and warming dish, delicately flavoured with the distinctive taste of Jerusalem artichokes, garlic and fresh thyme.

SERVES 3–4

INGREDIENTS
400g/14oz Jerusalem artichokes
40g/1½oz/3 tbsp butter
15ml/1 tbsp olive oil
1 onion, finely chopped
1 garlic clove, crushed
275g/10oz/1½ cups risotto rice
120ml/4fl oz/½ cup fruity white wine
1 litre/1¾ pints/4 cups simmering vegetable stock
10ml/2 tsp chopped fresh thyme
40g/1½oz/½ cup grated Parmesan cheese, plus extra to serve
salt and ground black pepper
thyme sprigs, to garnish

1 Peel the artichokes, cut them into pieces and immediately add them to a pan of lightly salted boiling water. Simmer until tender, then drain well and mash with 15g/½oz/1 tbsp of the butter. Add a little more salt, if needed.

2 Heat the oil and the remaining butter in a pan and fry the onion and garlic for 5–6 minutes until soft. Add the rice and cook over a medium heat for about 2 minutes until the grains are translucent around the edges. Pour in the wine, stir until it has been absorbed, then add the stock, a ladleful at a time, making sure each quantity has been absorbed before adding more.

3 When you have only one ladleful of stock still to add, stir in the artichokes and thyme. Season. Continue cooking until the risotto is creamy. Stir in the Parmesan. Remove from the heat, cover the pan and leave to rest for a few minutes. Spoon into a serving dish, garnish with thyme, and serve with extra Parmesan.

MARINATED SQUID RISOTTO WITH RED CHILLI

Squid needs to be cooked either very quickly or very slowly. Here the squid is marinated in lime and kiwi fruit, which tenderizes the flesh beautifully before it is pan-fried very quickly.

SERVES 3–4

INGREDIENTS
about 450g/1lb squid
about 45ml/3 tbsp olive oil
15g/½oz/1 tbsp butter
1 onion, finely chopped
2 garlic cloves, crushed
1 fresh red chilli, seeded and finely sliced
275g/10oz/1½ cups risotto rice
175ml/6fl oz/¾ cup dry white wine
1 litre/1¾ pints/4 cups simmering fish stock
30ml/2 tbsp chopped fresh coriander (cilantro)
salt and ground black pepper

FOR THE MARINADE
2 ripe kiwi fruit, chopped and mashed
1 fresh red chilli, seeded and finely sliced
30ml/2 tbsp fresh lime juice

1 If not already cleaned, prepare the squid by cutting off the tentacles at the base with a sharp knife and pulling to remove the quill. Discard the quill and intestines and pull away the thin outer skin. Rinse the body under cold running water, pat dry with kitchen paper and cut into thin strips. Cut the tentacles into short pieces, discarding the beak and eyes.

2 Make the marinade. Mash the kiwi fruit in a bowl, then stir in the chilli and lime juice. Add the squid, stirring to coat all the strips in the mixture. Season with salt and ground black pepper, cover with clear film (plastic wrap), place in the refrigerator and leave to marinate for 4 hours or overnight.

3 Drain the squid. Heat 15ml/1 tbsp of the olive oil in a frying pan and cook the strips, in batches if necessary, for about 30–60 seconds over a high heat. (It is essential that the squid cooks very quickly.) Transfer the cooked squid to a plate and set aside. Don't worry if some of the marinade clings to the squid, but if too much juice accumulates in the pan, pour this into a jug (pitcher) and add more olive oil when cooking the next batch, so that the squid fries rather than simmers.

4 Heat the remaining olive oil with the butter in a large pan and gently fry the onion and garlic for 5–6 minutes until soft. Add the sliced chilli to the pan and fry for 1 minute more.

5 Add the rice to the pan. Cook for a few minutes, stirring, until the rice is coated with oil and is slightly translucent around the edges, then stir in the white wine until it has been absorbed.

6 Gradually add the hot stock and the reserved cooking liquid from the squid a ladleful at a time, stirring the rice constantly and waiting until each quantity of stock has been absorbed before adding the next.

7 When the rice is about three-quarters cooked, stir in the squid and continue cooking the risotto until all the stock has been absorbed and the rice is tender, but retains a bit of "bite". Stir in the chopped coriander, cover with the lid or a dishtowel, and leave to rest for a few minutes before serving.

COOK'S TIP
Although fish stock underlines the flavour of the squid, a light chicken or vegetable stock would also work well in this recipe.

SEAFOOD PAELLA

There are many versions of this classic Mediterranean dish. It is perfect for a special occasion because it looks spectacular. Bring the steaming paella pan, filled with rice and seafood, to the table and let guests help themselves.

SERVES 4

INGREDIENTS
60ml/4 tbsp olive oil
225g/8oz monkfish or cod fillets, skinned and cut into chunks
3 prepared baby squid, body cut into rings and tentacles chopped
1 red mullet, filleted, skinned and cut into chunks (optional)
1 onion, chopped
3 garlic cloves, finely chopped
1 red (bell) pepper, seeded and sliced
4 tomatoes, peeled and roughly chopped
225g/8oz/generous 1 cup risotto rice
450ml/³/₄ pint/scant 2 cups fish stock
150ml/¹/₄ pint/²/₃ cup white wine
4–5 saffron strands soaked in 30ml/2 tbsp hot water
115g/4oz cooked peeled prawns (shrimp), thawed if frozen
75g/3oz/³/₄ cup frozen peas
8 fresh mussels, scrubbed
salt and ground black pepper
4 cooked Mediterranean prawns (shrimp), in the shell, and fresh parsley sprigs,
   to garnish
lemon wedges, to serve

COOK'S TIP
Before adding the mussels to the rice mixture, check that they are all closed. Any that are open should close when sharply tapped; any that fail to do this must be discarded.

1 Heat half the oil in a paella pan or a large frying pan and add the monkfish or cod, the squid, and the red mullet if using. Stir-fry for 2 minutes, then tip the contents of the pan into a bowl and set aside.

2 Heat the remaining oil in the pan and add the onion, garlic and pepper. Fry for 6–7 minutes, stirring frequently, until softened.

3 Stir the tomatoes into the onion and pepper mixture and fry for 2 minutes, then add the rice. Stir to coat the grains with oil, then cook for 2–3 minutes. Pour over the fish stock, white wine and saffron water. Season with plenty of salt and ground black pepper, and mix well.

4 Gently stir in the reserved cooked fish (with all the juices), then add the peeled prawns and the peas and stir to combine. Push the prepared mussels into the rice. Cover and cook over a gentle heat for about 30 minutes, or until the stock has been absorbed but the rice mixture is still relatively moist. Discard any mussels that have not opened.

5 Remove the pan from the heat, and leave the paella to stand, covered, for about 5 minutes. Arrange the whole prawns on top of the paella, sprinkle with parsley and serve with the lemon wedges for squeezing over.

ALMOND & CHICKEN RISOTTO

This risotto has its origins in Spain. It uses brown basmati rice, which gives the dish an almost nutty taste and texture. The addition of spicy chorizo sausage contributes to the Spanish flavour and feel and makes it a substantial and satisfying dish.

SERVES 4

INGREDIENTS
1 orange
8 chicken thighs
seasoned plain (all-purpose) flour, for dusting
45ml/3 tbsp olive oil
1 large Spanish onion, roughly chopped
2 garlic cloves, crushed
1 red (bell) pepper, seeded and sliced
1 yellow (bell) pepper, seeded and sliced
115g/4oz chorizo sausage, sliced
50g/2oz/½ cup flaked (slivered) almonds
225g/8oz/generous 1 cup brown basmati rice
about 600ml/1 pint/2½ cups chicken stock
400g/14oz can chopped tomatoes
175ml/6fl oz/¾ cup dry white wine
generous pinch of dried thyme
salt and ground black pepper
thyme sprigs, to garnish

1 Pare a thin strip of peel from the orange and set it aside. Peel the orange, then cut it into segments, working over a bowl to catch the juice, and discard the membrane. Dust the chicken thighs with the seasoned flour.

2 Heat the oil in a large frying pan and fry the chicken pieces on both sides until evenly brown. Transfer to a plate. Add the onion and garlic to the pan and fry for 4–5 minutes until the onion begins to brown. Add the red and yellow peppers and fry, stirring occasionally, until slightly softened.

3 Add the chorizo sausage to the pan, stir-fry for a few minutes, then sprinkle the almonds and rice into the mixture. Cook, stirring, for 1–2 minutes.

4 Pour the chicken stock, tomatoes and white wine into the pan and add the orange strip and thyme. Season well with salt and black pepper. Bring to simmering point, stirring, then return the chicken pieces to the pan.

5 Cover the pan tightly and cook over a very low heat for 1–1¼ hours until the rice and chicken are tender. Just before serving, add the orange segments and cook briefly until warmed through. Garnish with fresh thyme and serve.

COOK'S TIP
The cooking times for this dish depend largely on the heat. If the rice seems to be drying out too quickly, add a little more chicken stock or white wine and reduce the heat. If, after 40 minutes or so, the rice is still barely cooked, increase the heat a little. Make sure the rice is kept below the liquid (the chicken can lie on the surface). Stir the rice occasionally if it seems to be cooking unevenly.

TURKISH LAMB PILAU

This rice dish is a typical Middle Eastern combination of meat, spices, nuts and fruit. The mix of sweet and savoury flavours and interesting textures is delicious.

SERVES 4

INGREDIENTS
40g/1½oz/3 tbsp butter
1 large onion, finely chopped
450g/1lb lamb fillet, cut into small cubes
2.5ml/½ tsp ground cinnamon
30ml/2 tbsp tomato purée (paste)
45ml/3 tbsp chopped fresh parsley
75g/3oz/¾ cup pistachio nuts
115g/4oz/½ cup ready-to-eat dried apricots, halved
450g/1lb long grain rice, rinsed
salt and ground black pepper
flat leaf parsley, to garnish

1 Heat the butter in a large heavy pan. Add the onion and cook until soft and golden. Add the cubed lamb and brown on all sides. Add the ground cinnamon and season with salt and pepper. Cover and cook gently for 10 minutes.

2 Add the tomato purée to the pan and pour over enough water to cover the meat. Stir in the parsley, bring to the boil, cover and simmer very gently for 1½ hours, until the meat is tender. Meanwhile, chop the pistachio nuts.

3 Add enough water to the pan to make up to about 600ml/1 pint/2½ cups liquid. Add the apricots, pistachio nuts and rice, bring to the boil, cover and simmer for 20 minutes, or until the rice is cooked. (Add more water if necessary.) Transfer to a warmed serving dish and garnish with parsley before serving.

EGYPTIAN RICE WITH LENTILS

Lentils are cooked with spices in many ways in the Middle East and are very good combined with rice. This dish can be served hot or cold.

SERVES 6

INGREDIENTS
350g/12oz/1½ cups large brown lentils, soaked overnight
2 large onions
45ml/3 tbsp olive oil
15ml/1 tbsp ground cumin
2.5ml/½ tsp ground cinnamon
225g/8oz/generous 1 cup long grain rice
salt and ground black pepper
flat leaf parsley, to garnish

1 Drain the lentils, rinse in cold water and put in a large pan. Add enough water to cover by 5cm/2in. Bring to the boil, cover and simmer for 40 minutes–1½ hours, or until tender. Drain thoroughly.

2 Finely chop one onion, and slice the other. Heat 15ml/1 tbsp oil in a pan, add the chopped onion and fry until soft. Add the lentils, cumin and cinnamon and season with salt and ground black pepper.

3 Tip the rice in a measuring jug (pitcher) and check the volume, then add to the lentil mixture with the same volume of water. Cover and simmer for about 20 minutes, or until both the rice and lentils are tender.

4 Heat the remaining oil in a frying pan, and cook the sliced onion until very dark brown. Tip the rice mixture into a serving bowl, sprinkle with the browned onion and serve hot or cold, garnished with flat leaf parsley.

SPICED VEGETABLE COUSCOUS

This grain is a cereal processed from semolina and is widely used throughout North Africa, but mostly in Morocco. In this recipe it is served with a vegetable and chickpea stew but it is also served with meat and poultry and with traditional Moroccan tagines.

SERVES 6

INGREDIENTS
30ml/2 tbsp vegetable oil
1 large onion, finely chopped
2 garlic cloves, crushed
15ml/1 tbsp tomato purée (paste)
2.5ml/½ tsp ground turmeric
2.5ml/½ tsp cayenne pepper
5ml/1 tsp ground coriander
5ml/1 tsp ground cumin
225g/8oz/1½ cups cauliflower florets
225g/8oz baby carrots, trimmed
1 red (bell) pepper, seeded and diced
4 beefsteak tomatoes
225g/8oz courgettes (zucchini), thickly sliced
400g/14oz can chickpeas, drained and rinsed
45ml/3 tbsp chopped fresh coriander (cilantro)
salt and ground black pepper
coriander (cilantro) sprigs, to garnish

FOR THE COUSCOUS
15ml/1 tbsp olive oil
5ml/1 tsp salt
450g/1lb/2⅔ cups couscous
50g/2oz/2 tbsp butter

1 Heat the vegetable oil in a large pan, add the onion and garlic, and cook until soft. Stir in the tomato purée, turmeric, cayenne, ground coriander and cumin. Cook, stirring, for about 2 minutes.

2 Add the cauliflower, carrots and pepper, with enough water to come halfway up the vegetables. Bring to the boil, then cover and simmer for 10 minutes.

3 Plunge the tomatoes into boiling water for 30 seconds, then refresh in cold water. Peel away the skins and chop the flesh. Add the sliced courgettes, chickpeas and tomatoes to the other vegetables and cook for 10 minutes. Stir in the fresh coriander and season with salt and pepper. Keep hot.

4 To cook the couscous, bring 475ml/16fl oz/2 cups water to the boil in a large pan. Add the oil and the salt. Remove from the heat, and add the couscous, stirring. Leave to stand for 2 minutes, then add the butter, and heat through gently, stirring with a fork to separate the grains.

5 Turn the couscous out on to a warm serving dish, and spoon the vegetable and chickpea stew on top, pouring over any liquid. Garnish with coriander sprigs and serve immediately.

COOK'S TIP
Beefsteak tomatoes have excellent flavour and are ideal for this recipe, but you can substitute six ordinary tomatoes or two 400g/14oz cans chopped tomatoes if you like.

LEBANESE KIBBEH WITH YOGURT DIP

This is the national dish of Syria and the Lebanon. Kibbeh *are a kind of meatball made from minced lamb and bulgur wheat. Raw* Kibbeh *is the most widely eaten type, but this version is very popular too.*

SERVES 6

INGREDIENTS
115g/4oz/³⁄₄ cup bulgur wheat
450g/1lb finely minced (ground) lean lamb
1 large onion, grated
15ml/1 tbsp melted butter
salt and ground black pepper
sprigs of mint, to garnish
rice, to serve

FOR THE FILLING
30ml/2 tbsp oil
1 onion, finely chopped
225g/8oz minced (ground) lamb or veal
50g/2oz/¹⁄₂ cup pine nuts
2.5ml/¹⁄₂ tsp ground allspice

FOR THE DIP
600ml/1 pint/2¹⁄₂ cups Greek (US strained plain) yogurt
2–3 garlic cloves, crushed
15–30ml/1–2 tbsp chopped fresh mint

1 Preheat the oven to 190°C/375°F/Gas 5. Place the bulgur wheat in a strainer and rinse under cold running water, then squeeze out the excess moisture.

2 In a large bowl, combine the lamb, onion and seasoning, kneading the mixture to make a thick paste. Add the bulgur wheat and mix well to combine.

3 To make the filling, heat the oil in a frying pan and fry the onion until golden. Add the lamb or veal and cook, stirring, until evenly browned, then add the pine nuts and allspice and season with salt and pepper.

4 Oil a large baking dish and spread half of the meat and bulgur wheat mixture over the base. Spoon over the filling and top with a second layer of meat and bulgur wheat, pressing down firmly with the back of a spoon.

5 Pour the melted butter over the top and then bake in the centre of the oven for 40–45 minutes until browned on top.

6 Meanwhile, make the yogurt dip. Blend together the yogurt and garlic, spoon into a serving bowl and sprinkle with the chopped mint.

7 Cut the cooked kibbeh into squares or rectangles and garnish with mint. Serve with rice and the yogurt dip.

VARIATION
In many parts of the Middle East, kibbeh are shaped into balls. The bulgur wheat mixture forms a case around the onion and meat filling. These ball-shaped kibbeh may be deep-fried or grilled (broiled). Making kibbeh in this way can be tricky and requires practice.

STUFFED KIBBEH

These tasty North African minced (ground) meat and bulgur wheat patties are sometimes stuffed with additional meat and then deep-fried. They are moderately spiced and are very good served with yogurt.

SERVES 4–6

INGREDIENTS
450g/1lb lean lamb or lean minced (ground) lamb or beef
225g/8oz/1⅓ cups bulgur wheat
1 fresh red chilli, seeded and roughly chopped
1 onion, roughly chopped
oil, for deep-frying
salt and ground black pepper
coriander (cilantro) sprigs, to garnish
avocado slices, to serve

FOR THE STUFFING
30ml/2 tbsp olive oil
1 onion, finely chopped
50g/2oz/⅔ cup pine nuts
7.5ml/1½ tsp ground allspice
60ml/4 tbsp chopped fresh coriander (cilantro)

1 If necessary, roughly cut up the lamb and process the pieces in a food processor or blender until minced. Divide the minced meat into two equal portions.

2 To make the kibbeh, place the bulgur wheat in a large bowl, pour over cold water and leave to soak for about 15 minutes. Drain well, then process in the food processor or blender with the chilli, onion, half the meat and plenty of salt and ground black pepper.

3 To make the stuffing, heat the oil in a frying pan, add the onion and pine nuts and cook for 5 minutes. Add the allspice and remaining minced meat and fry gently, breaking up the meat with a wooden spoon, until browned. Stir in the coriander and a little seasoning.

4 Turn the kibbeh mixture out on to a work surface and, using your hands, shape into a round cake. Cut into 12 wedges.

5 Shape one wedge into a ball and flatten in the palm of your hand. Spoon a little stuffing into the centre, then bring the edges of the kibbeh up over the stuffing to enclose it. Make the stuffed kibbeh into a firm egg-shape between the palms of the hands, ensuring that the filling is completely encased. Repeat with the other 11 wedges of kibbeh mixture.

6 Heat the oil to a depth of 5cm/2in a large pan until a few kibbeh crumbs sizzle on the surface. Using a slotted spoon, lower half the kibbeh into the oil and fry for about 5 minutes, or until golden. Lift out of the pan with a slotted spoon. Drain on kitchen paper and keep hot while cooking the remainder. Garnish with coriander sprigs and serve hot with avocado slices.

FALAFEL

In North Africa these spicy fritters are made using dried broad beans, but chickpeas are much easier to obtain. They are lovely served as a snack with garlicky yogurt or stuffed into warmed pitta bread.

SERVES 4

INGREDIENTS
150g/5oz/³⁄₄ cup dried chickpeas, soaked overnight
1 large onion, roughly chopped
2 garlic cloves, roughly chopped
60ml/4 tbsp roughly chopped parsley
5ml/1 tsp cumin seeds, crushed
5ml/1 tsp coriander seeds, crushed
2.5ml/½ tsp baking powder
oil, for deep-frying
salt and ground black pepper
pitta bread, salad and natural (plain) yogurt, to serve

1 Drain the chickpeas, place in a large pan and cover with fresh water. Bring to the boil then boil rapidly for 10 minutes. Reduce the heat and simmer for about 1 hour, or until soft. Drain.

2 Place the chickpeas in a food processor or blender with the onion, garlic, parsley, cumin, coriander and baking powder. Add salt and black pepper. Process until the mixture forms a firm paste.

3 Wet your hands and shape the mixture into walnut-size balls, then flatten slightly. In a deep pan, heat 5cm/2in oil until a little of the chickpea mixture sizzles on the surface. Fry the falafel in batches until golden. Lift out of the pan with a slotted spoon and drain on kitchen paper. Keep hot while frying the remainder. Serve warm in pitta bread, with salad and yogurt.

VERMICELLI WITH LEMON

This is a quick and easy Italian dish with a fresh and tangy flavour. It makes an excellent lunch or supper dish or could be served as an appetizer for a dinner party. Choose lemons that feel heavy for their size.

SERVES 4

INGREDIENTS
350g/12oz dried vermicelli
juice of 2 large lemons
50g/2oz/¼ cup butter
200ml/7fl oz/scant 1 cup double (heavy) cream
115g/4oz/1⅓ cups grated Parmesan cheese
salt and ground black pepper

1 Cook the vermicelli in salted boiling water according to the instructions on the packet. Meanwhile, pour the lemon juice into a pan. Add the butter and cream, then season to taste. Bring to the boil, then lower the heat and simmer for about 5 minutes, stirring occasionally, until the cream reduces slightly.

2 When the pasta is cooked, drain it, then return to the pan. Add the grated Parmesan, then taste the sauce for seasoning, adjusting if necessary, and pour it over the pasta. Toss quickly over a medium heat until the pasta is evenly coated with the sauce. Divide among four warmed bowls and serve immediately.

VARIATIONS
• *Use spaghettini or spaghetti, or small pasta shapes such as fusilli instead of vermicelli.*
• *For an even tangier taste, add a little grated lemon rind to the sauce when you add the butter and the cream to the pan in Step 1.*

SPAGHETTI WITH TOMATOES & PANCETTA

This sauce comes from Umbria in Italy. It is a fresh, light sauce in which the tomatoes are cooked for just a short time, so it should only be made in summer when tomatoes are ripe and have a good flavour.

SERVES 4

INGREDIENTS
350g/12oz ripe Italian plum tomatoes
150g/5oz pancetta or rindless streaky (fatty) bacon, diced
30ml/2 tbsp olive oil
1 onion, finely chopped
350g/12oz fresh or dried spaghetti
2–3 marjoram sprigs, leaves stripped
salt and ground black pepper
shredded fresh basil, to garnish
grated Pecorino cheese, to serve

1 With a sharp knife, cut a cross on the base of each plum tomato. Plunge them into boiling water, a few at a time, and refresh in cold water. Peel off the skins and finely chop the flesh.

2 Put the pancetta or streaky bacon in a pan with the olive oil. Stir over a low heat until the fat runs. Add the onion and stir to mix. Cook gently for about 10 minutes, stirring.

3 Add the tomatoes to the pan and season with salt and pepper to taste. Stir well and cook, uncovered, for about 10 minutes. Meanwhile, cook the pasta according to the instructions on the packet.

4 Remove the sauce from the heat, stir in the marjoram and check the seasoning. When cooked, drain the pasta and tip it into a warmed serving bowl. Pour the sauce over the pasta and toss well. Serve immediately, sprinkled with shredded basil. Hand round grated Pecorino separately.

FUSILLI WITH WILD MUSHROOMS & HERBS

This is a very rich dish with an earthy flavour and lots of garlic. It makes an ideal main course for vegetarians, especially if it is followed by a crisp green salad.

SERVES 4

INGREDIENTS
½ × 275g/10oz jar wild mushrooms in olive oil
25g/1oz/2 tbsp butter
225g/8oz/2 cups fresh wild mushrooms, sliced if large
5ml/1 tsp finely chopped fresh thyme
5ml/1 tsp finely chopped fresh marjoram or oregano, plus extra to garnish
4 garlic cloves, crushed
350g/12oz/3 cups fresh or dried fusilli
200ml/7fl oz/scant 1 cup double (heavy) cream
salt and ground black pepper

1 Drain about 15ml/1 tbsp of the olive oil from the bottled mushrooms into a pan. Slice or chop any large bottled mushrooms into bitesize pieces; leave smaller ones whole.

2 Add the butter to the oil in the pan and place over a low heat until sizzling. Add the bottled and fresh mushrooms, the chopped herbs and the garlic, with salt and pepper to taste. Simmer over a medium heat, stirring frequently, for 10 minutes, or until the fresh mushrooms are soft and tender. Meanwhile, cook the pasta in salted boiling water according to the instructions on the packet.

3 As soon as the mushrooms are cooked, increase the heat to high and toss the mixture with a wooden spoon to drive off any excess liquid. Pour in the cream and bring to the boil, stirring, then taste and add more salt and pepper if needed.

4 When the pasta is cooked, drain it, then tip into a warmed serving bowl. Pour the mushroom sauce over the pasta and toss well. Serve at once, sprinkled with marjoram or oregano.

LINGUINE WITH HAM & MASCARPONE

The soft white cheese masquerades as cream in this recipe. Its thick, unctuous consistency makes it perfect for sauces. Have the water boiling, ready for the pasta, before you start making the sauce, because everything cooks so quickly.

SERVES 6

INGREDIENTS
25g/1oz/2 tbsp butter
150g/5oz/³⁄4 cup mascarpone cheese
90g/3¹⁄2oz cooked ham, cut into thin strips
30ml/2 tbsp milk
45ml/3 tbsp grated Parmesan cheese, plus extra to serve
500g/1¹⁄4lb fresh linguine
salt and ground black pepper

1 Melt the butter in a pan, add the mascarpone cheese, ham and milk and stir well over a low heat until the mascarpone has melted. Add 15ml/1 tbsp of the grated Parmesan and plenty of pepper and stir well.

2 Cook the linguine in a large pan of boiling salted water for 2–3 minutes or until al dente. Drain the pasta well and tip it into a warmed serving bowl.

3 Pour the sauce over the pasta, add the remaining Parmesan cheese and toss well. Check the seasoning, adding more salt and pepper if necessary, and serve the pasta immediately. Hand round more ground black pepper and extra grated Parmesan cheese separately.

COOK'S TIP
Give this dish an authentic Italian flavour by using either a cooked or cured Italian ham such as Parma ham or San Daniele.

SICILIAN SPAGHETTI WITH SARDINES

This is a traditional dish from Sicily using local ingredients. It is very simple and the unusual combination of sardines and sweet, juicy raisins is delicious.

SERVES 4

INGREDIENTS
12 fresh sardines, cleaned and boned
250ml/8fl oz/1 cup olive oil
1 onion, chopped
25g/1oz dill sprigs
50g/2oz/½ cup pine nuts
25g/1oz/2 tbsp raisins, soaked in water
50g/2oz/½ cup fresh white breadcrumbs
450g/1lb spaghetti
flour, for dusting
salt

1 Wash the sardines and pat dry on kitchen paper. Open them out flat, then cut in half lengthways.

2 Heat 30ml/2 tbsp of the oil in a pan, add the onion and fry until golden. Add the dill and cook gently for 1–2 minutes. Add the pine nuts and raisins and season with salt. In another pan, dry-fry the breadcrumbs, stirring constantly, until golden. Remove from the heat and set aside.

3 Cook the spaghetti in boiling salted water according to the instructions on the packet, until *al dente*. Heat the remaining oil in a pan. Dust the sardines with flour and fry in the hot oil for 2–3 minutes. Drain on kitchen paper.

4 When cooked, drain the spaghetti and return to the pan. Add the onion mixture and toss well. Transfer to a serving platter and arrange the fried sardines on top. Sprinkle with the breadcrumbs and serve immediately.

Pappardelle with Olive, Anchovy & Caper Paste

This home-made pasta is flavoured with sun-dried tomato paste. The results are well worth the effort, but bought pasta can be substituted for a really quick supper dish.

Serves 4

Ingredients
275g/10oz/2½ cups plain (all-purpose) flour
1.5ml/¼ tsp salt
3 eggs
45ml/3 tbsp sun-dried tomato paste

For the sauce
115g/4oz/⅔ cup pitted black olives
75ml/5 tbsp capers
5 canned anchovy fillets, drained
1 fresh red chilli, seeded and roughly chopped
60ml/4 tbsp roughly chopped fresh basil
60ml/4 tbsp roughly chopped fresh parsley
150ml/¼ pint/⅔ cup olive oil
4 ripe tomatoes
salt and ground black pepper
flat leaf parsley or basil, to garnish
Parmesan cheese shavings, to serve

1 To make the pasta, sift the flour and salt into a large bowl and make a well in the centre. Lightly beat the eggs with the sun-dried tomato paste, then pour the mixture into the well.

2 Mix the ingredients together using a round-bladed knife. Turn out on to a work surface and knead for 6–8 minutes until the dough is very smooth and soft. Work in a little more flour if the dough becomes sticky. Wrap in foil and chill in the refrigerator for 30 minutes.

3 To make the sauce, put the olives, capers, anchovies, chilli, basil and parsley in a food processor or blender with the oil. Process briefly until the ingredients are finely chopped. (Alternatively, you can finely chop the ingredients and then mix with the olive oil.) Plunge the tomatoes into boiling water for 30 seconds, then refresh in cold water. Peel away the skins, remove the seeds and dice the flesh.

4 Roll out the dough very thinly on a floured surface. Sprinkle with a little flour, then roll up like a Swiss roll. Cut across into 1cm/½in slices. Then unroll the pasta and lay out on a clean dishtowel for about 10 minutes to dry.

5 Bring a large pan of salted water to the boil. Add the pasta and cook for about 2 minutes, or until just tender. Drain immediately and return to the pan.

6 Add the olive mixture, tomatoes and salt and black pepper to taste, then toss together gently over a medium heat for about 1 minute until heated through. Garnish with parsley or basil and serve scattered with Parmesan shavings.

TAGLIOLINI WITH CLAMS & MUSSELS

This dish makes good use of the superb shellfish found in the Mediterranean. For a stunning presentation, serve on white china. The sauce can be prepared a few hours ahead of time, then the pasta cooked and the dish assembled at the last minute.

SERVES 4

INGREDIENTS
450g/1lb fresh mussels
450g/1lb fresh clams
60ml/4 tbsp olive oil
1 small onion, finely chopped
2 garlic cloves, finely chopped
large handful fresh flat leaf parsley, plus extra chopped parsley to garnish
175ml/6fl oz/¾ cup dry white wine
250ml/8fl oz/1 cup fish stock
1 small fresh red chilli, seeded and chopped
350g/12oz squid ink tagliolini or tagliatelle
salt and ground black pepper

1 Scrub the mussels and clams under cold running water and discard any that are open or damaged, or that do not close when tapped sharply.

2 Heat half of the oil in a large pan, add the onion and cook gently for about 5 minutes until softened. Sprinkle in the garlic, then add about half the parsley, with salt and pepper to taste. Add the mussels and clams and pour in the wine. Cover with the lid and bring to the boil over a high heat. Then cook for about 5 minutes, shaking the pan frequently, until the shellfish have opened.

3 Tip the mussels and clams into a fine sieve set over a bowl and let the liquid drain through. Discard the aromatics in the sieve, together with any mussels or clams that have failed to open.

4 Return the liquid to the cleaned pan and add the fish stock. Chop the remaining parsley finely and add it to the liquid with the chilli. Bring to the boil, then simmer, stirring, for a few minutes until slightly reduced. Turn off the heat.

5 Remove and discard the top shells from half the mussels and clams. Put all the mussels and clams in the pan of liquid and seasonings, then cover the pan tightly and set aside.

6 Cook the pasta according to the instructions on the packet. Drain well, then return to the cleaned pan and toss with the remaining olive oil. Put the pan of shellfish over a high heat and toss to heat the shellfish through and combine with the liquid and seasonings.

7 Divide the pasta among four warmed plates, spoon the shellfish mixture over and around, then serve immediately, sprinkled with chopped parsley.

Seafood Conchiglie

Serve this warm salad composed of scallops, pasta and fresh rocket flavoured with roasted pepper, chilli and balsamic vinegar for a special supper.

SERVES 4

INGREDIENTS
8 large fresh scallops
300g/11oz/2¾ cups dried conchiglie
15ml/1 tbsp olive oil
15g/½oz/1 tbsp butter
120ml/4fl oz/½ cup dry white wine
90g/3½oz rocket leaves, stalks trimmed
salt and ground black pepper

FOR THE VINAIGRETTE
60ml/4 tbsp extra virgin olive oil
15ml/1 tbsp balsamic vinegar
1 piece bottled roasted (bell) pepper, drained and finely chopped
1–2 fresh red chillies, seeded and chopped
1 garlic clove, crushed
5–10ml/1–2 tsp clear honey

1 Cut each scallop into 2–3 pieces. If the corals (roe) are attached, pull them off and cut each piece in half. Season the scallops and corals with salt and pepper.

2 To make the vinaigrette, put the oil, vinegar, chopped pepper and chillies in a jug (pitcher) with the garlic. Whisk well, adding honey to taste.

3 Cook the pasta according to the instructions on the packet. Meanwhile, heat the oil and butter in a non-stick frying pan until sizzling. Add half the scallops and toss over a high heat for 2 minutes. Remove and keep warm. Repeat with the rest. Add the wine to the pan and stir over a high heat until reduced to a few tablespoons. Remove and keep warm.

4 Drain the pasta; tip into a warmed serving bowl. Add the rocket, scallops, cooking juices and vinaigrette; toss well and serve at once.

BLACK PASTA WITH SQUID SAUCE

This sophisticated-looking dish is perfect for a dinner party. Long, slow cooking ensures that the squid is deliciously tender. Chilli provides an added bite.

SERVES 4

INGREDIENTS
105ml/7 tbsp olive oil
2 shallots, chopped
3 garlic cloves, crushed
45ml/3 tbsp chopped fresh parsley
675g/1½lb cleaned squid, cut into rings and rinsed
150ml/¼ pint/⅔ cup dry white wine
400g/14oz can chopped tomatoes
2.5ml/½ tsp dried chilli flakes or powder
450g/1lb squid ink tagliatelle
salt and ground black pepper

1 Heat the oil in a pan and add the shallots. Cook until pale golden, then add the garlic. When the garlic colours a little, add 30ml/2 tbsp of the parsley, stir, then add the squid and stir again. Cook for 3–4 minutes, then add the wine.

2 Simmer the sauce for a few seconds, then add the tomatoes and chilli and season with salt and pepper. Cover and simmer gently for about 1 hour, until the squid is tender. Add more water if the mixture looks too dry.

3 Cook the pasta in plenty of boiling salted water according to the instructions on the packet, until *al dente*. Drain and return the tagliatelle to the pan. Add the squid sauce and mix well. Sprinkle each serving with the remaining chopped parsley and serve at once.

COOK'S TIP
Tagliatelle flavoured with squid ink tastes delicious and looks very pretty, particularly on a white plate. You can find it in most good Italian delicatessens and some larger supermarkets.

PIZZAS & BREADS

Throughout the Mediterranean region, yeasted and unyeasted dough forms the foundation of many dishes from cheese-topped pizzas and savoury flatbreads to decorative celebration breads. Traditionally, pizzas are associated with Italy, but other countries have their own versions including Onion and Anchovy Pizza from Spain and filled Marrakesh Pizza from Morocco. Breads vary enormously and can be sweet or savoury. This chapter offers a selection of classic recipes including Olive Bread, rustic Pan de Cebada from Spain, Pitta Bread and Greek Easter Bread. Mallorcan Ensaimadas are traditionally eaten for breakfast with a cup of strong coffee, while Spanish Twelfth Night Bread is baked to celebrate the Christian festival of Epiphany.

MARRAKESH PIZZA

Rather than sprinkling flavourings on top of the bread dough like a classic Italian pizza, Moroccan cooks tend to place flavourings inside the bread. This pizza has a wonderfully tasty filling of onion, tomato and cheese, flavoured with herbs and spices. This version is lightly fried rather than baked.

MAKES 4 PIZZAS

INGREDIENTS
5ml/1 tsp sugar
10ml/2 tsp dried yeast
*450g/1lb/4 cups white flour or a mixture of white and wholemeal
  (whole-wheat) flour*
10ml/2 tsp salt
melted butter, for brushing, plus extra for drizzling (optional)
rocket salad and black olives, to serve
rock salt, for sprinkling

FOR THE FILLING
1 small onion, very finely chopped
2 tomatoes, peeled, seeded and chopped
25ml/1½ tbsp chopped fresh parsley
25ml/1½ tbsp chopped fresh coriander (cilantro)
5ml/1 tsp paprika
5ml/1 tsp ground cumin
50g/2oz vegetable suet, finely chopped
40g/1½oz Cheddar cheese, grated
salt and ground black pepper

1 Place 150ml/¼ pint/⅔ cup warm water in a small bowl or jug (pitcher), stir in the sugar and then sprinkle with the yeast. Stir once or twice, then set aside in a warm place for about 10 minutes until the mixture is frothy.

2 Meanwhile, make the filling. In a large bowl, mix together the chopped onion, tomatoes, parsley, coriander, paprika, cumin, suet and cheese, then season with a little salt and set aside.

3 In a large bowl, mix together the flour and salt. Add the yeast mixture and enough warm water to make a fairly soft dough (about 250ml/8fl oz/1 cup). Knead the mixture into a ball and then knead on a floured work surface for 10–12 minutes until the dough is firm and elastic.

4 Break the dough into four pieces and roll each out into a rectangle measuring 20 × 30cm/8 × 12in. Place the filling down the centre of each rectangle, then fold into three, to form a rectangle measuring 20 × 10cm/8 × 4in.

5 Roll out the dough again, until the same size as before and again fold into three to make a smaller rectangle. (The filling will be squashed out in places, but don't worry – just push it back inside the dough.)

6 Place the pizzas on a buttered baking sheet, cover with oiled clear film (plastic wrap) and leave in a warm place for about 1 hour until slightly risen.

7 Heat a griddle and brush with melted butter. Prick the pizzas with a fork five or six times on both sides and fry for about 8 minutes on each side until crisp and golden. Serve immediately, with a little melted butter drizzled over, if liked, accompanied by rocket salad and black olives and with rock salt for sprinkling.

ONION & ANCHOVY PIZZA

This pizza is flavoured with ingredients brought to Spain from North Africa – including pine nuts and dried fruit – which are used in many classic Spanish recipes.

SERVES 6–8

INGREDIENTS
400g/14oz/2½ cups plain bread flour
2.5ml/½ tsp salt
15g/½oz easy-blend dried yeast
120ml/4fl oz/½ cup olive oil
150ml/¼ pint/⅔ cup milk and water, in equal quantities, mixed together
3 large onions, thinly sliced
50g/2oz can anchovies, drained and roughly chopped
30ml/2 tbsp pine nuts
30ml/2 tbsp sultanas (golden raisins)
5ml/1 tsp dried chilli flakes or powder
salt and ground black pepper

1 Sift the flour and salt together into a large bowl. Stir in the yeast. Make a well in the centre and add 60ml/4 tbsp of the olive oil and a little of the milk and water. Bring the flour mixture and liquid together, gradually adding the remaining milk and water, until a dough is formed.

2 Turn the dough out on to a floured work surface and knead for about 10 minutes. Return to the bowl, cover with a clean dishtowel and leave in a warm place to rise for about 1 hour until doubled in bulk.

3 Heat the remaining oil in a large frying pan, add the onions and cook for about 7 minutes until soft. Preheat the oven to 240°C/475°F/Gas 9.

4 Knock back (punch down) the dough, and roll out to a rectangle about 30 × 38cm/12 × 15in. Place the dough on an oiled baking sheet. Cover with the onions. Scatter over the anchovies, pine nuts, sultanas and chilli flakes or powder and season well with plenty of salt and ground black pepper. Bake for 10–15 minutes, until the edges are beginning to brown. Serve hot.

MUSHROOM & PESTO PIZZA

Home-made Italian-style pizzas are well worth the effort. This filling contains dried and fresh mushrooms with basil, pine nuts and Parmesan cheese.

SERVES 4

INGREDIENTS
350g/12oz/3 cups white bread flour
1.5ml/¼ tsp salt
15g/½oz easy-blend dried yeast
15ml/1 tbsp olive oil
50g/2oz dried porcini mushrooms
25g/1oz/¾ cup fresh basil
25g/1oz/⅓ cup pine nuts
40g/1½oz Parmesan cheese, thinly sliced
105ml/7 tbsp olive oil
2 onions, thinly sliced
225g/8oz chestnut mushrooms, sliced
salt and ground black pepper

1 For the dough, put the flour in a bowl with the salt, dried yeast and olive oil. Add 250ml/8fl oz/1 cup hand-hot water and mix to a dough. Knead on a floured work surface for 5 minutes. Place in a clean bowl, cover with clear film (plastic wrap) and leave in a warm place for about 1 hour until doubled in bulk.

2 For the topping, put the porcini in a small bowl, pour over hot water to cover and leave to soak for about 20 minutes. Drain. Place the basil, pine nuts, Parmesan and 75ml/5 tbsp of the oil in a food processor or blender and process to a smooth paste. Set aside. Fry the onions in the remaining oil for 3–4 minutes until just colouring. Add the chestnut mushrooms and fry for about 2 minutes. Stir in the drained porcini and season.

3 Preheat the oven to 220°C/425°F/Gas 7. Roll out the dough on a floured surface to a 30cm/12in round. Place on a large greased baking sheet. Spread the pesto mixture to within 1cm/½in of the edges. Spread the mushroom mixture on top. Bake for 35–40 minutes until risen and golden.

RED ONION FOCACCIA

This pizza-like Italian flat bread is characterized by its soft dimpled surface. It is sometimes dredged simply with coarse salt, herbs or olives, but here it has a tasty red onion topping, which takes on a wonderfully mellow, sweet flavour when the bread is cooked. It tastes delicious served warm with soups and stews.

MAKES TWO 25CM/10IN LOAVES

INGREDIENTS
675g/1½lb/6 cups plain bread flour
2.5ml/½ tsp salt
2.5ml/½ tsp caster (superfine) sugar
15ml/1 tbsp easy-blend dried yeast
60ml/4 tbsp extra virgin olive oil, plus extra for drizzling
450ml/¾ pint/1⅞ cups hand-hot water
2 red onions, thinly sliced
15ml/1 tbsp coarse salt

1 Sift the flour, salt and sugar into a large bowl. Stir in the dried yeast, olive oil and water and mix to a dough using a round-bladed knife. (Add a little extra water if the dough is too dry.)

2 Turn the dough out on to a lightly floured surface and knead for 10 minutes, or until it becomes smooth and elastic.

3 Place the dough in a clean, lightly oiled bowl and cover with lightly oiled clear film (plastic wrap). Leave to rise in a warm place for about an hour, or until doubled in bulk.

4 Place two 25cm/10in plain metal flan rings on baking sheets. Oil the insides of the rings and the baking sheets.

5 Preheat the oven to 200°C/400°F/Gas 6. Halve the dough and, working on a floured surface, roll each piece to a 25cm/10in round with a floured rolling pin. Press into the flan rings, cover with a dampened dishtowel and leave to rise for about 30 minutes.

6 Remove the dishtowel and, using your fingers, press deep holes, about 2.5cm/ 1in apart, in the dough. Replace the dampened dishtowel and leave to rise for a further 20 minutes.

7 Remove the dishtowel and scatter the dough with the sliced onions and generously drizzle over about 45ml/3 tbsp olive oil. Sprinkle with the coarse salt, then a little cold water, to stop a crust from forming.

8 Bake for about 25 minutes, sprinkling with water again during cooking. Cool slightly on a wire rack and serve warm.

VARIATIONS
• If you like, use another mild-tasting onion for the bread such as the yellow-skinned Spanish onion. Alternatively, use a mixture of the two.
• Scatter some crushed garlic over the rounds of dough before you add the sliced onion for a more pungent flavour.
• Scatter a handful of pitted black olives over the red onions, if you like.

SUN-DRIED TOMATO BREAD

In the south of Italy many people make their own sun-dried tomatoes. First they are dried off in the hot sun, then they are either preserved in oil or hung up in strings in the kitchen, to use in the winter. They are delicious baked in bread.

MAKES 4 SMALL LOAVES

INGREDIENTS
675g/1½lb/6 cups plain bread flour
10ml/2 tsp salt
25g/1oz/2 tbsp caster (superfine) sugar
25g/1oz fresh yeast
400–475ml/14–16fl oz/1⅔–2 cups warm milk
15ml/1 tbsp tomato purée (paste)
75ml/5 tbsp oil from the jar of sun-dried tomatoes
75ml/5 tbsp extra virgin olive oil
75g/3oz/¾ cup drained sun-dried tomatoes, chopped
1 large onion, chopped

1 Sift the flour, salt and sugar into a bowl, and make a well in the centre. Crumble the yeast, mix with 150ml/¼ pint/⅔ cup of the warm milk and add to the flour.

2 Mix the tomato purée into the remaining milk, until evenly blended, then add to the flour with the tomato oil and olive oil. Gradually mix the flour into the liquid ingredients to form a dough.

3 Turn the dough out on to a floured surface and knead for about 10 minutes until smooth and elastic. Return to the cleaned bowl, cover with a dishtowel, and leave to rise in a warm place for about 2 hours.

4 Knock the dough back, and add the tomatoes and onion. Knead until evenly distributed through the dough. Shape into four rounds and place on a greased baking sheet. Cover with a dishtowel and leave to rise again for about 45 minutes.

5 Preheat the oven to 190°C/375°F/Gas 5. Bake the bread for 45 minutes, or until the loaves sound hollow when tapped underneath. Leave to cool on a wire rack. Eat warm or toasted.

OLIVE BREAD

This is popular all over the Mediterranean. For this Greek recipe use rich, oily olives or those marinated in herbs rather than canned ones. Black olives impart a deep, rich flavour while green olives produce a fresher taste.

MAKES TWO 675G/1 ½LB LOAVES

INGREDIENTS
2 red onions
30ml/2 tbsp olive oil
225g/8oz/1⅓ cups pitted black or green olives
750g/1¾lb/7 cups plain bread flour
7.5ml/1½ tsp salt
20ml/4 tsp easy-blend dried yeast
45ml/3 tbsp roughly chopped parsley, coriander (cilantro) or mint

1 Slice the red onions thinly, then fry them in the olive oil until soft but not browned. Remove from the heat. Roughly chop the olives.

2 Put the flour, salt, yeast and parsley, coriander or mint in a large bowl with the fried onions and olives and pour in 475ml/16fl oz/2 cups hand-hot water. Mix to a dough using a round-bladed knife, adding a little more water if the mixture feels too dry.

3 Turn the dough out on to a lightly floured work surface and knead for about 10 minutes until smooth and elastic. Put in a clean bowl, cover with lightly oiled clear film (plastic wrap) and leave to rise in a warm place for about 1 hour until doubled in bulk.

4 Preheat the oven to 220°C/425°F/Gas 7. Lightly grease two baking sheets. Turn the dough on to a floured surface and cut in half. Shape into two rounds and place on the baking sheets. Cover loosely with lightly oiled clear film and leave until doubled in size.

5 Slash the tops of the loaves with a knife, then bake for about 40 minutes or until the loaves sound hollow when tapped underneath. Transfer to a wire rack to cool a little before serving warm.

Pan de Cebada

Cebada is Spanish for barley, and this country bread has a close, heavy texture that will satisfy even those with a larger appetite. It incorporates three types of flour, which give it a deeply rich flavour.

Makes 1 large loaf

Ingredients
maize meal, for dusting
20g/³⁄₄oz fresh yeast
45ml/3 tbsp lukewarm water
225g/8oz/2 cups wholemeal (whole-wheat) bread flour
15ml/1 tbsp salt

For the sourdough starter
175g/6oz/1½ cups maize meal
560ml/scant 1 pint/scant 2½ cups water
225g/8oz/2 cups wholemeal (whole-wheat) bread flour
75g/3oz/³⁄₄ cup barley flour

1 To make the sourdough starter, mix the maize meal with half the water in a pan, then blend in the remainder. Cook over a gentle heat, stirring continuously, until thickened. Transfer to a large bowl and set aside to cool.

2 Add the wholemeal flour and barley flour to the maize meal dough. Turn out on to a lightly floured surface and knead for 5 minutes. Return to the bowl, cover with lightly oiled clear film (plastic wrap) and leave the starter in a warm place for 36 hours.

3 Dust a baking sheet with maize meal. In a small bowl, cream the yeast with the water for the dough. Mix the yeast mixture into the starter with the wholemeal flour and salt and work to a dough. Turn out on to a lightly floured surface and knead for 4–5 minutes until smooth and elastic.

4 Transfer the dough to a lightly oiled bowl, cover with lightly oiled clear film or an oiled plastic bag and leave in a warm place for 1½–2 hours to rise, or until nearly doubled in bulk.

5 Knock back (punch down) the dough and turn out on to a lightly floured surface. Shape into a plump round and sprinkle with a little maize meal.

6 Place the shaped bread on the prepared baking sheet. Cover with a large upturned bowl. Leave to rise in a warm place for about 1 hour, or until nearly doubled in bulk. Place an empty roasting pan in the bottom of the oven. Preheat the oven to 220°C/425°F/Gas 7.

7 Pour 300ml/½ pint/1¼ cups cold water into the roasting pan. Lift the bowl off the risen loaf and immediately place the baking sheet in the oven. Bake the bread for 10 minutes. Remove the tin of water, reduce the oven temperature to 190°C/375°F/Gas 5 and bake for about 20 minutes. Cool on a wire rack.

PAN GALLEGO

This is a typical round bread with a twisted top from Spain. Olive oil gives a soft crumb and the millet, pumpkin and sunflower seeds scattered through the loaf provide a wonderfully nutty flavour and an interesting mix of textures. This bread is excellent served with cheese.

MAKES 1 LARGE LOAF

INGREDIENTS
maize meal, for dusting
350g/12oz/3 cups unbleached white bread flour
115g/4oz/1 cup wholemeal (whole-wheat) bread flour
10ml/2 tsp salt
20g/³⁄₄oz fresh yeast
275ml/9fl oz/generous 1 cup lukewarm water
30ml/2 tbsp olive oil or melted lard (shortening)
30ml/2 tbsp pumpkin seeds
30ml/2 tbsp sunflower seeds
15ml/1 tbsp millet

COOK'S TIP
If you prefer, use a 6g/¹⁄₄oz sachet of easy-blend dried yeast instead of fresh yeast. Stir the dried yeast into the white and wholemeal flour in Step 1, then pour in the warm water and olive oil or melted lard and continue as before.

---

1 Sprinkle a baking sheet with maize meal. Mix the white and wholemeal flours and the salt together in a large bowl.

2 Mix the yeast with the water in a small bowl and stir until smooth. Add to the centre of the flours with the olive oil or melted lard and mix to a firm dough. Turn out on to a lightly floured work surface and knead for about 10 minutes until smooth and elastic. Place in a lightly oiled bowl, then cover with lightly oiled clear film (plastic wrap) and leave to rise in a warm place for about 1½–2 hours, or until the dough has doubled in bulk.

3 Knock back (punch down) the dough and turn out on to a lightly floured surface. Gently knead in the pumpkin seeds, sunflower seeds and millet. Re-cover and leave to rest for about 5 minutes.

4 Shape the dough into a round ball and twist the centre to make a cap. Transfer the shaped dough to the prepared baking sheet and dust with maize meal. Cover with a large upturned bowl and leave to rise in a warm place for about 45 minutes, or until doubled in bulk.

5 Meanwhile, place an empty roasting pan in the bottom of the oven. Preheat the oven to 220°C/425°F/Gas 7. Pour about 300ml/½ pint/1¼ cups cold water into the roasting pan. Lift the bowl off the risen loaf and immediately place the baking sheet in the oven, above the roasting pan. Bake the bread for 10 minutes.

6 Remove the pan of water and bake the bread for a further 25–30 minutes, or until well browned and sounding hollow when tapped underneath. Transfer to a wire rack to cool.

GREEK EASTER BREAD

*Traditionally the Easter celebrations are very important in Greece, and involve much
preparation in the kitchen. This bread is sold in all the bakers' shops, and also made
at home. It is usually decorated with red dyed eggs.*

MAKES 1 LOAF

INGREDIENTS
25g/1oz fresh yeast
120ml/4fl oz/½ cup warm milk
675g/1½lb/6 cups white bread flour
2 eggs, beaten
2.5ml/½ tsp caraway seeds
15ml/1 tbsp caster (superfine) sugar
15ml/1 tbsp brandy
50g/2oz/4 tbsp butter, melted
1 egg white, beaten

FOR THE DECORATION
2–3 hard-boiled (hard-cooked) eggs, dyed red
50g/2oz/½ cup split almonds

1 Crumble the yeast into a bowl. Mix with one or two tablespoons of warm
water, until softened. Add the warm milk and 115g/4oz/1 cup of the flour and
mix to a creamy consistency. Cover with a dishtowel, and leave to stand in a warm
place for about 1 hour.

2 Sift the remaining flour into a large bowl and make a well in the centre. Pour
the risen yeast into the well, and draw in a little of the flour from the sides. Add
the eggs, caraway seeds, sugar and brandy. Gradually incorporate the remaining
flour, until the mixture begins to form a dough. Mix in the melted butter.

3 Turn the dough out on to a floured work surface, and knead for 10 minutes
until smooth and elastic. Return the dough to the bowl and cover with a
dishtowel. Leave to stand in a warm place for about 3 hours.

4 Preheat the oven to 180°C/350°F/Gas 4. Knock back (punch down) the dough,
turn out on to a floured work surface and knead for 1–2 minutes.

5 Divide the dough into three equal pieces, and roll each piece into a long sausage. Twist the three pieces of dough into a plait (braid) and place the loaf on a greased baking sheet.

6 Tuck the ends of the plait under the loaf and brush with the egg white. Gently press the dyed eggs on to the loaf and scatter over the split almonds to decorate. Bake for about 1 hour, or until the loaf sounds hollow when tapped underneath. Leave to cool on a wire rack.

COOK'S TIP
You can often buy fresh yeast from bakers' shops and some larger supermarkets that have an in-store bakery. It should be pale cream in colour with a firm but crumbly texture.

CHRISTOPSOMO

This Greek Christmas bread is decorated with an aniseed-flavoured Byzantine cross and walnuts (for good fortune). The light, butter enriched bread contains orange rind, cinnamon and cloves, giving it a spicy, aromatic taste.

MAKES 1 LOAF

INGREDIENTS
15g/½oz fresh yeast
140ml/scant ¼ pint/scant ⅔ cup lukewarm milk
450g/1lb/4 cups unbleached white bread flour
2 eggs
75g/3oz/6 tbsp caster (superfine) sugar
2.5ml/½ tsp salt
75g/3oz/6 tbsp butter, softened
grated rind of ½ orange
5ml/1 tsp ground cinnamon
1.5ml/¼ tsp ground cloves
a pinch of crushed aniseed
8 walnut halves
beaten egg white, for glazing

1 Lightly grease a large baking sheet. In a large bowl, mix the yeast with the milk until the yeast is dissolved, then stir in 115g/4oz/1 cup of the flour to make a thin batter. Cover with lightly oiled clear film (plastic wrap) and leave in a warm place for about 30 minutes.

2 Beat the eggs and sugar until light and fluffy. Beat these into the yeast mixture. Gradually mix in the remaining flour and salt to form a soft dough. Add in the softened butter and knead to a soft but not sticky dough. Knead on a lightly floured work surface for 8–10 minutes until smooth. Place in a lightly oiled bowl, cover with lightly oiled clear film and leave in a warm place for 1½ hours, until the dough has doubled in bulk.

3 Turn out on to a lightly floured work surface and knock back (punch down). Cut off about 50g/2oz of dough, cover and set aside. Gently knead the orange rind, ground cinnamon and cloves into the large piece of dough and shape into a round loaf. Place on the baking sheet.

4 Knead the aniseed into the remaining dough. Cut the dough in half and shape each piece into a 30cm/12in long rope. Cut through each rope at either end by one-third of its length. Place the two ropes in a cross on top of the loaf, then curl each cut end into a circle, in opposite directions.

5 Place a walnut half inside each circle. Cover the loaf with lightly oiled clear film and leave to rise for 45 minutes, or until doubled in size. Meanwhile, preheat the oven to 190°C/375°F/Gas 5. Brush the loaf with the egg white and bake for 40–45 minutes, or until golden. Cool on a wire rack.

COOK'S TIP
Don't be tempted to shorten the proving times for the dough. If it has not doubled in size, leave it for a bit longer, otherwise the baked bread will be heavy rather than light and fluffy.

TWELFTH NIGHT BREAD

Epiphany or the Day of the Three Kings, on 6 January, is celebrated in Spain as a time for exchanging presents. Historically this date was when the Three Wise Men arrived bearing gifts for Christ. An ornamental bread ring is specially baked for the occasion. The traditional version contains a silver coin, china figure or dried bean hidden inside, and the lucky recipient is declared King of the festival.

MAKES 1 LARGE LOAF

INGREDIENTS
450g/1lb/4 cups unbleached white bread flour
2.5ml/½ tsp salt
25g/1oz fresh yeast
140ml/scant ¼ pint/scant ⅔ cup mixed lukewarm milk and water
75g/3oz/6 tbsp butter
75g/3oz/6 tbsp caster (superfine) sugar
10ml/2 tsp finely grated lemon rind
10ml/2 tsp finely grated orange rind
2 eggs
15ml/1 tbsp brandy
15ml/1 tbsp orange flower water
silver coin or dried bean (optional)
beaten egg white, for glazing
a mixture of crystallized and glacé (candied) fruit slices, and flaked (slivered)
    almonds, to decorate

1 Lightly grease a large baking sheet. Sift the flour and salt together into a large bowl. Make a well in the centre.

2 In a small bowl or jug (pitcher), mix the yeast with the lukewarm milk and water until the yeast has dissolved. Pour the yeast mixture into the centre of the flour and stir in enough of the flour from around the sides of the bowl to make a thick batter.

3 Sprinkle a little of the remaining flour over the top of the batter and leave in a warm place for about 15 minutes, or until frothy.

4 Using an electric whisk or a wooden spoon, beat the butter and sugar together in a bowl until soft and creamy, then set aside.

5 Add the citrus rinds, eggs, brandy and orange flower water to the flour mixture and use a wooden spoon to mix to a sticky dough.

6 Beat the mixture by hand until it forms a fairly smooth dough. Gradually beat in the reserved butter mixture and beat for a few minutes until the dough is smooth and elastic. Cover with lightly oiled clear film (plastic wrap) and leave to rise in a warm place for about 1½ hours, or until doubled in bulk.

7 Knock back (punch down) the dough and turn out on to a lightly floured surface. Gently knead for 2–3 minutes, incorporating the coin or bean, if using.

8 On a floured work surface, roll out the dough into a long strip measuring about 66 × 13cm/26 × 5in. Roll up the dough from one long side like a Swiss roll to make a long sausage shape. Place seam side down on the prepared baking sheet and seal the ends together to form a ring. Cover with lightly oiled clear film and leave to rise in a warm place for 1–1½ hours, or until doubled in size.

9 Meanwhile, preheat the oven to 180°C/350°F/Gas 4. Brush the dough ring with beaten egg white and decorate with candied and glacé fruit slices, pushing them slightly into the dough. Sprinkle with almond flakes and bake for 30–35 minutes, or until risen and golden. Turn out on to a wire rack to cool.

COOK'S TIP
If you like, this bread can be baked in a lightly greased 24cm/9½in ring-shaped cake tin (pan) or savarin mould. Place the dough seam side down into the tin or mould and seal the ends together.

MOROCCAN HOLIDAY BREAD

The addition of maize meal and a cornucopia of seeds gives this superb loaf an interesting flavour and texture.

MAKES 1 LOAF

INGREDIENTS
275g/10oz/2½ cups unbleached white bread flour
50g/2oz/½ cup maize meal
5ml/1 tsp salt
20g/¾oz fresh yeast
120ml/4fl oz/½ cup lukewarm water
120ml/4fl oz/½ cup lukewarm milk
15ml/1 tbsp pumpkin seeds
15ml/1 tbsp sesame seeds
30ml/2 tbsp sunflower seeds

VARIATIONS
• Incorporate all the seeds in the dough in step 5 and leave the top of the loaf plain.
• Alternatively, use sesame seeds instead of sunflower seeds for the topping and either incorporate the sunflower seeds in the loaf or leave them out.

1 Lightly grease a baking sheet. Sift the flours and salt into a large bowl. Cream the yeast with a little of the water in a jug (pitcher). Stir in the remainder of the water and the milk. Pour into the centre of the flour and mix to a soft dough.

2 Turn the dough out on to a lightly floured work surface and knead it for about 5 minutes until smooth and elastic. Place in a lightly oiled bowl, cover with lightly oiled clear film (plastic wrap) and leave to rise in a warm place for about 1 hour, or until doubled in bulk.

3 Turn the dough out on to a lightly floured work surface and knock back (punch down). Gently knead the pumpkin and sesame seeds into the dough. Shape the dough into a round ball and flatten slightly.

4 Place on the prepared baking sheet, cover with lightly oiled clear film or slide into a large, lightly oiled plastic bag and leave to rise in a warm place for about 45 minutes, or until doubled in bulk.

5 Meanwhile, preheat the oven to 200°C/400°F/Gas 6. Brush the top of the loaf with water and sprinkle evenly with the sunflower seeds. Bake the loaf for 30–35 minutes, or until it is golden and sounds hollow when tapped on the base. Transfer the loaf to a wire rack to cool.

PITTA BREAD

These Turkish breads are a firm favourite in the eastern Mediterranean. The bread forms a pocket as it cooks – perfect for filling with vegetables, salads or meats.

MAKES 6 PITTA BREADS

INGREDIENTS
225g/8oz/2 cups unbleached white bread flour
5ml/1 tsp salt
15g/½oz fresh yeast
140ml/scant ¼ pint/scant ⅔ cup lukewarm water
10ml/2 tsp extra virgin olive oil

1 Sift the flour and salt into a bowl. Dissolve the yeast in the water, then stir in the oil and pour into a large bowl. Gradually beat the flour into the yeast mixture, then knead to make a soft dough.

2 Turn out on to a lightly floured surface and knead for 5 minutes until smooth. Place in a large clean bowl, cover with lightly oiled clear film (plastic wrap) and leave to rise in a warm place for about 1 hour, or until doubled in bulk.

3 Knock back the dough. On a lightly floured surface, divide it into 6 equal pieces and shape into balls. Cover with oiled clear film; leave to rest for 5 minutes.

4 Roll out each ball of dough to an oval 5mm/¼in thick and 15cm/6in long. Place on a floured dishtowel and cover with lightly oiled clear film. Leave to rise for 20–30 minutes. Meanwhile, preheat the oven to 230°C/450°F/Gas 8. Place 3 baking sheets in the oven.

5 Place two pitta breads on each baking sheet and bake for 4–6 minutes, or until puffed up; they do not need to brown. If preferred, cook the pitta bread in batches. It is important that the oven has reached the recommended temperature before the pitta breads are baked to ensure that they puff up.

6 Transfer the pittas to a wire rack to cool until warm, then cover with a dishtowel to keep them soft.

MALLORCAN ENSAIMADAS

These spiral-shaped rolls are a popular Spanish breakfast treat. Lard (shortening) was once brushed over the dough, but now butter is preferred.

MAKES 16 ROLLS

INGREDIENTS
225g/8oz/2 cups unbleached white bread flour
2.5ml/½ tsp salt
50g/2oz/¼ cup caster (superfine) sugar
15g/½oz fresh yeast
75ml/5 tbsp lukewarm milk
1 egg
30ml/2 tbsp sunflower oil
50g/2oz/¼ cup butter, melted
icing (confectioners') sugar, for dusting

1 Grease 2 baking sheets. Sift the flour and salt into a large mixing bowl. Stir in the sugar and make a well in the centre. Cream the yeast with the milk, pour into the flour mixture, then sprinkle a little of the flour mixture evenly over the top of the liquid. Leave in a warm place for about 15 minutes, or until frothy.

2 Beat the egg and oil together. Add to the flour mixture and mix to a smooth dough. Turn out on to a lightly floured surface and knead for 8–10 minutes until smooth and elastic. Place in a lightly oiled bowl, cover with lightly oiled clear film (plastic wrap) and leave to rise in a warm place for 1 hour, or until doubled in bulk.

3 Turn out the dough on to a lightly floured surface. Knock back (punch down) the dough; divide into 16 equal pieces. Shape into thin ropes about 38cm/15in long. Dip into the melted butter to coat. On the baking sheets, curl each rope into a loose spiral; tuck the ends under. Cover with lightly oiled clear film and leave in a warm place for about 45 minutes or until doubled in size.

4 Meanwhile, preheat the oven to 190°C/375°F/Gas 5. Brush the rolls with water and dust with icing sugar. Bake for 10 minutes, or until light golden brown. Cool on a wire rack. Dust again with icing sugar and serve warm.

DESSERTS, CAKES & PASTRIES

Although Mediterranean meals are often finished simply with fresh fruit, there are a number of desserts that are enjoyed on special occasions. Ices and ice creams are popular and easy to prepare – try pretty Iced Oranges from the south of France or Italian Coffee Granita. Also popular are rich and creamy desserts such as Crema Catalana and the classic French Lemon Tart, fruit desserts such as Apricots stuffed with Almond Paste, and milk-based puddings such as Moroccan Rice Pudding. Wonderful cakes and pastries such as Moroccan Serpent Cake and Baklava also play an important part in the Mediterranean cuisine and are often enjoyed with a cup of coffee.

ICED ORANGES

These little sorbets are served in the hollowed-out orange skin and were originally sold in the beach cafés in the south of France. They are very pretty and easy to eat and are great for an al fresco lunch.

SERVES 8

INGREDIENTS
150g/5oz/²⁄₃ cup granulated sugar
juice of 1 lemon
14 oranges, plus orange juice or extra oranges for squeezing
8 fresh bay leaves, to decorate

1 Put the granulated sugar in a heavy pan, then add half the lemon juice and 120ml/4fl oz/½ cup water. Cook over a low heat until all the sugar has dissolved. Then increase the heat, bring to the boil, and boil for 2–3 minutes until the syrup is clear. Set aside and leave to cool.

2 Slice the tops off eight of the oranges. Scoop out the flesh of the oranges, and reserve. Put the empty orange shells and "lids" on a tray and place in the freezer until needed.

3 Grate the rind of the remaining oranges and add to the cooled syrup. Squeeze the juice from the oranges and from the reserved flesh. You will need to have 750ml/1¼ pints/3 cups. Squeeze another orange or add bought orange juice, if you have not made enough.

4 Stir the orange juice and remaining lemon juice, with 90ml/6 tbsp water into the syrup. Taste, adding more lemon juice or sugar, as desired. Pour the mixture into a shallow freezerproof container and freeze for 3 hours.

5 Turn the semi-frozen mixture into a bowl, and whisk vigorously with a fork to break up the ice crystals. Return to the freezer and freeze for a further 4 hours, until quite firm but not solid.

6 Pack the sorbet into the orange shells, mounding it up, and set the orange skin lids on top. Freeze until ready to serve. Just before serving, push a skewer into the tops of the lids and push in a bay leaf.

Mango & Passion Fruit Gelato

This tropical ice cream has a delicate perfume and fresh and fruity flavour. Passion fruit tend to vary in size. If you can locate the large ones, four will be plenty for this dish. You can make the gelato by hand or using an ice cream maker.

Serves 4

Ingredients
4 large mangoes
grated rind and juice of 1 lime
50g/2oz/¼ cup caster (superfine) sugar
300ml/½ pint/1¼ cups whipping cream
4 – 6 passion fruit

1 Cut a thick slice from either side of the stone (pit) on each unpeeled mango. Using a sharp knife, make criss-cross cuts in the mango flesh, cutting down as far as the skin but not right through.

2 Turn the slices inside out so that the pieces of mango stand proud of the skin, then scoop the flesh into a food processor or blender, using a spoon. Cut the remaining flesh away from the stones and add it to the rest. Process the mango flesh until smooth, then add the lime rind, lime juice and sugar and process briefly.

3 Whip the cream until it is just thick but will still fall from a spoon. Fold in the puréed mango and lime mixture, then pour into a freezerproof container. Freeze for 4 hours until semi-frozen.

4 Cut the passion fruit in half and scoop the seeds and pulp into the ice cream mixture, mix well and freeze for 2 hours until firm enough to scoop.

Cook's Tip
To use an ice cream maker, churn the mango purée for 10–15 minutes, add the cream and continue to churn until the mixture is thick. Scrape it into a plastic tub, stir in the passion fruit pulp and freeze.

COFFEE GRANITA

This semi-frozen sorbet consists of larger particles of ice. It is very refreshing, particularly in the summer. Granitas may also be made with fruit, but the coffee version is perhaps the most popular.

SERVES 6–8

INGREDIENTS
30ml/2 tbsp granulated sugar
350ml/12fl oz/1½ cups hot strong espresso coffee
250ml/8fl oz/1 cup double (heavy) cream
10ml/2 tsp caster (superfine) sugar

1 Stir the granulated sugar into the hot coffee until dissolved. Leave to cool, then chill. Pour into a shallow plastic or metal freezerproof container, then cover and freeze for about 1 hour.

2 The coffee should have formed a frozen crust around the rim of the container. Scrape this away with a spoon and mix with the rest of the coffee. Repeat this process every 30 minutes, using the spoon to break up the clumps of ice.

3 After about 2½ hours, the granita should be ready. It will have the appearance of small, fairly uniform ice crystals. Whip the cream with the caster sugar until stiff. Serve the granita in tall glasses, each topped with a spoonful of cream.

TURKISH DELIGHT ICE CREAM

*This luxurious ice cream gives a modern twist to traditional Turkish Delight. It is
especially good served with thin almond cookies, or try home-made meringues.
Serve scattered with rose petals, if you have them.*

SERVES 6

INGREDIENTS
4 egg yolks
115g/4oz/½ cup caster (superfine) sugar
300ml/½ pint/1¼ cups milk
300ml/½ pint/1¼ cups double (heavy) cream
15ml/1 tbsp rose water
175g/6oz rose-flavoured Turkish Delight, chopped

1 Beat the egg yolks and caster sugar until light and airy. In a pan, bring the milk
to the boil. Pour into the egg and sugar in a stready stream, stirring constantly,
then return to the cleaned pan.

2 Continue stirring the custard over a low heat until the mixture coats the back
of a spoon. Do not boil, or it will curdle. Remove from the heat and leave to
cool, then stir in the cream and rose water.

3 Put the Turkish Delight in a pan with 30–45ml/2–3 tbsp water. Heat gently
until almost completely melted, with just a few small lumps. Remove from the
heat and stir into the cooled custard.

4 Leave the rose-flavoured custard to cool completely, then pour it into a shallow
plastic or metal freezerproof container. Freeze for 3 hours until just frozen all
over. Spoon the mixture into a bowl.

5 Using a whisk, beat the mixture well, then return to the freezerproof container
and freeze for 2 hours more. Repeat the beating process, then return to the
freezer for about 3 hours, or until firm. Remove the ice cream from the freezer
about 20–25 minutes before serving so that it softens slightly.

PISTACHIO NUT ICE CREAM

This Mediterranean favourite owes its enduring popularity to its delicate pale green colour and distinctive yet subtle flavour.

SERVES 4–6

INGREDIENTS
4 egg yolks
75g/3oz/6 tbsp caster (superfine) sugar
5ml/1 tsp cornflour (cornstarch)
300ml/½ pint/1¼ cups semi-skimmed (low-fat) milk
115g/4oz/1 cup pistachio nuts, plus extra to decorate
300ml/½ pint/1¼ cups whipping cream
a little green food colouring
chocolate dipped waffle cones, to serve (optional)

1 Place the egg yolks, sugar and cornflour in a bowl and whisk until the mixture is thick and foamy. Pour the milk into a heavy pan, bring gently to the boil, then gradually whisk it into the egg yolk mixture.

2 Return the mixture to the cleaned pan and stir over a gentle heat until the custard thickens and is smooth. Pour it back into the bowl, set aside to cool, then chill in the refrigerator until required.

3 Shell the pistachio nuts and put them in a food processor or blender. Add 30ml/2 tbsp of the cream and grind the mixture to a coarse paste. Pour the rest of the cream into a small pan. Bring to the boil, stir in the pistachio paste, then remove from the heat and leave to cool.

4 Mix the chilled custard and pistachio cream together and tint the mixture delicately with a few drops of food colouring.

5 Pour the mixture into a plastic tub or similar freezerproof container. Freeze for about 6 hours, beating once or twice with a fork or in an electric mixer to break up the ice crystals. To serve, scoop the ice cream into cones or dishes and sprinkle each portion with a few extra pistachio nuts.

Fresh Figs with Honey

This classic Mediterranean combination of fresh figs, wine and honey, served with vanilla-flavoured cream is absolutely delicious.

Serves 6

Ingredients
450ml/¾ pint/1⅞ cups dry white wine
75g/3oz/⅓ cup clear honey
50g/2oz/¼ cup caster (superfine) sugar
1 small orange
8 whole cloves
450g/1lb fresh figs
1 cinnamon stick
300ml/½ pint/1¼ cups double (heavy) cream
1 vanilla pod (bean)
5ml/1 tsp caster (superfine) sugar
mint sprigs or fresh bay leaves, to decorate

1 Put the wine, honey and sugar in a heavy pan and heat gently until the sugar has completely dissolved. Stud the orange with the cloves and add to the syrup with the figs and cinnamon. Cover and simmer very gently for 5–10 minutes until the figs are softened. Transfer to a serving dish and leave to cool.

2 Put 150ml/¼ pint/⅔ cup of the cream in a small pan and add the vanilla pod. Bring almost to the boil, then leave to cool and infuse for 30 minutes.

3 Remove the vanilla pod. Mix all the cream together in a bowl, stir in the sugar and whip lightly. Decorate with mint or bay leaves and serve with the figs.

Cook's Tip
Choose plump, ripe figs and use as soon as possible as they do not keep well. The length of cooking time depends on the ripeness of the fruit; less ripe fruit will need slightly longer cooking.

CREMA CATALANA

This delicious Spanish dessert is a cross between a crème caramel and a crème brûlée.
Like crème brulée, it has a caramelized sugar topping.

SERVES 4

INGREDIENTS
475ml/16fl oz/2 cups milk
pared rind of ½ lemon
1 cinnamon stick
4 egg yolks
105ml/7 tbsp caster (superfine) sugar
25ml/1½ tbsp cornflour (cornstarch)
grated nutmeg, for sprinkling

1 Put the milk in a pan with the lemon rind and cinnamon stick. Bring to the boil, then simmer for 10 minutes. Remove the lemon peel and cinnamon. Place the egg yolks and 45ml/3 tbsp of the sugar in a bowl, and whisk until pale yellow. Add the cornflour and mix well.

2 Stir in a few tablespoons of the hot milk, then add this mixture to the remaining milk. Return to the heat and cook gently, stirring, for about 5 minutes, until thickened and smooth. Do not let it boil.

3 Pour the mixture into four shallow ovenproof dishes, about 13cm/5in in diameter. Leave to cool, then place in the refrigerator for a few hours, overnight if possible, until firm.

4 Before serving, preheat the grill (broiler) to high. Sprinkle each pudding with a tablespoon of caster sugar and a little grated nutmeg. Place the custards under the grill, on the highest shelf, and cook until the sugar caramelizes. This will only take a few seconds. Leave to cool for a few minutes before serving. (The caramel will only stay hard for about 30 minutes.)

LEMON TART

This is one of the classic French desserts, and it is difficult to beat. A rich lemon curd filling is encased in crisp pastry. Serve with crème fraîche.

SERVES 6

INGREDIENTS
6 eggs, beaten
350g/12oz/1½ cups caster (superfine) sugar
115g/4oz/½ cup unsalted (sweet) butter
grated rind and juice of 4 lemons
icing (confectioners') sugar, for dusting

FOR THE PASTRY
225g/8oz/2 cups plain (all-purpose) flour
115g/4oz/½ cup butter
30ml/2 tbsp icing (confectioners') sugar
1 egg
5ml/1 tsp vanilla essence (extract)

1 Preheat the oven to 200°C/400°F/Gas 6. Make the pastry. Sift the flour into a large bowl, add the butter, cut into small pieces, and work with your fingertips until the mixture resembles fine breadcrumbs. Stir in the icing sugar.

2 Add the egg, vanilla essence and a scant tablespoon of cold water to the flour mixture, then work to a dough. Roll the pastry out on a floured surface and use to line a 23cm/9in tart tin (pan). Line with foil or baking parchment and fill with dried beans or baking beans. Bake for 10 minutes. Leave the oven on.

3 Put the beaten eggs, sugar and butter into a pan, and stir over a low heat until the sugar has dissolved. Add the lemon rind and juice, and continue cooking, stirring, until slightly thickened, then pour into the pastry case. Bake for 20 minutes until just set. Transfer to a wire rack to cool. Dust with icing sugar and serve.

GLAZED PRUNE TART

Generously glazed, creamy custard tarts are a pâtisserie favourite in France. Plump prunes, heavily laced with brandy, add a wonderful taste and texture to this deliciously sweet and creamy filling.

SERVES 8

INGREDIENTS
225g/8oz/1 cup ready-to-eat prunes
60ml/4 tbsp brandy
150ml/¼ pint/⅔ cup double (heavy) cream
150ml/¼ pint/⅔ cup milk
1 vanilla pod (bean)
3 eggs
50g/2oz/¼ cup caster (superfine) sugar
60ml/4 tbsp apricot jam
15ml/1 tbsp brandy
icing (confectioners') sugar, for dusting

FOR THE PASTRY
175g/6oz/1½ cups plain (all-purpose) flour
pinch of salt
115g/4oz/½ cup unsalted (sweet) butter
25g/1oz/2 tbsp caster (superfine) sugar
2 egg yolks

1 Put the prunes in a bowl, pour over the brandy and leave to stand for about 4 hours until most of the liquid has been absorbed.

2 To make the pastry, sift the flour and salt into a bowl. Add the butter, cut into small pieces, and rub in with the fingertips. Stir in the sugar and egg yolks and mix to a dough using a round-bladed knife. Turn the dough out on to a lightly floured surface and knead to a smooth ball. Wrap closely in clear film (plastic wrap) and chill for 30 minutes.

3 Preheat the oven to 200°C/400°F/Gas 6. Roll out the pastry on a lightly floured surface and use to line a 24–25cm/9½–10in loose-based flan tin (tart pan).

4 Line with baking parchment and fill with dried beans or baking beans. Bake for about 15 minutes until golden. Remove the beans and parchment and bake for a further 5 minutes. Leave the oven on.

5 Arrange the soaked prunes, evenly spaced, in the pastry case, reserving any brandy left in the bowl.

6 To make the custard filling, put the cream and milk in a pan with the vanilla pod and bring to the boil. Turn off the heat and leave the mixture to infuse for about 15 minutes.

7 Whisk together the eggs and sugar in a bowl. Remove the vanilla pod from the cream and return the cream to the boil. Pour into the egg and sugar mixture in a steady stream, whisking constantly to make a smooth custard.

8 Leave the custard to cool slightly, then pour over the prunes. Bake the tart for about 25 minutes until the filling is lightly set and just turning golden around the edges.

9 Press the apricot jam through a sieve into a small pan. Add the brandy and heat through gently. Use to glaze the tart. Serve warm or cold, dusted with icing sugar.

COOK'S TIP
The vanilla pod can be washed and dried and used again at another time. Alternatively, use 5ml/1 tsp vanilla or almond essence (extract).

Pear & Almond Cream Tart

This French tart is equally successful made with other kinds of fruit. Try making it with nectarines, peaches, apricots or apples.

Serves 6

Ingredients

350g/¾lb shortcrust or sweet shortcrust pastry
100g/3½oz/¾ cup blanched whole almonds
50g/2oz/¼ cup caster (superfine) sugar
70g/2½oz/5 tbsp butter
1 egg, plus 1 egg white
a few drops of almond essence (extract)
3 firm pears
lemon juice
15ml/1 tbsp peach brandy
60ml/4 tbsp peach preserve, strained

1 Roll out the pastry and use to line a 23cm/9in flan tin (tart pan). Chill. To make the almond cream filling, put the almonds and sugar in a food processor and pulse until finely ground. Add the butter and process until smooth and creamy; mix in the egg, egg white and almond essence.

2 Place a baking sheet in the oven and preheat to 190°C/375°F/Gas 5. Peel the pears, halve them, remove the cores and rub with lemon juice. Put the pear halves cut side down and slice thinly crossways, keeping the slices together.

3 Pour the almond cream filling into the pastry case. Slide a metal spatula under one pear half and press the top with your fingers to fan out the slices. Transfer to the tart, placing the fruit on the filling like spokes of a wheel.

4 Place the tart on the hot baking sheet and bake for 50–55 minutes until the filling is set and well browned. Cool on a wire rack.

5 Meanwhile, heat the brandy and peach preserve in a small pan, then brush over the top of the hot tart to glaze. Serve at room temperature.

DATE & ALMOND TART

Sweet and chewy dark brown dates make an unusual but delicious filling for a tart.
The influences here are French and Middle Eastern – a true Mediterranean fusion.

SERVES 6

INGREDIENTS
90g/3½oz/scant ½ cup butter
90g/3½oz/7 tbsp caster (superfine) sugar
1 egg, beaten
90g/3½oz/scant 1 cup ground almonds
30ml/2 tbsp plain (all-purpose) flour
30ml/2 tbsp orange flower water
12–13 fresh dates, halved and stoned (pitted)
60ml/4 tbsp apricot jam

FOR THE PASTRY
175g/6oz/1½ cups plain (all-purpose) flour
75g/3oz/6 tbsp butter
1 egg

1 Preheat the oven to 200°C/400°F/Gas 6. Place a baking sheet in the oven. Make the pastry. Sift the flour into a bowl, add the butter and work with your fingertips until the mixture resembles fine breadcrumbs. Add the egg and 15ml/ 1 tbsp cold water, then work to a smooth dough. Roll out on a lightly floured surface and use to line a 20cm/8in tart tin (pan). Prick the base with a fork and chill.

2 To make the filling, cream the butter and sugar until light, then beat in the egg. Stir in the ground almonds, flour and 15ml/1 tbsp of the orange flower water. Spread the mixture in the pastry case. Arrange the dates, cut side down, on top. Place on the hot baking sheet and bake for 10–15 minutes. Reduce the heat to 180°C/350°F/Gas 4. Bake for a further 15–20 minutes until light golden and set.

3 Transfer the tart to a wire rack to cool. Gently heat the jam in a small pan and press through a sieve. Add the remaining orange flower water. Brush the tart with the jam and serve at room temperature.

Honey & Pine Nut Tart

This unusual tart comes from the south of France. It is particularly good served warm with crème fraîche or vanilla ice cream.

Serves 6

Ingredients
115g/4oz/½ cup unsalted (sweet) butter, diced
115g/4oz/½ cup caster (superfine) sugar
3 eggs, beaten
175g/6oz/⅔ cup sunflower or other flower honey
grated rind and juice of 1 lemon
225g/8oz/2⅔ cups pine nuts
pinch of salt
icing (confectioners') sugar for dusting

For the pastry
225g/8oz/2 cups plain (all-purpose) flour
115g/4oz/½ cup butter
30ml/2 tbsp icing (confectioners') sugar
1 egg

1 Preheat the oven to 180°C/350°F/Gas 4. Make the pastry. Sift the flour into a bowl, add the butter and work with your fingertips until the mixture resembles fine breadcrumbs. Stir in the icing sugar. Add the egg and 15ml/1 tbsp water and work to a firm dough that leaves the bowl clean. Roll out the pastry on a floured surface and use to line a 23cm/9in tart tin (pan). Prick the base with a fork then chill for 10 minutes. Line with baking parchment and fill with dried beans or baking beans. Bake for 10 minutes. Remove the baking parchment and beans.

2 In a bowl, cream together the butter and caster sugar until light. Beat in the eggs. Heat the honey in a small pan until runny; add to the butter mixture with the lemon rind and juice. Stir in the pine nuts and salt. Pour into the pastry case. Bake for about 45 minutes, until the filling is lightly browned and set. Leave to cool slightly in the tin, then dust generously with icing sugar. Serve warm.

CHERRY CLAFOUTI

This classic French batter pudding is perfect when fresh cherries are in season.
It makes an ideal dessert for any occasion, served with a little cream.

SERVES 6

INGREDIENTS
675g/1½lb fresh cherries
50g/2oz/½ cup plain (all-purpose) flour
pinch of salt
4 eggs, plus 2 egg yolks
115g/4oz/½ cup caster (superfine) sugar
600ml/1 pint/2½ cups milk
50g/2oz/¼ cup melted butter
caster (superfine) sugar, for dusting (optional)
pouring cream, to serve

1 Preheat the oven to 190°C/375°F/Gas 5. Lightly butter the base and sides of a shallow ovenproof dish. Stone (pit) the cherries and place in the dish.

2 Sift the flour and salt into a bowl. Add the eggs, egg yolks, sugar and a little of the milk and whisk to a smooth batter.

3 Gradually whisk the rest of the milk and the butter into the batter, then strain the batter over the cherries. Bake for 40–50 minutes until golden and just set. Serve warm, dusted with caster sugar if you like. Hand pouring cream separately.

VARIATIONS
• *If fresh cherries are not available, use 2 × 425g/15oz cans stoned (pitted) black cherries, thoroughly drained instead.*
• *For an extra special dessert, add 45ml/3 tbsp brandy or kirsch to the batter.*

Nut & Raisin Pudding

This sweet Egyptian dessert comprises layers of crisp crumbled filo pastry, nuts and raisins baked in a custard delicately flavoured with rose water. Serve with cream.

SERVES 4

INGREDIENTS
10–12 sheets filo pastry
600ml/1 pint/2½ cups milk
250ml/8fl oz/1 cup double (heavy) cream
1 egg, beaten
30ml/2 tbsp rose water
50g/2oz/½ cup each chopped pistachio nuts, almonds and hazelnuts
115g/4oz/⅔ cup raisins
15ml/1 tbsp ground cinnamon, for sprinkling

1 Preheat the oven to 160°C/325°F/Gas 3. Unroll the filo pastry and place on a baking sheet. Bake for 15–20 minutes until crisp. Remove from the oven and raise the temperature to 200°C/400°F/Gas 6.

2 Scald the milk and cream in a pan by heating it very gently until hot but not boiling. Slowly add the beaten egg and the rose water. Cook over a very low heat until the mixture begins to thicken, stirring constantly.

3 Crumble the pastry, then spread in layers with the nuts and raisins in a shallow baking dish. Pour the custard over the nut and pastry base. Bake for 20 minutes until golden. Sprinkle with the cinnamon and serve.

APRICOTS STUFFED WITH ALMOND PASTE

Almonds are widely used in Moroccan cooking. They have a delightful affinity with apricots and this popular dessert is delicious.

SERVES 6

INGREDIENTS
75g/3oz/scant ½ cup caster (superfine) sugar
30ml/2 tbsp lemon juice
115g/4oz/1 cup ground almonds
50g/2oz/½ cup icing (confectioners') sugar or caster (superfine) sugar
a little orange flower water (optional)
25g/1oz/2 tbsp melted butter
2.5ml/½ tsp almond essence (extract)
900g/2lb fresh apricots
fresh mint sprigs, to decorate

1 Preheat the oven to 180°C/350°F/Gas 4. Place the sugar, lemon juice and 300ml/½ pint/1¼ cups water in a small pan and bring to the boil, stirring occasionally until the sugar has dissolved completely. Simmer gently for 5–10 minutes to make a thin sugar syrup.

2 In a small bowl, blend together the ground almonds, icing or caster sugar, orange flower water, if using, butter and almond essence to make a smooth paste.

3 Wash the apricots, pat dry with kitchen paper, then make a slit in the flesh and ease out the stone (pit). Take small pieces of the almond paste, roll into balls and press one into each of the apricots.

4 Arrange the stuffed apricots in a shallow ovenproof dish and carefully pour the sugar syrup around them. Cover with foil and bake in the oven for about 25 minutes. Serve the apricots hot or warm with a little of the syrup, if liked, decorated with sprigs of mint.

LEMON RICE PUDDING

This dish is traditionally served cold, but it is also delicious warm. It is very simply flavoured with lemon rind, then dusted with cinnamon before being served with lemon wedges for squeezing over.

SERVES 4–6

INGREDIENTS
175g/6oz/scant 1 cup short grain pudding rice
600ml/1 pint/2½ cups creamy milk
2 or 3 strips pared lemon rind
65g/2½oz/5 tbsp butter, in pieces
115g/4oz/½ cup caster (superfine) sugar
4 egg yolks
salt
ground cinnamon, for dusting
lemon wedges, to serve

1 Cook the rice in a pan of lightly salted water for about 5 minutes. Drain well, then return to the cleaned pan. Add the milk, lemon rind and the butter. Stir, then bring to the boil over a low–medium heat. Cover, reduce the heat and simmer for 20 minutes, or until the rice is thick and creamy.

2 Remove the pan from the heat and leave to cool slightly. Remove the lemon rind, then stir in the sugar and the egg yolks. Divide among four to six serving bowls and dust with ground cinnamon. Serve cool, with lemon wedges.

MOROCCAN RICE PUDDING

This is a simple and delicious alternative to a traditional rice pudding. The rice is cooked in almond-flavoured milk and delicately spiced with cinnamon and orange flower water. It is best eaten hot.

SERVES 6

INGREDIENTS

25g/1oz/¼ cup blanched almonds, chopped
450g/1lb/2¼ cups pudding rice
25g/1oz/¼ cup icing (confectioners') sugar
7.5cm/3in cinnamon stick
50g/2oz/¼ cup butter
pinch of salt
1.5ml/¼ tsp almond essence (extract)
175ml/6fl oz /¾ cup milk
175ml/6fl oz/¾ cup condensed milk
30ml/2 tbsp orange flower water
toasted flaked (slivered) almonds and ground cinnamon, to decorate

1 Put the almonds in a food processor or blender with 60ml/4 tbsp of very hot water. Process, then push through a sieve into a bowl. Return to the food processor or blender, add a further 60ml/4 tbsp very hot water, and process again. Push through the sieve into a pan.

2 Add 300ml/½ pint/1¼ cups water to the almond "milk" and bring to the boil. Stir in the rice, sugar, cinnamon, half the butter, the salt and almond essence. In a jug (pitcher), combine the milk and condensed milk and pour half into the pan.

3 Bring the mixture to the boil, then simmer, covered, for about 30 minutes, adding more milk if necessary. Continue to cook the rice, stirring, and adding the remaining milk, until it becomes thick and creamy. Stir in the orange flower water, then taste for sweetness, adding extra sugar if necessary.

4 Pour the rice pudding into a serving bowl, and sprinkle with the flaked almonds. Dot with the remaining butter and dust with cinnamon. Serve hot.

SPANISH DOUGHNUTS

These sweet Spanish twists are known as Churros. *They are commercially deep-fried in huge coils and broken off into smaller lengths for selling. Serve this home-made version freshly cooked with hot chocolate or strong coffee.*

MAKES 12–15

INGREDIENTS
200g/7oz/1¾ cups plain (all-purpose) flour
1.5ml/¼ tsp salt
30ml/2 tbsp caster (superfine) sugar
60ml/4 tbsp olive or sunflower oil
1 egg, beaten
caster (superfine) sugar and ground cinnamon, for dusting
oil, for deep-frying

1 Sift the flour, salt and sugar on to a plate. In a pan, bring 250ml/8fl oz/1 cup water with the oil to the boil. Tip in the flour mixture and beat with a wooden spoon until the mixture forms a stiff paste. Leave to cool for 2 minutes.

2 Gradually beat the egg into the paste until smooth. Oil a large baking sheet. Sprinkle plenty of sugar on to a plate and stir in a little cinnamon.

3 Put the dough in a large piping bag fitted with a 1cm/½in plain piping nozzle. Pipe little coils or "s" shapes on to the baking sheet.

4 Heat 5cm/2in of oil in a large pan to 168°C/336°F or until a little dough sizzles on the surface. Using an oiled fish slice (spatula), lower several of the piped shapes into the oil and cook for about 2 minutes until light golden. Lift out of the oil with a slotted spoon.

5 Drain the doughnuts on kitchen paper, then coat with the sugar and cinnamon. Cook the remaining doughnuts in the same way and serve immediately.

ALMOND FINGERS

These very simple Middle Eastern sweetmeats are known as Seinab's Fingers. They comprise of a sweetly scented nut filling wrapped in filo pastry which is then baked until golden and crisp.

MAKES 40–50

INGREDIENTS
200g/7oz/2¼ cups ground almonds
50g/2oz/½ cup ground pistachio nuts
50g/2oz/¼ cup granulated sugar
15ml/1 tbsp rose water
2.5ml/½ tsp ground cinnamon
12 sheets of filo pastry
115g/4oz/½ cup melted butter
icing (confectioners') sugar, to decorate
coffee, to serve

1 Preheat the oven to 160°C/325°F/Gas 3. To make the filling, mix together the almonds, pistachio nuts, sugar, rose water and cinnamon in a bowl.

2 Cut each sheet of filo pastry into four rectangles. Work with one rectangle at a time, and cover the remaining rectangles with a damp dishtowel.

3 Brush one of the rectangles of filo pastry with a little melted butter and place a heaped teaspoonful of the nut filling in the centre.

4 Fold in the sides of the pastry and roll into a finger or cigar shape. Continue making fingers until all the filling has been used.

5 Place the fingers on a buttered baking sheet and bake in the oven for about 30 minutes, or until lightly golden. Remove from the oven and leave to cool, then dust with icing sugar before serving with hot coffee.

Moroccan Serpent Cake

This is perhaps the most famous of all Moroccan pastries, filled with lightly fragrant almond paste. It is coiled on to the baking sheet before being cooked.

Serves 8

Ingredients
100g/4oz/8 tbsp butter, melted
225g/8oz/2 cups ground almonds
2.5ml/½ tsp almond essence (extract)
50g/2oz/½ cup icing (confectioners') sugar
egg yolk, beaten
8 sheets of filo pastry
1 egg, beaten
5ml/1 tsp ground cinnamon
icing (confectioners') sugar, for dusting

1 Make the almond paste. In a bowl, blend half of the butter with the ground almonds and almond essence. Add the sugar and egg yolk, mix well and knead until soft and pliable. Chill for about 10 minutes, then break into 10 balls and roll into 10cm/4in sausages. Chill again.

2 Preheat the oven to 180°C/350°F/Gas 4. Place two sheets of filo pastry on the work surface so that they overlap to form an 18 × 56cm/7 × 22in rectangle. Brush the overlapping pastry with butter to secure, then brush all over. Cover with another two sheets of filo and brush again with butter.

3 Place five sausages of almond paste along the lower edge of the filo sheet and roll up the pastry tightly, tucking in the ends. Shape the roll into a loose coil. Repeat with the remaining filo and almond paste, so that you have two coils. Brush a large baking sheet with butter and place the coils together to make an "S" shape.

4 Beat together the egg and half of the cinnamon. Brush over the pastry, then bake for 20–25 minutes until golden. Carefully invert the snake on to another baking sheet and return to the oven for 5–10 minutes until golden. Place on a serving plate. Dust with icing sugar, then sprinkle with cinnamon. Serve warm.

GAZELLES' HORNS

Kaab el Ghzal is a favourite in Morocco and elsewhere. The horn-shaped, filled pastries are commonly served at wedding ceremonies.

MAKES ABOUT 16

INGREDIENTS
200g/7oz/scant 2 cups ground almonds
115g/4oz/1 cup icing (confectioners') sugar or caster (superfine) sugar
60ml/4 tbsp orange flower water
50g/2oz/2 tbsp melted butter
3 egg yolks, beaten
2.5ml/½ tsp ground cinnamon
200g/7oz/1¾ cups plain (all-purpose) flour
pinch of salt
icing (confectioners') sugar, for dusting

1 In a bowl, mix the almonds, sugar, half of the orange flower water, half of the butter, 2 egg yolks and the cinnamon to a paste. Set aside.

2 Combine the flour and a little salt in a bowl and stir in the remaining butter and orange flower water, and three-quarters of the remaining egg yolk. Stir in cold water, a little at a time, to make a soft dough. Knead for about 10 minutes, then roll out as thinly as possible. Cut into long strips about 7.5cm/3in wide.

3 Preheat the oven to 180°C/350°F/Gas 4. Take small pieces of the almond paste and roll them into thin sausages about 7.5cm/3 in long with tapering ends. Place in a line along one side of the pastry strips, about 3cm/1¼in apart.

4 Dampen the pastry edges with water and fold the other half of the strip over the filling, pressing the edges together. Using a pastry wheel, cut around each sausage to make a crescent shape.

5 Prick the crescents with a fork or a needle and place on a buttered baking sheet. Brush with the remaining beaten egg yolk and bake for 12–16 minutes until lightly coloured. Cool, then dust with icing sugar before serving.

GREEK FRUIT & NUT PASTRIES

Aromatic sweet pastry crescents, known as Moshopoungia *in Greece, are packed with candied peel and walnuts that have been soaked in a coffee syrup.*

MAKES 16

INGREDIENTS
60ml/4 tbsp clear honey
60ml/4 tbsp strong brewed coffee
75g/3oz/½ cup mixed candied citrus peel, finely chopped
175g/6oz/1 cup walnuts, chopped
1.5ml/¼ tsp grated nutmeg
milk, to glaze
caster (superfine) sugar, for sprinkling

FOR THE PASTRY
450g/1lb/4 cups plain (all-purpose) flour
2.5ml/½ tsp ground cinnamon
2.5ml/½ tsp baking powder
pinch of salt
150g/5oz/10 tbsp unsalted (sweet) butter
30ml/2 tbsp caster (superfine) sugar
1 egg
120ml/4fl oz/½ cup chilled milk

1 Preheat the oven to 180°C/350°F/Gas 4. To make the pastry, sift the flour, ground cinnamon, baking powder and salt into a bowl. Rub in the butter until the mixture resembles fine breadcrumbs. Stir in the sugar until well combined and make a well in the centre.

2 In a jug (pitcher), beat together the egg and milk and pour into the well in the dry ingredients. Mix to a soft dough. Divide the dough into two and wrap each in clear film (plastic wrap). Chill in the refrigerator for 30 minutes.

3 Meanwhile, make the filling. In a bowl, combine the honey and coffee. Add the candied citrus peel, walnuts and nutmeg. Stir well, cover and leave to stand for at least 20 minutes.

4 Roll out a portion of chilled dough on a lightly floured surface until about 3mm/⅛in thick. Stamp out rounds using a 10cm/4in round pastry cutter.

5 Place a heaped teaspoonful of filling on one side of each round. Brush the edges with a little milk, then fold over and press the edges together to seal. Repeat with the remaining pastry until all the filling is used.

6 Put the pastries on lightly greased baking sheets, brush with milk and sprinkle with caster sugar. Carefully make a steam hole in each pastry with a skewer. Bake for 35 minutes, or until lightly browned. Cool on a wire rack.

DATE & NUT PASTRIES

The sweet filling of fruit and nuts is encased in soft, rose-water-flavoured pastry.
These pastries make a delicious treat served with strong coffee.

MAKES 35–40

INGREDIENTS
225g/8oz/1¼ cups dates, stoned (pitted) and chopped
175g/6oz/1¼ cups walnuts, finely chopped
115g/4oz/¼ cup blanched almonds, chopped
50g/2oz/½ cup pistachio nuts, chopped
120ml/4fl oz/½ cup water
115g/4oz/½ cup sugar
10ml/2 tsp ground cinnamon

FOR THE PASTRY
450g/1lb/4 cups plain (all-purpose) flour
225g/8oz/1 cup unsalted (sweet) butter, cubed
45ml/3 tbsp rose water
60–75ml/4–5 tbsp milk
icing (confectioners') sugar, for sprinkling

1 Preheat the oven to 160°C/325°F/Gas 3. Place the dates, walnuts, almonds, pistachio nuts, water, sugar and cinnamon in a small pan and cook over a low heat until the dates are soft and the water has been absorbed.

2 To make the pastry, place the flour in a large bowl and add the butter, working it into the flour with your fingertips until the mixture resembles fine breadcrumbs. Stir in the rose water and milk, then knead the dough until soft.

3 Pull off walnut-size lumps of dough. Roll each into a ball and make a hollow in the middle with your thumb. Pinch the sides. Place a spoonful of date mixture in the hollow, then press the dough back over the filling to seal.

4 Arrange the pastries on a large, greased baking sheet. Press to flatten them slightly. Make little dents with a fork on the pastry. Bake in the oven for 20 minutes. Do not let them change colour or the pastry will become hard. Cool slightly, then sprinkle with icing sugar and serve.

BAKLAVA

Turkish coffee is black, thick, very sweet and often spiced. It is used to flavour this pastry confection that is popularly enjoyed in Turkey.

MAKES 16

INGREDIENTS
50g/2oz/½ cup blanched almonds, chopped
50g/2oz/½ cup pistachio nuts, chopped
75g/3oz/scant ½ cup caster (superfine) sugar
115g/4oz filo pastry
75g/3oz/6 tbsp unsalted (sweet) butter, melted and cooled

FOR THE SYRUP
115g/4oz/generous ½ cup caster (superfine) sugar
7.5cm/3in piece cinnamon stick
1 whole clove
2 cardamom pods, crushed
75ml/5 tbsp strong brewed coffee

1 Preheat the oven to 180°C/350°F/Gas 4. Mix the nuts and sugar together in a bowl. Cut the pastry to fit a tin (pan) measuring 18 × 28cm/7 × 11in. Brush the tin with a little butter. Lay a sheet of pastry in the tin and brush with melted butter. Repeat with three more sheets and spread with half the nut mixture.

2 Layer three more sheets of pastry in the tin, lightly brushing with butter between the layers, then spread the remaining nut mixture over them, smoothing it over the entire surface. Top with the remaining pastry and butter. Gently press down the edges to seal.

3 With a sharp knife, mark the top into diamonds. Bake for 20–25 minutes until golden brown and crisp. Meanwhile, put the syrup ingredients in a small pan and heat gently until the sugar has dissolved. Cover the pan with a lid and leave to infuse for 20 minutes.

4 Remove the baklava from the oven. Reheat the coffee and spice syrup and strain over the pastry. Leave to cool in the tin. Using a sharp knife, cut into diamonds, remove from the tin and serve.

ALMOND & DATE PASTRIES WITH FRAGRANT HONEY

It is worth investing in a good-quality honey in which to dip these delicious Moroccan pastries, which are known as briouates. *Serve with strong coffee.*

MAKES ABOUT 30

INGREDIENTS
15ml/1 tbsp sunflower oil
225g/8oz/1⅓ cups blanched almonds
115g/4oz/⅔ cup stoned (pitted) dates
25g/1oz/2 tbsp butter, softened
5ml/1 tsp ground cinnamon
1.5ml/¼ tsp almond essence (extract)
40g/1½oz/⅓ cup icing (confectioners') sugar
about 30ml/2 tbsp orange flower water or rose water
10 sheets of filo pastry
50g/2oz/4 tbsp melted butter
120ml/4fl oz/½ cup fragrant honey
dates, to serve (optional)

1 Heat the oil in a small pan and fry the almonds for a few minutes until golden, stirring all the time. Drain on kitchen paper. When cool, grind in a coffee or spice mill. Pound the dates by hand or process in a food processor or blender.

2 Spoon the ground almonds into a mixing bowl or into the food processor or blender with the dates and blend with the butter, cinnamon, almond essence, icing sugar and a little orange flower or rose water to taste. If the mixture feels stiff, work in a little extra flower water.

3 Preheat the oven to 180°C/350°F/Gas 4. Brush a sheet of filo pastry with melted butter and cut into three equal strips, keeping the remaining sheets covered.

4 Place a walnut-size piece of almond paste at the bottom of each strip. Fold one corner over the filling to make a triangle and then fold up, in triangles, to make a neat package. Brush again with a little butter. Repeat to make about 30 pastries.

5 Place the pastries on a greased baking sheet and bake for 30 minutes until golden. If possible, cook in batches, as once cooked they should be immediately immersed in the honey while still very hot.

6 While the briouates are cooking, pour the honey and a little orange flower or rose water into a pan and heat very gently to melt the honey. When the pastries are cooked, lower them one by one into the pan and turn them in the honey so that they are thoroughly coated. Transfer to a plate and cool a little before serving, with extra dates if you wish.

Semolina & Nut Halva

Semolina is a very popular ingredient in many desserts in the eastern Mediterranean.
Here it provides a spongy base for soaking up a deliciously fragrant spicy syrup.

SERVES 10

INGREDIENTS
115g/4oz/½ cup unsalted (sweet) butter, softened
115g/4oz/½ cup caster (superfine) sugar
finely grated rind of 1 orange, plus 30ml/2 tbsp juice
3 eggs
175g/6oz/1 cup semolina
10ml/2 tsp baking powder
115g/4oz/1 cup ground hazelnuts
50g/2oz/½ cup unblanched hazelnuts, toasted and chopped
50g/2oz/½ cup blanched almonds, toasted and chopped
shredded rind of 1 orange, to decorate
lightly whipped cream, to serve (optional)

FOR THE SYRUP
350g/12oz/1½ cups caster (superfine) sugar
2 cinnamon sticks, halved
juice of 1 lemon
60ml/4 tbsp orange flower water

> COOK'S TIP
> *Be sure to use a deep solid-based cake tin (pan),*
> *rather than one with a loose base, otherwise the syrup*
> *might seep out. If you only have a loose-based tin,*
> *place on a large plate before pouring over the syrup.*

1 Preheat the oven to 220°C/425°F/Gas 7. Grease and line the base of a deep 23cm/9in square solid-based cake tin (pan).

2 Lightly cream the butter in a bowl. Add the sugar, orange rind and juice, eggs, semolina, baking powder and ground hazelnuts and beat until smooth.

3 Turn into the prepared tin and level the surface. Bake for 20–25 minutes until just firm and golden. Leave to cool in the tin.

4 To make the syrup, put the sugar in a small heavy pan with 575ml/18fl oz/ 2¼ cups water and the halved cinnamon sticks. Heat gently, stirring, until the sugar has dissolved completely.

5 Bring the mixture to the boil and boil fast, without stirring, for about 5 minutes. Carefully remove the cinnamon sticks. Measure half the boiling syrup into a jug (pitcher) and add the lemon juice and orange flower water to it. Pour over the halva. Reserve the remainder of the syrup in the pan.

6 Leave the halva in the tin until the syrup is absorbed, then turn it out on to a plate and cut diagonally into diamond-shaped portions. Scatter with the nuts.

7 Boil the remaining syrup until slightly thickened, then pour over the halva. Scatter the shredded orange rind evenly over the cake. Serve with lightly whipped cream, if you like.

INDEX

moussaka, 182–3

sautéed lamb with
  yogurt, 176

skewered lamb with herb
  yogurt, 188

skewered lamb with red
  onion salsa, 189

Turkish lamb with apricot
  and cashew nut rice, 180–1

Turkish lamb pilau, 238

lemons, 16

  avgolemono, 67

  chicken with lemons and
    olives, 199

  lemon rice pudding, 300

  lemon tart, 291

  vermicelli with lemon, 247

lentils, 12, 227

  Egyptian rice with lentils, 239

  green lentil soup, 69

linguine with ham and
  mascarpone, 250

lobster: Spanish fish
  stew, 164–5

M

macaroni, Corsican beef stew
  with, 170–1

mace, 21

Mallorcan ensaimadas, 281

mango and passion fruit
  gelato, 285

marjoram, 19

Marrakesh pizza, 260–1

Marsala, pork with juniper
  and, 191

mascarpone, 11

  linguine with ham and
    mascarpone, 250

meat, 10

meatballs in tomato sauce, 175

melons, 17

  prawn and melon salad, 133

mint, 18

  yogurt and cucumber soup
    with fresh mint, 61

mojama, 8

monkfish, 8

  monkfish with tomatoes, 144

Moroccan holiday
  bread, 278–9

Moroccan serpent cake, 304

mouclade of mussels, 161

moussaka, 182–3

mozzarella, 11

mullet, 8

  grilled red mullet with
    herbs, 142

  pan-fried red mullet with
    basil and citrus sauce, 137

  Turkish cold fish, 136

  see also tarama

mushrooms, 15

  broad bean, mushroom and
    chorizo salad, 122

  fusilli with wild mushrooms
    and herbs, 249

  garlic mushrooms, 85

  marinated mushrooms, 84

  mushroom and pesto
    pizza, 263

mussels, 9

  grilled mussels with parsley
    and Parmesan, 139

  mouclade of mussels, 161

  Spanish fish stew, 164–5

  spiced mussel soup, 77

  tagliolini with clams and
    mussels, 254–5

N

navy beans see haricot beans

nectarines, 16

nutmeg, 21

nuts, 17

  date and nut pastries, 308

  nut and raisin pudding, 298

  see also types of nut

O

octopus, 9

  octopus and red wine
    stew, 160

okra, 15

  okra with coriander and
    tomatoes, 100

olive oil, 22

olives, 15

  chicken with lemons and
    olives, 199

  duck stew with olives, 219

  olive bread, 267

  pappardelle with olive,
    anchovy and caper
    paste, 252–3

  Provençal beef and olive
    daube, 168–9

  tapas of almonds, olives and
    cheese, 36–7

  tapenade and herb aioli with
    summer vegetables, 32–3

onions, 14

  red onion focaccia, 264–5

  skewered lamb with red
    onion salsa, 189

  sweet and sour onion
    salad, 127

orange flower water, 23